The Best Catholics in the World

The Best Catholics in the World

The Irish, the Church and the End of a Special Relationship

DEREK SCALLY

SANDYCOVE

an imprint of

PENGUIN BOOKS

SANDYCOVE

UK | USA | Canada | Ireland | Australia
India | New Zealand | South Africa

Sandycove is part of the Penguin Random House group of companies
whose addresses can be found at global.penguinrandomhouse.com.

First published 2021

003

Copyright © Derek Scally, 2021

The moral right of the author has been asserted

Lines on page 53 from Seamus Heaney's 'St Kevin and the Blackbird' from
The Spirit Level (Faber, 1996), copyright Heaney estate, used with permission.

Every effort has been made to contact copyright holders and to obtain their permission
for the use of copyright material. There are instances where we have been unable to
trace or contact the copyright holder. If notified, the publisher will be pleased to
rectify any errors or omissions at the earliest opportunity.

Set in 12/14.75 pt Bembo Book MT Std
Typeset by Jouve (UK), Milton Keynes
Printed and bound in Great Britain by Clays Ltd, Elcograf S.p.A.

The authorized representative in the EEA is Penguin Random House Ireland,
Morrison Chambers, 32 Nassau Street, Dublin D02 YH68

A CIP catalogue record for this book is available from the British Library

ISBN: 978-1-844-88526-8

www.greenpenguin.co.uk

Penguin Random House is committed to a
sustainable future for our business, our readers
and our planet. This book is made from Forest
Stewardship Council® certified paper.

To my parents, Frances and Joe, with thanks for their belief. And to Till, for hope.

'The name of the game was Salvation, the object
to get to Heaven and avoid Hell. It was like Snakes
and Ladders . . . everything was subject to spiritual
accounting . . . there was a snake called Presumption
that was just as fatal as the one called Despair.
(It really was a most ingenious game.)'

David Lodge, *How Far Can You Go?*

Contents

Prologue

It is high noon near Dublin's Heuston Station and I've paused to take in the scene. The low, grey summer sky promises drizzle any minute. From all directions, the trickle of papal Mass-goers is turning into a flood. The last time people marched this way for a Pope, the quays of the River Liffey were in what seemed like terminal decline – the once proud red-brick houses lined the river like broken-down teeth with shattered window cavities; half-demolished brick piles held together by braces, and gaps filled with scrub and rubbish.

Waiting on the footpath, I survey the Dublin I see before me, and consider how utterly it has changed from the city that was once my hometown. The ruins are renovated and, at ground level, occupied with shops that signal the new prosperity. When Irish people celebrate the breaking of bread today, it is more likely to be sourdough and produced by tattooed hipsters in faux artisanal bakeries than silent nuns in convents. Passion is the word used to sell Ireland's new holy water – coffee – rather than to remind the faithful that Jesus Christ died on the cross for the salvation of their souls. The decrepit old Strumpet City is cleaned up and is now a playground of nail bars, tanning salons, cupcakes and CrossFit.

Once Dublin streets echoed with street-trader voices, like a profane Gregorian chant – *'Pears – foive-for-feeeefty. Herdled or Press.'* I never noticed the chorus had vanished until hearing it again – the voices back for one day only. *'Pope Fraaancis posters, plaques and scaaaarves.'* But business is as slack as the papal flags, hanging limp in the heavy air. Many of the Mass-goers learned their lesson at a concert for the Pope in Croke Park the night before, when flags they bought on the way in were confiscated moments later because the plastic flagpoles posed a security risk. In Ireland's twenty-first-century Rock-Scissors-Paper game of belief systems, Health and Safety always wins.

Health and Safety has also imposed a huge security cordon outside the already sprawling Phoenix Park and people are converging having walked for up to eight kilometres to get here. Over 250,000 tickets have been distributed for the Mass, a quarter of the number that attended in 1979. Those who attended the 1979 Mass tell me it felt like a triumph. In retrospect, it was a final dip in a font of holy water before the water evaporated, leaving a residue of filth in its wake. While this 2018 Mass is a comfort to some, for many in Ireland that it's happening at all is a provocation.

With my mind wandering idly, it takes a moment to take in fully the approaching anachronism – a nun in full habit who looks about my age. Sr Deirdre Tymon tells me she is originally from Roscommon but lives and works as a Carmelite in a home for the aged and infirm in Germantown, upstate New York. She has five nieces with her, tweens and teens, all with long reddish hair, freckles and in leggings. They are taking a break, too, before the uphill march through the Parkgate Street entrance to the park.

Sr Deirdre has been in the US for twenty years and is back especially for the papal Mass. Swirling in my head is a list of questions and issues I'd like to put to her but I am here today as an observer, I tell myself, not a journalist on a deadline to file a 'colour' piece. No leading questions, I decide, just open ones.

Now that she's back, what does she make now of the mood?

'There's a real anger,' she says. The anger comes from a continued failure by Ireland's Catholic Church to address fully the clerical child sexual abuse scandal, she says. Neighbours in Co. Roscommon who used to be very pious are now 'giving out yards' about the Church. The abuse, the cover-ups, the state collusion, the apologies, the pain, the wasted lives, the broken families. In sum: the agony of grappling today with what was once Catholic Ireland. Then, without a moment's hesitation, or any leading questions from me, something pours out of this young Sister that she has clearly been reflecting on for some time.

'There is anger,' she repeats, 'but I sense it is an old anger.' Some of the anger directed outward, she thinks, is from people who are unable to rid themselves of an inner rage that has been building in themselves at something inherited from Famine or Penal times, or perhaps even earlier.

'People put the priests and bishops on a pedestal and they are angry now at themselves for doing it,' she says. 'The current younger generation is taking them down but the anger at the past remains.'

But when I look at the crowd passing me – papal Mass-goers and apathetic Dubliners out for some Sunday shopping – no one looks angry. Can you be both angry and apathetic? I wonder. Or angry yet calm? On my way here this morning I have been struck many times by the easy, gentle demeanour of the Mass-going crowd. I felt it when crammed into the Luas tram and as we glided, without a murmur of protest or a sharp remark or elbow, through the city centre to today's last stop, Smithfield. The driver, aware of the trudge down the quays ahead of us, told the passengers apologetically, 'I can get you no closer to the Pope.' Everyone chuckled as they disembarked. Like the singsong voices of the street traders, this softer spirit is part of the atmosphere of my childhood, something that I didn't notice disappearing.

These people remind me of a quieter Ireland that no longer exists. Like Sr Deirdre, I have been out of the country for two decades. The Ireland I return to is a second home now. A place of good chats, bad organization and gentle social control that I can handle for about a week, no problem. It has taken twenty years but I no longer have strong feelings about the place. It just is the way it is, and I decided it wasn't for me.

I still have very mixed feelings towards the Irish Catholic Church, but I'm no longer angry with it. That has taken a while, too. It is as it is, in seemingly terminal decline, and I have the luxury, living in Berlin, of not being exposed to it every day. I didn't have to get children baptized just to get them into a local school. Away from the daily reality of life in Ireland, and its Church, I am what you would call a grappling Catholic: unsure of church doctrine and uneasy about its effect on my life, yet better able now to appreciate the beauty, and see how many of the toxic elements I remember were as much Irish as Catholic.

As Sr Deirdre steers her nieces off towards the park, a new announcement comes over the loud speakers. With ninety minutes to Mass-time, the colour-coded routing system imposed by Health and Safety has been abandoned. Anyone can enter by any gate, regardless of their ticket. I laugh at the mild anxiety I was feeling about being turned away from the most convenient – red – entrance though I hold a green ticket. The years in Germany, where systems are imposed and must be obeyed regardless of need or common sense, have left their mark. In contrast, Ireland likes to devise systems and rules that are rarely enforced, or so flawed they are abandoned when the collective embarrassment or chaos outweighs the collective value.

And yet these deep deposits of common sense and pragmatism in our national DNA didn't prevent the Catholic Church from being able to dominate this land completely and absolutely for most of the twentieth century. Why, I wonder, did we, as a nation, let it? How did the Church establish and consolidate power with its rules and systems? Were we browbeaten into obedience, in all places, at all times, as a modern narrative goes? Or did we accommodate ourselves with it because, often, it suited us? Was our unquestioning deference to the bishop a Catholic thing or a part of our inherited colonial deference to power? Even in the modern age, by which time humans had learned to split the atom and splice DNA, why was it impossible for so long to separate the Catholic and Irish elements of our identity?

Heading into the Phoenix Park, it occurs to me that I could be on holiday in the Alps, reading a mindless thriller with a pot of tea. But instead I am here among the crowd of papal extras asking myself impossible questions. Trudging forward, under a purple sky worthy of a Cecil B. DeMille biblical epic, I feel a storm brewing.

Walking through the park I look left and right, wondering where Tony Walsh had his hideaway here for abusing boys. In journalist Mary Raftery's explosive 2002 television documentary *Cardinal Secrets*, Darren McGavin recalled the priest bringing him to this park on his ninth birthday and pushing him over on to his stomach.

'He just went straight into me and he just kept going . . . for fucking ever,' he said, recalling how the priest wiped his bottom with a purple sash and brought him home.

Catching sight of the looming steel cross, a souvenir of the 1979 papal Mass in the park, I wonder how many gathering here accept that the legacy of abuse – of children, of power – is as much a part of our country's history as the 35-metre-high cross.

At a time like this, perhaps distance is the most potent form of protest. The story of this papal visit will not be how many came to the events, but how many stayed away. The previous day, walking through the city centre, I noticed a modest crowd gathered behind barriers on O'Connell Street to wave at the passing Pope on his arrival. I walked northwards, along the east side of Parnell Square and on to North Frederick Street where a man was dancing in a spontaneous pavement protest. Blaring from speakers in his van was Australian singer Tim Minchin's explicit 'Pope Song' about allegations that Pope Benedict XVI helped cover up abuse claims during his predecessor's time as Pope. After angry references to apostates and papists, the man is now bouncing around to Minchin's lyrics that, if the Pope covered up child abuse, he's as bad as the paedophile priest.

On Parnell Square, at the Garden of Remembrance, a protest has been called in parallel to the Phoenix Park Mass. Around 5,000 people hold cards reading 'Truth, Justice, Love'. Performance poet Sarah Clancy reads:

Cherish the shame they implanted in whole generations.
Cherish the suicides – collateral damage in an otherwise virtuous struggle.
Cherish the ring-kissers who made it all possible . . .

There were lots of ring-kissers then, even in my own profession. From my bag I dig out the reissue of the September 1979 edition of the *Sunday Independent* that covered Pope John Paul's visit – reproduced nearly thirty-nine years later to mark this second papal visit – and read a headline with a now ambiguous papal exclamation: ' "I am expressing my sense of what Ireland deserves." '

'He came to us yesterday from the east across the river of time,' an unnamed reporter wrote, 'the son of Poland held out his arms for the embrace of Mother Ireland and she grasped him to her bosom as if welcoming home a long lost child.' As I read on, wearing my professional hat, I can't decide if it would be better if the reporter believed what he was writing, or didn't believe it but wrote it to capture the public mood. When I ask people who were present in 1979, many admit feeling part of an elated collective – a memory that some would now prefer to forget.

I have the perfect excuse for my absence in 1979: I was in the terrible twos and, from what I hear, a potential danger to the public. Had I been covering the event back then, though, I can easily imagine myself writing copy to capture the mood as I gauged it – while quietly seething at the social pressure to be present and enthused. Had I been there privately, maybe I would have cheered along like everyone else.

Even if the crowd knew we were not as we presented ourselves to the Polish Pope in 1979, perhaps we liked being seen as he apparently chose to see us? How would I feel now, I wonder, if I saw my face in a still image of the largest mass gatherings in Irish history – a local version of Leni Riefenstahl's *Triumph of Will*, captured in bright John Hinde colours?

I meet a shop-owner acquaintance who stayed as far away from Pope Francis as he did from his Polish predecessor. However, unlike in 1979, when strangers came in to berate him for keeping his shop open, business was brisk during the 2018 Mass. 'I wonder,' he says, laughing, 'how many of those who went along in 1979 are acting as moral arbiters of those who choose to go now?'

Saturday evening. Pope Francis has been in Dublin for about eight hours as I take my place in the Cusack Stand in Dublin's Croke Park. I'm at the Festival of Families, a concert to mark the Pope's arrival at the 2018 World Meeting of Families (WMOF). This second-ever visit of a Pope to Ireland has none of the significance of the first. Pope John Paul II's visit was staged as a triumphalist celebration of Irish spiritual exceptionalism. This visit is turning out to be more of an attestation of Irish spiritual indifference. Apart from those who have bothered to get out and protest, that is – those angry about the Church's abuse legacy, its treatment of women, and the WMOF organizers' views of family that, in their eyes, excludes those who identify as LGBTI.

Still, many Irish Catholics have embraced the five-day WMOF event as a chance to take stock and meet like-minded people in what many find an increasingly hostile atmosphere. 'Practising Catholics in Ireland are a minority now,' says Ann from Mayo, sitting between me and her nodding husband. I watch them watching the evening, drawing comfort from its messages about the value of faith and traditional families in times of crisis. They hold hands when Andrea Bocelli sings 'Nessun Dorma' and 'Ave Maria'.

Their first big cheer of the evening, with the rest of the crowd of 80,000, is to greet Pope Francis into the stadium as actor Patrick Bergin sings Leonard Cohen's 'Anthem'. After a slow circuit in his Popemobile, the Pope settles onstage. He seems slightly distracted – perhaps dazed from his ninety-minute meeting with clerical abuse survivors which ended barely an hour before his arrival here.

There are prayers, more songs and videos of traditional families discussing Catholic faith in their lives. But the final, loudest cheer of the evening is for a stirring performance of *Riverdance*. As the professional dancers onstage build to the finale, they are joined by hundreds of amateurs lining the pitch perimeter. The footwork, logistics and stage craft delight the audience. As the evening air turns chilly, they wrap themselves gladly in its cultural comfort blanket.

I leave my seat and battle through the nostalgic haze, looking for the exit, thinking of how much Ireland has changed since *Riverdance* first exploded. Back then, it was sold to us as Irish dance rediscovering its mojo, the looseness and vitality it had before killjoy Catholic bishops imposed stiff bodies and arms to avoid 'occasions of sin'. A quarter of a century later, looking back, *Riverdance* seems more like a last jig at the Catholic crossroads. A few months before *Riverdance*'s premiere in Dublin, as the interval act at the 1994 Eurovision Song Contest, Fr Brendan Smyth of the Norbertine order was charged with a range of child sexual abuse offences in Northern Ireland; by the end of that year, delays over his extradition to the North contributed to the collapse of the government in Dublin. And exactly a year after the *Riverdance* spectacle, in April 1995, Andrew Madden became the first victim of clerical child sexual abuse to go public in Ireland. Neither Ireland nor the Catholic Church were ever the same again.

The following afternoon in the Phoenix Park, I have lots to contend with: Mass-goers around me, drizzle above me and Daniel O'Donnell's voice within me. As Catholic Ireland's favourite crooner finishes his set under the papal cross, I try to shake off the raindrops – and my continuing feeling of ambivalence.

The sky is leaden with cloud but the crowd is bright with chatter. What's striking is how so many conversations – without any prompting from me – drift to the abuse legacy. A woman from Sutton, near where I grew up, tells me in a matter-of-fact voice how she often had Fr Ivan Payne, a notorious offender (Andrew Madden's abuser), at her kitchen table. When I ask her how she feels about that now, she falls silent.

Things are about to get going but even judging from ground level, it's a low turnout. Later it is estimated at just 150,000, down 85 per cent on the 1979 numbers. The largest group in Ireland today is clearly the stay-at-homes.

For me, the 2018 papal Mass is a sombre affair. In his opening words, Archbishop of Dublin Diarmuid Martin speaks of Ireland's fragile faith and the 'hope of a spring for the Irish Church . . . that does not wish to cover up the harshness of dark days'.

That prompts the most memorable moment, when Pope Francis departs from the usual opening liturgy to read a handwritten note. It is his personal, unparsed response to his meeting with clerical abuse survivors the previous day. Having listened to their stories individually, he described abusing clergy and religious as 'filth'. Improvising in the Phoenix Park, he turns the Penitential Act of the Mass back on the Church itself. Instead of asking the crowd to reflect on their sins, he asks for the Church to be forgiven: for abuses of power, abuse of conscience, sexual abuses and religious who looked away. But few notice what he's doing.

In conclusion, Francis heeds the advice given to him the day before by Clodagh Malone, a woman born in a mother and baby home and adopted at ten weeks: he asks forgiveness for 'all the times single mothers had been told that to seek their children, whom they had been separated from, was a mortal sin, and sons and daughters who were told the same'.

'This is not a mortal sin,' he says, to rising applause.

For younger ears it is an anachronistic aside but for older listeners, in particular women separated from their newborn children, it is hugely important. Many survivors say afterwards hearing these words from the Pope is a huge relief. I find myself wondering why it has taken so long – and an Argentinian Pope, a self-described 'man from the end of the earth' – to say what these damaged people needed to hear? After years of apologies, genuine and qualified, what prevented Irish bishops from making this apology?

It gets to Communion and I watch as dozens of old white men in white vestments and cellophane rain ponchos parade through the crowd in columns to distribute the host. I've seen enough and leave. It feels like a requiem – and I hate being anywhere at the end.

Catholic Ireland – adjective and noun – shaped us as a people more than we will ever know. In the last twenty-five rancorous years of scandals – pursuing overdue justice for victims and survivors of abusive clerics and religious – there has been little time or capacity to reflect on the trauma that remains.

One ascendant camp of Irish society rejoices at Catholic Ireland's slide; the other camp, once in the majority, mourns its decline. Between these camps, though, I see many silent people, as bewildered by the fall as the rise. When I ask these people about the recent past, I hear what sounds like the same uneasy silence that's in my own mind. Something about this past is gnawing at me. Despite full exposure, as a member of the last generation to have a full Irish Catholic childhood, I have a very shaky grasp on Roman Catholicism. I feel too young to grasp the sorrowful mystery that was Catholic Ireland, or carry any significant scars, yet old enough to feel its lingering effects.

Two decades living in Germany has given me distance – and an idea. I wonder would it be possible to apply to our Irish Catholic story some principles of German *Vergangenheitsbewältigung* – the process of coming to terms with the past? The basic rule underlying that tonguetwister of a word was learned the hard way by Germany in the last century: you cannot be blamed for a past beyond your reach, but that does not absolve you of responsibility to try and understand it, either. I want to understand how my Catholic past went from rigid reality to vanishing act – now you see it, now you don't. To do that, though, I need to understand how Catholic Ireland rose to glory and shrivelled up in shame. Until I do that, I cannot have a proper parting.

PART ONE

The Leaning Tower of Piety

1.   The feathers of scandal

'Beneath the trees where nobody sees
They'll hide and seek as long as they please . . .'

Jimmy Kennedy and John W. Bratton, 'The Teddy Bears' Picnic'

Dead leaves follow me through Edenmore, the wind carrying them on a final, scratchy dance. It's a cold January day and, somewhere nearby, I hear the ice-cream truck on an optimistic round, kerb-crawling for trade. The warbling melody takes me back thirty years, echoing through Edenmore, winter or summer. The tune's pitch, I always noticed, is distorted by wind and motion – and now by memory. I've always disliked 'The Teddy Bears' Picnic', particularly the creepy lyrics by Omagh native Jimmy Kennedy. In hindsight, I hate it even more.

If you go down in the woods today
You're sure of a big surprise
If you go down in the woods today
You'd better go in disguise!

I pass my old primary school St Malachy's, a three-storey concrete bunker. Opposite is St Eithne's Girls' School and the local pub, The Concorde, which has now outlived its grander, aircraft namesake by twenty years. It occurs to me that I've never been inside, reminding me how I have always felt a sense of belonging and not belonging to this place.

I was raised, one of five children, in an in-between place. Our family home was built on the outskirts of Raheny, a suburban village on the north side of Dublin. Our street of private houses was built around the corner from the Dublin Corporation's 1960s housing development named Edenmore. At St Malachy's in Edenmore, I sat alongside boys from the corporation houses. I didn't really fit in. I was bookish, not sporty. I liked serving at Mass. I didn't understand the rules of the street as they did. The Edenmore boys and I never quite clicked. The class question was there, but unspoken.

My tenuous sense of connection to Edenmore has lessened further after two decades away. And yet here I am, walking streets that have always been both familiar and strange: Edenmore Avenue, Edenmore Drive, Edenmore Gardens . . . almost 1,000 plain houses with pebble-dash facades.

I keep walking and thinking. I pass a shrine to Our Lady for victims of the 1981 nightclub fire that killed forty-eight people, and then enter a park that was once a landfill site. The grass here gets waterlogged when it rains heavily. Who knows what's under there? I always meant to ask more.

There is a lot buried in Edenmore that I have always meant to ask about. Above all, the unfinished business of our past. When I raise it, people say it's ancient history or didn't affect them. Sometimes I sense a gap between the awful facts they mention in passing and their matter-of-fact tone. Something happened here that didn't affect people. Or it did affect them and they're not interested, not able or not willing to talk. I'm here to give it a final go.

St Monica's Church is an elongated prism of brick, glass and tile that once had seven weekend Masses and full pews. But in the late 1990s, things flipped from religious parish to secular neighbourhood. Today the church capacity has been reduced, and still the three weekend Masses are half-empty, attended mainly by older people who won't be here in ten or twenty years' time. Attendance is dropping so fast that, at some Masses, the brass memorial plaques on the pews outnumber the attendees. People come and go, as much out of habit and social outlet as faith. Even Christmas Mass two weeks previously was a dispiriting affair: a sparse crowd, fluorescent lights that cast a curious green glow, a three-sentence sermon.

As I gaze at the building, I'm wondering why the slump here happened so fast, and with so little fuss. And will anything be left here in twenty years' time? Does anyone here care? Before this part of my past dies, I would like to know what finished it off. Not to apportion blame or pronounce sentence, just to understand.

St Monica's was only supposed to be a temporary church but, over half a century later, it's still in use. Monday morning Mass is just finishing as I enter. With its blond wood benches and pink carpet, it's more functional than frills. And yet, when I allow it, I notice how much emotion this place stirs in me. The church is steeped in memory, particularly of my time as an altar boy.

I walk up through the church and through a door to the left of the altar into the low-ceilinged sacristy. A modest space of drawers and cupboards, seeing the yellow marble-effect counter top prompts the first flashback. My first panicked taste of alcohol: a careless altar boy trying to sup up the Mass wine I'd spilled on the counter before it dripped on to the floor.

Leading off the sacristy and down a narrow corridor behind the altar, a space like the backstage of a theatre, I reach the dim, disused area that was once the altar boys' changing room. It's like a passage tomb now. There are no altar boys. Even the altar girl phenomenon has died out. And yet everything else is still here, covered in dust and grime. In the corner is the small nook with a sink, used to fix up the altar flowers. Whenever I was in here on my own, I liked to mess with the green blocks (the trade name Oasis pops back into my head) used to arrange the flowers. When saturated with water, the green substance held the flowers in place and kept them alive. Dried out, you could stick your finger into a block or break off a corner and rub it between your fingers. With very little effort, something that seemed firm could be reduced to dust. It's an apt image for what has happened here: this church is dried out, a block of dust held together by habit.

Once, St Monica's was just another suburban Dublin parish that looked salt-of-the-earth solid. For me, the oasis began to crumble in the summer of 1997. I was working in New York City on a J1 student visa when I received a letter from my younger brother. I found it recently. Scrawled and ripped from a spiral notepad, scraggly bits of paper at the top, a bulletin of form-follows-function urgency:

Father McGennis has been given an 18-month jail sentence and another 9-month sentence to run concurrently for indecently assaulting a 13-year-old girl in hospital in 1960 . . . I have to say I don't know how I feel about it.

Over twenty years later, ambivalence remains in Edenmore about Paul McGennis, his past and how it caught up with him during his time here. Three decades before he came to us, as a young chaplain in Our Lady's Hospital for Sick Children in Crumlin, he had sexually abused and taken obscene pictures of a young patient called Marie Collins. The abuse ruined her life for decades. But then she came forward to press charges, one of Ireland's first clerical sexual abuse survivors to do so. Another woman from another parish did the same. The McGennis conviction helped tip Catholic Ireland, already primed for collapse, into a tailspin – and St Monica's with it.

There are just two slim blue files on St Monica's in the Dublin diocesan archives. Housed in a wing of Holy Cross College, the former seminary for Dublin, the archive is a treasure trove of a vanished world. Even the sparse documents held on my parish speak volumes about midcentury Irish Catholicism, its untroubled confidence, its ways and means of establishing itself on the map, and in people's minds.

More than a century before it became a Dublin suburb – and parish – the Parliamentary Gazetteer of 1844–45 describes Raheny and neighbouring districts rather grandly as 'brilliant and beautiful, at once in natural luxuriance, in artificial decoration and in free command of a most lovely and gorgeous landscape'.

Behind Dollymount beach were meadows, orchards and quiet country roads linking the grand houses associated with famous names like the brewing dynasties Guinness and Jameson, and hotelier Thomas Gresham.

That all changed in 1954, diocesan files show, when Dublin Corporation's chief planner sent Archbishop John Charles McQuaid a full report into the corporation's development plans for Edenmore, including details of compulsory purchase orders. At the time the Catholic Church was the main provider of health and education in the Republic, and this correspondence is an indicator of how this close co-operation with the state functioned in its first decades of independence. The nuns came first, in 1956. The Poor Servants of the Mother of God bought land to build a convent. It's still there, with an adjoining nursing home. Then in 1962, Dublin Corporation sold the archdiocese sites in Edenmore for schools and a church, at cost price: £4,575.

A few days later I visit the Dublin City Archives on Pearse Street to view the plans for the rest of Edenmore: ambitious, unrealized blueprints on crunchy tracing paper for a library, a circular 'sunken piazza', and a monumental cinema with a tall clock tower. None of these were built, as architectural optimism yielded to cost-conscious reality. By the late 1960s the real Edenmore had emerged: a windy, open-air shopping precinct and terraces of corporation houses on a triangular area, bordered by three main roads. Families moved out here from inner-city tenements, others were new arrivals from outside Dublin.

At the heart of the new community was a site for a permanent church. It was never built and neither city nor diocesan archives have any blueprints for this phantom structure. In July 1966 Archbishop McQuaid consecrated the modest temporary structure after St Monica. There are no details on file about that occasion but the diocesan papers contain a programme for a school consecration on 17 December 1968. It spells out the pecking order of that time: the architect was to hand the key of St Malachy's Boys' School to the archbishop who would, in turn, hand the key to an unnamed Department of Education official. The state had funded around 85 per cent of the school capital cost – but it was built on church land, albeit purchased at cost after notification from Dublin Corporation's chief planner. The transition from unspoiled meadow to concrete reality called St Monica's is more than just an example of close church–state co-operation. Such a term sounds mysterious and abstract: this was Irish people – mostly men – in various institutions, working closely to establish structures of control in a new community.

After the handing over of the key, the programme for the school consecration instructs parishioners to proceed to a Mass in St Monica's Church (*'Rise as Archbishop enters and kneel as he passes up centre aisle . . . '*).

From then on, only one topic dominates the diocesan files on St Monica's – money. Or, more precisely, what to do about the £58,564 overdraft the new parish had inherited. In anxious letters to the archbishop Fr Foley, the first parish priest, tells the archbishop how the bank is 'pressing for regular payments' from the new, indebted parish. Salvation comes in a glossy brochure, a copy of which is still in the file, carrying the name 'Planned Giving' and laying out plans for a door-to-door envelope collection. The brochure, to be delivered to every household in the parish, explains in friendly but firm terms what is to happen in order to make giving a planned part of life in St Monica's. The text urges parishioners to open their homes to a visiting local man who 'comes as a friend . . . [and] does not come to beg, nor to pry into your affairs . . . His purpose is to help you, if you need help, in deciding how much you should give.'

Considering this is a voluntary collection, the brochure has remarkably robust views on how much to contribute.

[A gift to the church] should have its rightful place in our budget . . . no gift can be worthy unless it costs us an effort – it must be something we will miss . . . Our gift should reflect our Catholic beliefs – that all we have comes from God; that we are only returning what is His; that we are responsible for the use of His gifts.

I'm reminded of the line from a fundraiser in the Eddie Murphy film *Coming to America*: 'We're happy to get the kind of money that jingles, but we'd rather the kind that folds.'

Reading further into these files, and copious follow-up reports, the Dublin Archdiocese's new parish model worked here as follows: it acquires land at cost from the city, builds a church with the bank's money, transfers the overdraft to the local parish, leans on parishioners to make sacrifices to pay off the debt, while insisting the buildings they are paying off – and the money they are using to do so – belong to God, or his earthly representatives.

The brochure also tells the tale of 1960s gender roles, with a photograph of smiling Edenmore women, sitting at school desks, who organized 'Loyalty Suppers'. 'Their task is now finished and our men take over,' the brochure says. The men aren't squeezed into desks for their photograph, I note. Instead they look dynamic as they pose in the church in their winter coats, perhaps on their way to visit the homes, as promised. How many of those men, I wonder, had compassionate eyes and ears and could sense people's struggles raising their young children, paying their corporation rent, and now facing financial demands from the parish?

The record shows that 965 families signed pledge cards and received a box of dated envelopes. It also flags 120 'non-participating families' who would require further attention. Fr Foley invited the archbishop to visit St Monica's volunteers for a 'pep-talk'.

'Very unwise procedure,' noted McQuaid on the letter. 'Has always failed. Follow Wells pattern.' This is a reference to the Wells Organization, a US-based professional fundraising outfit engaged by the Dublin Archdiocese – including for the St Monica's 'Planned Giving' drive. A visit by the archbishop might impress the locals, but it could shatter illusions, too. The brochure's familiar tone implies the local fundraising campaign was grassroots. The implementation was, but operating to an outside template bought in from outside and imposed from above.

Reading the slim St Monica's file is illuminating, showing a professional approach to fundraising of which few in the parish were aware. In its final report the Wells Organization consultant, who oversaw planning meetings in St Monica's, praises the local men recruited by the parish priest. They went door to door, as the 'real core of the Church [with] a deep sense of fellowship'. The file doesn't contain anything to indicate the Wells Organization's cut of the proceeds for its services.

After an enthusiastic start, not everything went to plan with 'Planned Giving' in St Monica's. Actual contributions fell short of pledges by a half. The archdiocese warned Fr Foley about the 'falling standard of giving' and suggested he agree to further professional fundraising drives.

Sitting in the Diocesan Archives, I don't know what I expected to find in the St Monica's files – but it wasn't this. Perhaps I was naïve to expect records of parish concerns, hopes or ambitions. Instead the folders contain a series of financial reports and a pile of letters that accompanied cheques for supplementary parish collections: Lateran Sunday (to support the Pontifical University in Rome); Holy Cross College, Clonliffe (to support the local seminary); Northern Ireland; Pakistan Relief; the Diocesan Central Fund . . . In their cover letters the priests note the level of contributions by per-thousand of population, suggesting that someone in Archbishop's House maintained a parish donation league table. Perhaps there was a diocesan map with green and red pins.

St Monica's parishioners, many raising large families on low incomes and struggling to make ends meet, were spared the humiliations of old: the priest reading out each parishioner's contribution from the pulpit, starting with the most generous and working his way down. The modern practice was more subtle and professionalized peer pressure with a local face. The message: *money may be tight, but that is no excuse.*

Edenmore's corporation house tenants were allowed to buy their homes eventually. The dwindling numbers of Mass-going parishioners, meanwhile, are still tenants in the church that they have paid for. Of course, someone had to pay the bills in St Monica's. (Today the parish debt is paid off but the envelope collection continues, alongside two Mass collections, to pay the priests, maintain their houses and cars, and run the parish, though with ever-diminishing returns.)

At half a century's distance, the 'Planned Giving' campaign imposed by the archdiocese on St Monica's looks to me more like planned taking. What traces, I wonder, has this early power play left on local parishioners?

There are few left in St Monica's who have seen everything, but the women of the parish choir, now in their seventies, have been here since the start. Sitting in a nearby shopping centre, far busier than the Sunday Mass minutes earlier, we find seats in a cafe and make small talk. As we get settled and pour our tea, I get the impression that no one's ever asked them what they've seen in St Monica's. Surrounded by six chatty women, I abandon any hope of asking questions and instead just listen. Soon they're rattling through a half-century cast of clerics: the snobby priest, the fussy priest, the drinking priest, the gentle priest, the sexy priest, the womanizing priest, the abusing priest and the obsessive-compulsive priest. They're mad for their priests. These women, Irish mothers in the 1960s and 1970s, took them all in their stride. They were an in-between generation: more free-spirited than their parents, who would never criticize 'God's holy anointed', yet still creatures of an upbringing and culture far more rigorous and hierarchical than my own.

This Ireland, disappearing over the horizon yet still within reach, was a world of church obedience, tacit signals and unwritten rules.

The rule-givers for these women were often the nuns who taught them. One of the choir women, Brenda, recalls one of the Sisters' many warnings, particularly: 'Giving scandal is like opening a pillow of feathers.' The saying is new to me but the women nod in familiarity; it was just one of many pronouncements religious used to cow and contain them.

The tales pour forth. Happy memories – and there are many – are soon punctuated by less happy ones. Without any prompting from me, talk turns to the humiliations, big and small, these women experienced at the hands of St Monica's passing padre cadre. The tales would be hilarious if they weren't so depressing. Like how the choir, of voluntary singers, was fired by a priest for 'disobedience'. Their crime: raising funds to replace the organ without asking his permission.

Brenda remembers another brush with disobedience. When she dared to demand the renovation of decrepit school rooms, she got a triple dressing-down. First, from the parish priest; then a general admonishment from the pulpit by another priest; and, finally, via barbed remarks from a visiting bishop, who had been told in advance who she was. Decades later, she still remembers sitting on her bed at home, weeping with frustration.

The other women nod in sympathy, and recognition, and tell similar stories. Theirs are shocking tales of everyday callousness and emotional violence told by the mothers of today's #metoo generation.

Did anyone push back?

Kay suggests 'somebody could have stood up and said no', but isn't sure who that somebody should have been.

'Nobody ever did, that's why it went as it did,' she says quietly.

The huge power discrepancy between priest and parishioners, the roots of control in parishes like St Monica's, was viewed as an order so natural it was rarely discussed or even consciously noted. It was just the way it was. Most of the women gathered here finishing off their tea realize, in hindsight, that the relationship between priests and people was based on an exchange of power and trust. Once abuse of the people's trust went too far – with the McGennis revelations – the clergy's power was undermined terminally. But everything that is clear in hindsight was less clear at the time.

The structures that once seemed impervious to challenge lie in ruins, but they have left a wincing legacy. In a resigned voice Rita says that there was 'a lot of fear in the Church. That's where all this anger came from, a huge backlash because they had such control.'

As they gather their things these women, all still practising Catholics, say their faith remains strong but private. A clergy that once dominated them now seems pitifully weak. Looking back, Brenda wonders if the priests were so arrogant because they were so revered.

'Weren't we very stupid,' she says, 'to believe everything they told us?'

Behind her bright tone, I hear pain.

Back at St Monica's Church, the morning Mass-goers are long gone, as is the priest. But sacristan Bridie Kelly is still here, just as she's been for fifty years. With salty Dublin humour to match her accent, she has mastered the art of motherly chastisement that gets the best results with Irish priests. The foolish priests cross her, the smart ones know to not even try.

As she tidies the sacristy, she tells me how a boy from St Malachy's school asked her recently, 'Missus, is this your church?'

' "Why?" says I.

'Says he, "Because you're always here." '

Bridie's seen it all here: an IRA funeral with an all-female armed guard of honour; a bomb scare; robbers who dragged her by her neck through the church, looking for the collection money. She stepped in once when a priest was a no-show for Mass, leading a prayer service with little fuss. She stepped in, too, when another priest's housekeeper ran out of his house, screaming that she had seen the Virgin Mary on the stairs. Her voice lowers when talk turns to 1997, when parishioners learned why Fr Paul McGennis was gone for good.

'We knew something was up, as he came and went from the parish, but few asked questions. We knew it was permanent when his name disappeared from his Confession box.'

Paul McGennis pleaded guilty to four counts of indecent assault. After an appeal he served nine months in prison. But the case has never really ended. Not for the now elderly priest, not for his victims, not for his sister – a teacher in a local school – and certainly not for the parishioners of St Monica's.

When her case became public, Marie Collins, abused by McGennis in 1960, told me she had begged Archbishop Desmond Connell to send counsellors to St Monica's. He never bothered.

'They left it up to poor old Fr Geaney,' says Bridie, sitting in the empty sacristy.

Michael Geaney was the parish priest at the time, a silver-haired, soft-spoken Corkman who struggled to impose any authority on Paul McGennis. He knew his curate was a strange one, but not a serious problem. Though McGennis got on famously with children, his demeanour and body language helped him keep adults out of his life – and his house. Not even his fellow priests got past his front door. After underestimating his curate, it fell to Michael Geaney to explain the unfolding McGennis horror to parishioners.

I was in New York at the time, but Bridie watched Fr Geaney's ordeal up close: 'He started to cry and ran out the back there, I had to run out after him into the field and bring him back. He nearly threw up. It was a terrible time, an awful time.'

I was born in 1977 and, though I worked alongside him closely as an altar boy, I remember little about Paul McGennis during his time in St Monica's. He was a shy, balding man in his mid-fifties, with greasy hair, thick glasses and a chronic inability to meet anyone's gaze. He was notorious among parishioners for his long, muttered Masses. Someone once said to me, 'If you want to understand the concept of eternity, go sit through one of his sermons.'

I actually quite liked his sermons. As I mentioned, I was a bookish child and, to me, his sermons' ideas about faith and God and the world – theology for beginners – appealed to me more than the other priests' more pastoral fare. Like the man himself, McGennis Masses were at odds with their surroundings.

Though he liked a long Mass, Paul McGennis also liked to cut it fine with time, roaring up behind the church at the last minute in a white VW Beetle, usually filled with children. As he readied himself for Mass, I often opened the sacristy door and watched them playing with the car lights, wipers, radio. Why were they not coming into Mass, I wondered, and where were their parents?

I saw the same children – or were they different ones? – when my mother sent me to his house to get his signature on papers for the school board of management, of which both were members. He never answered the door, a child always did. Looking into the dim hallway, I saw more children dangling from the bannister or looking down from the upstairs landing. How many had he taken in? I felt as little connection to these children, mostly girls, as I did to the boys from the corporation houses in my class at school. One part of my brain found it all deeply strange, but another part accepted it. The set-up felt like the 1980s television sitcom *Diff'rent Strokes*, but with an edge rather than laughs.

My younger brother felt the same. In his 1997 letter, he said that he suspected 'there was more to it than just those two offences'. He wrote:

I always remember the [*surname omitted*] and [*surname omitted*] kids in his house regularly. I knew about this two months ago but didn't want to say anything lest I slander the man. It's quite a sordid affair but at the same time I find it very interesting how different people are reacting.

My brother doesn't remember now who had what reaction then. By the time I returned from New York in September, ready to learn more about the greatest scandal ever to rock our sleepy parish, I was surprised and disappointed to find it had been buried. McGennis was not referred to, as if he – and the scandal – had never happened.

I'm curious to know more, at two decades' distance, about the motivation to close down debate.

Were people afraid to scatter the nuns' metaphorical feathers of scandal – or were they concerned some of the feathers might blow back on them?

2.   The lies we tell ourselves

'. . . he had no problem with little boys but, "if he had
a problem, it was with little girls . . ." '

Murphy Report

They call Des Lynch the Pope of Edenmore. Born in 1926 in Kilmes-
san, Co. Meath, he's lived locally since 1963. You'll still find him
sitting at the back of the church after Sunday Mass, fresh and full of
chat. I meet him in his living room, surrounded by photographs and
memories.

Des helped set up the local GAA club and approached the first parish priest, Fr Foley, about using a field behind the church as a pitch.
He doesn't know if Fr Foley even owned the land, but in those days
you went to a priest on matters like this.

'Fr Foley told us "possession is nine-tenths of the law" and we had
goalposts in that evening,' laughs Des.

He raised six children and saw the parish hold together despite the
challenges of drugs, joyriding and crime. Those all made the papers,
he says, less so the community spirit that was always stronger. Until
the McGennis saga triggered a slump in Mass attendance – and the
door-to-door church collection he once helped organize.

'The money went down from £900 to £200 or £300, and that was
a lot,' he says.

He remembers challenging Paul McGennis about the children in
his car, but more as a warning than an accusation: 'I says to him, "All
it'd take is one of them to say something . . ." '

Des remembers Paul McGennis not meeting his gaze and saying
the children were minding the car for him.

'And I didn't think of anything else,' says Des.

Sacristan Bridie Kelly clashed regularly with Paul McGennis over the young local girls in his car, his house and his life. She was furious that he allowed them to count the weekly collection money.

'He'd say, "Ah, Bridie, they could be standing on a street corner," ' she remembers. 'I told him, "They should be in bed." But I never saw the man doing anything, that's the truth of God.'

Goretti Groves remembers the priest, who lived next door to her, as a rude man who would knock you down reversing out of his drive if you weren't careful. Her mother-in-law complained to Fr Geaney about children in the McGennis house during school hours, she says, but got nowhere. Sitting in her kitchen, Goretti can't understand why I'm feeling uneasy about both seeing and not seeing what was going on with Paul McGennis.

'We were closer to him than you are, living right next door, and there's no way in the world . . . I wouldn't blame myself,' she says.

She was often annoyed by the girls sitting on the priest's wall, running in and out of the house, laughing and joking. She says she never let her children into his house but isn't sure why not.

Grazing my way through the biscuits she's placed before me, I tell her I'm not interested in blame but a wider understanding of the time. I'm not quite sure I'm even convincing myself, though, so I decide to leave her kitchen and continue my walk.

As I leave, she repeats her advice to me – at least I think it was addressed to me – 'I wouldn't blame myself for something I didn't know was going on.'

I continue my circuit of Edenmore, somewhere I rarely walked before, on the hunt for answers to questions that have me here and not in Berlin. If the McGennis past doesn't bother people here, who have lived with it, maybe that should be good enough for me. To my outsider's eye, though, the approach here to dealing with the past resembles not dealing with it.

For over forty years Breda Doyle has helped run the St Monica's youth club. Back in the early 1990s, young local girls began telling her stories about how Fr McGennis took them swimming – but made them change in his house. For Breda the girls' tales were strange but she thought no more of them until her sister, on hearing them, urged Breda to report her concerns to the parish. Breda told the young curate, Fr Eugene Taaffe. After a year and no progress, she says she pressed him again after Mass in the sacristy.

'He said to me, "Get out! I'm sick listening to you. I told you I reported it!"' says Breda in her living room, her voice trembling at the memory.

'I said to him, "I'm going, Fr Taaffe, to the Eastern Health Board to report it. I hope you can sleep at night, I know I will."'

She filed a report to the health board around the same time as Marie Collins was filing her complaint to the Garda and the net closed on Paul McGennis.

When I track down Fr Taaffe in his current parish, he says he has no memory of that confrontation.

Breda had general concerns about children hanging around the house, Taaffe recalls, things he says now were 'common knowledge in the neighbourhood' at the time.

'At no stage, with God as my judge, did Breda ever say anything specific to me about Paul McGennis,' says Fr Taaffe. He says he reported the concerns, and some of his own, to parish priest Michael Geaney, who seemed either unable or unwilling to do anything. Today, with two decades' distance, Fr Taaffe says he felt trapped: between the kind but conflict-averse parish priest and McGennis, a strange loner.

Like many in the parish the late Fr Geaney viewed McGennis as odd, nothing more, says Fr Taaffe, and there was nothing more to be done.

'I feel for the people that were hurt,' he says, 'but if I had known more at the time I would have moved hell and high water to make something happen.'

Breda, still a daily Mass-goer, is as unimpressed with Fr Taaffe's memory of their conversations as she is with former McGennis neighbours she remembers approaching her quietly after he was arrested.

'They said they knew all about the children but were afraid to do anything,' she said.

The conflicting versions of what happened in Edenmore in the 1990s may never be resolved, at least not as long as the silence prevails. That silence – familiar to other parishes around Ireland – keeps a lid on discussion and inhibits reflection over who knew what about what was going on, who acted, who didn't and why.

★

Breda Doyle, by going to the health board, got attention. But others who complained to the priests got none. Some felt helpless, or power-less to speak, fearful of spreading scandal where there might have been nothing. Some had been humiliated by priests in the past, others put priests in their place. Others didn't care, or couldn't afford to. And there was the social snobbery factor, familiar even in places like Edenmore, where some children are cherished less than others.

Ask around in Edenmore even today and a sharp tone prevails when talk turns to the children who spent time in the McGennis house. They threw stones, says one woman; they called other chil-dren names, says a second; they were 'little bitches', says a third.

In Edenmore, there is no sympathy for McGennis but not much more for the minors seen most often in his company. Some thought it was nice he was bringing deprived children swimming and buying them sweets. Others say they saw nothing odd in the McGennis set-up, once it wasn't their children.

In the garden behind his house, 'John' (not his real name)* is feed-ing his pigeons in their shiny garden chalet. As he closes the door, leaving the radio blaring for them, I notice his tattoos and his wariness when I mention the name McGennis. And then he starts to talk.

He fathered thirteen children and raised them in a three-bedroom corporation house. He was an alcoholic until five years ago, he says, matter-of-factly. Everyone in Edenmore knew that some of his children – as well as children from at least two other disadvantaged families – were regular visitors to the McGennis house which was nearby. John's family all did odd jobs for McGennis: he did wall-papering and painting; his wife washed the priest's curtains. She doesn't want to talk, insisting she didn't know the priest. John didn't go to Mass, he says, but McGennis still helped them out, just as a local nun financed the roof of an extension to the family home.

'The girls were in and out of the house but never said much, I never knew anything until he was charged,' he says. 'One used to be with him. She died.'

That daughter took her life; a son died sleeping rough.

* As well as using a pseudonym for 'John' some details of his story have been changed here to protect his family's privacy.

A heavy silence lies between us as we stand in the back garden, a burden of unmanageable grief and regret – stretching right back to his early years. John is drifting back now, talking about being sent as a teenager to St Conleth's reformatory school in Daingean, Co. Offaly. He remembers cutting turf on the bog and watching a Christian Brother, 'a mad fucker', beating boys with an iron bar.

'I don't forget, but you're making me feel brutal,' he says, eyes welling up. We grew up a short walk from each other, I realize during that silence, but in different worlds. Between the deep breaths I see deep pain, violence and no language to express any of it. For me, this past is a puzzle; for him it is a deep wound. What right do I have to poke around in there?

'Mary' is one of the girls from the McGennis house. It was girls like her, from large, often struggling, families in the corporation houses, who trooped in and out and were chosen by him to 'mind' his car while he said Mass. She has mixed memories of St Monica's in the 1980s. On the one hand she remembers a close community, with people out on the streets, mothers chatting, children playing rounders. On the other hand, her memories of school are mainly the stark contrast between the nuns' behaviour towards girls like her and those from the nearby private housing estates.

'The girls from Edenmore were treated horrifically, like dirt. The girls from the private estates were treated well – and this from nuns, people of the Church,' she says.

In the 1980s Edenmore was a place of huge social problems. For the most vulnerable families, McGennis was a one-man social worker: giving children somewhere to go, bringing them to the beach, buying girls dresses and boys shoes. As a young girl, Mary felt drawn to the man in the flat navy cloth cap. Yet she knew something was wrong every time he looked at her from the corner of his eye.

'He tried to touch me on the leg, but I pushed him off. He kept away from the streetwise children like me,' she says. Instinctively, she knew not to stay around McGennis for extended periods. That spared her, but she is less sure about girls she used to know – girls, like her, reared at the bottom of the St Monica's social pecking order, but less able to look out for themselves. 'He knew which girls to pick on. My mam told us not to be going around his house, everyone knew it was weird.'

Old, buried memories flow back into her mind. Like the belt game, where McGennis would tie a belt around his waist, she says, and get the girls to swing around. She has another image of a girl with Down's syndrome bouncing happily on an upstairs bed in the McGennis house, her skirt flying up in the air.

'He was just standing there looking at her. I remember calling her down and bringing her home,' says Mary.

Still, Mary insists that she witnessed no sexual or physical abuse. Her strangest memory is of the discovery she made in the sitting room one day, when a sudden movement of light drew her attention to the wall.

'He'd drilled a hole right through to the back sitting room and covered it with some kind of glass dome or lens,' she said. 'There was a wire coming out the back and a bulky camera. I remember saying to a friend, "He's some kind of weirdo pervert!" and the two of us laughing as we ran up the road to the park.'

Mary still lives in Edenmore and, when she looks back on her time around Paul McGennis as a young girl in the 1980s, it is with a muted concern and sense of distance. She still has her faith and knows of many good priests and nuns, she says, but stays away from St Monica's. She likes where she lives but is wary of a place where the social hierarchy left girls from homes like hers as fair game for a priest.

'He knew to pass up those higher up the ranks,' she said. Even in a working-class parish like St Monica's the link between social status and the likelihood of facing clerical abuse is complicated and causes conflict, Mary says. 'So we'd rather just brush it under the carpet.'

And what does Mary make of Bridie Kelly's fears about the girls McGennis had helping him with the church collection?

'If I'm one hundred per cent honest with you, me and my friends used to rob him,' says Mary. 'He'd have us counting the Mass collection and we'd take a pound or two out of the packets and buy sweets. We'd be delighted because we wouldn't see sweets from one end of the month to another.'

The house once occupied by Paul McGennis is now home to Fr Dave Lumsden, a popular local priest some call the glue holding together a frayed parish. In the living room – freshly decorated and with a furniture showroom feel – he talks about how familiar Edenmore is to him.

He grew up in Walkinstown in south-west Dublin and remembers the spoken and unspoken of the working-class Catholic childhood. The memories people discuss, he says, are the quiet generosity and community spirit, sharing the little there was. Memories less discussed include social control, alcoholism and violence. Authority and power from outside was feared and Fr Dave can still recall the name of the local school attendance officer, Mr Rice, who could send mitching boys to Artane Industrial School. 'If you don't behave,' Fr Dave's parents would say, 'we'll send you to Artane.' For generations of Dubliners, Artane was a byword for hell, a threat existing in that limbo of knowing and not knowing. Other parts of the country have their own Artanes.

'We knew nothing of Artane but my parents knew it was a place of brutality,' he says. 'They weren't threatening Butlin's on us.'

The priest is familiar, too, with the unspoken language of Irish clerical sexual abuse of children. While posted to Ballyfermot he helped young local men file criminal complaints against the serial abuser Fr Tony Walsh. The men were clearly grateful for his support: they stayed in the Church and Fr Dave baptized their children. It's not hard to see why he earned their respect. Fr Dave is a different sort of priest: a late vocation, street-smart and nobody's fool. He is wary of talking about the McGennis era. Perhaps because he knows he came too late to fix anything.

Of all the priests to send to St Monica's immediately after the McGennis trauma, the archdiocese chose to send Fr Eddie Griffin. Fr Griffin had no interest in discussing the case, working through the damage done or even attempting a fix. Quite the opposite: Eddie Griffin, who followed Michael Geaney as parish priest, was the least likely man in the entire archdiocese to be interested in this difficult job. In the 1980s, when Marie Collins had plucked up the courage to reveal what Paul McGennis had done to her twenty years earlier, she confided in her local priest. That priest was Fr Griffin. He dismissed her story of abuse, she says, and set her back ten years. In that lost decade, Paul McGennis was in circulation in Edenmore.

Eddie Griffin divided opinion in Edenmore. Some found him

cheery, and are thankful for how he renovated the run-down church. Others resent him for, as one parishioner told me, 'buying new carpet and brushing the McGennis thing under it'.

Fr Griffin, now retired, declined my interview requests.

St Monica's parish rose and fell in tandem with the recent fortunes of the official Church. If it is to be revived it will, like the Church itself, need to be led by the people. There are many in Edenmore trying to do their best for the area. But this time it's on their terms.

Theresa Kelly is an example of this local leadership. She is the kind of person every neighbourhood needs: engaged and energetic, with a campaigner's impatience for social injustice and political bullshit. On another trip to Dublin we sit together in 'Special Occasions', her pop-up shop in Edenmore Shopping Centre, surrounded by donated Communion dresses. This year's Communion dress trend, I read in a newspaper a few weeks previously, is 'Audrey Hepburn'. However, the people who come here have no time, or money, for new trends. Instead they come here for one of the donated dresses that are all new, Theresa says, and just as beautiful. Locals can kit out their children for their big day for €50 – or nothing, if they can't afford it.

It's an idea Theresa had after overhearing two mothers of Communion-age children discussing money lenders. She isn't a Mass-goer, thanks in part to a wounding remark from a priest years ago. But Theresa says her religion is 'rock solid' and she loves bouncing ideas off Fr Dave to rebuild the community. Theresa and Fr Dave have worked together on a memorial tree for the dead; a church plaque for stillborn babies; children's Christmas hampers; and a sensory garden for the elderly and disabled.

After two frozen decades, good things are happening again in Edenmore. Rather than expecting top-down priest action, and parishioner obedience, Theresa and others are doing things themselves. Her phone never stops ringing as we chat. She wants to give back. As much as if not more than many Mass-goers, she is living the Christian spirit.

'We're trying to get away from what happened down there,' she says, nodding towards the nearby house once occupied by Paul McGennis.

Is it possible, I ask her, to revisit that time and resolve the unresolved?

'I don't know if too much time has elapsed to go back there, or if people bottling it up need to let it out.'

You'll find May Gray at the back of St Monica's Church selling Catholic newspapers and magazines. Today, though, I'm sitting in her kitchen and we're studying an old parish directory from the early 1990s. Printed just before the McGennis revelations, the directory is evidence of how everything here was once linked to the parish church, from the cub scouts to the horticultural society. Now in her eighties, May has the quiet, kind but firm air that reminds me of nuns I've known. Over tea and buns, she recalls living opposite Paul McGennis.

From her front window she remembers looking over and seeing children sitting on his wall, waiting for him to come back. Her only thought at the time: *That man is going to get himself into shocking trouble.* She is clear about one thing: she never thought he was the problem.

'I just thought he should have some cop-on. I didn't suspect, in my innocence . . .' she says.

As she sips hot tea she explains her view of the last two decades. The revelations never rattled her own faith, but she sees how they catalysed the general decline in Mass attendance.

'People were looking for an opportunity to put their coats on and go,' she says. 'They blamed it all on the priests, everyone was painted with the same brush.'

A day later I bump into her again. She's been thinking about our conversation and worries she was too negative. The Church is struggling now, she says, but she's confident it will come back stronger. But she's not sure what the Church has to sort out, or where it needs to begin.

She urges me not to reproach myself over the Paul McGennis episode.

'Get that out of your head because, in the first place, you were young and no one would have believed you if you had known anything,' she says. 'I wouldn't dwell on it. What's to be gained?'

★

St Monica's is no different to dozens of parishes around Ireland that have known abusing clerics, and it has at least three histories. In one history, McGennis was just one more thing piled on top of deprivation, unemployment, drugs, limited social services. In another history, the sparse diocesan files documenting St Monica's early days are all about money, debt and control. And St Monica's third, unwritten history is one of kindness, comfort and compassion. The parish church filled the many gaps left by the Irish state. Many of the priests and nuns here – on this locals agree – were kind, patient and selfless people. Others were strange, while some were nursing serious problems.

And there were many abusing and abusive priests in Edenmore besides Paul McGennis. A man tells me all about another priest who I remember, who often ejaculated all over him. He is happy for me to tell his story in detail but, when I am unwilling to pay for it, rescinds permission. A well-known Irish figure who grew up in our parish tells me how a priest groped her sister as they were gathered around their dying mother, but she'd rather not go on the record. Another woman from Edenmore I meet by chance, now living outside Ireland, tells me how the same priest groped her when she was fourteen, then refused to marry her in the church because she admitted not going to Mass. She decided to push back.

'I told him that I was doing the church wedding for my mother and gran. "We'll all be there and if you're not, I'll tell them what you did to me." I'm not proud of what I said, but the priest was there.'

The more stones of the past I lift, the more emerges from below. The more you look the more you see, but who wants to go back willingly to struggle with what they heard and didn't hear, saw and didn't see, knew and didn't know?

St Monica's is unique in some ways yet typical in others for what was once Catholic Ireland. From wounding remarks to far worse, the traumas of abuse – verbal, physical, sexual as well as abuses of power – hang over the parish and its residents, past and present.

When I returned to Edenmore from New York in 1997 the McGennis episode had appeared buried. And yet, twenty years on, no one has forgotten.

I have been away so long, always predestined to leave, that I may have forfeited my right to probe the motivations of those who stayed, to intrude on their pain. Perhaps my preoccupation with the McGennis episode is about me and not Edenmore. Judging by the apathy towards the Church, the empty pews on Sundays, people have made up their minds and voted with their feet. Nothing to see here. How much truth, I wonder, can a parish like St Monica's handle? The people here have been through a lot. Sometimes it's easier – necessary – to keep going rather than looking deeper. But at what cost?

After the McGennis debacle, no one from the archdiocese ever came out to explain what had happened, or offered help with the pain. Archbishop Diarmuid Martin tells me he once visited, much later, and delivered a homily. Perhaps it helped. He seems to think so. Honouring the archdiocese's broken promise to Marie Collins – of therapists and other assistance – would have been better. The moment for that has passed now.

The parish of St Monica's Edenmore lives on, but not as John Charles McQuaid intended: tied tightly around the church and serving priests. Even a relatively modern, urban parish like ours felt the tractor beam of clerical control, radiating out and manifesting itself in people's lives, framing what they saw, or felt they could say.

Edenmore has produced drug dealers and joyriders, but also sculptors and several journalists. People respond to their past in a way that is best for them. I've been gone from this place for two decades, but it won't let me go. Because it has changed me, and I'm not yet sure how. Our parish experienced a kind of violence that leaves direct and indirect traces which, in turn, colour memories of the past. I wonder, if we put these pieces together – in Edenmore and beyond – would a more complex picture of Ireland's recent past emerge than the one currently on offer?

The black and white, us-and-them narrative – created immediately in the aftermath of abuse revelations – was natural, necessary and even useful. It shattered taboos and allowed criminal investigation and state inquiries into clerical sexual abuse, and those who tried to cover it up. But such inquiries, in particular establishing the guilt of individuals, are limited by their very nature. They are no substitute for revisiting the past collectively, to explore how the pain and shame experienced then lingers on in us today. Going back challenges us to face what US therapist Elvin Semrad described as the greatest source of human suffering: 'the lies we tell ourselves'.

A precondition for a meaningful conversation about our past is admitting that this past is ours, all of it. But even if we agreed to own our Catholic past – and, as I will learn, that is a big 'if' for some – do we even know what this past entails? I certainly don't. I thought Edenmore was the beginning of the story but now I realize it's time to head back to the real start.

3. Into the Celtic mist

'For all we Irish, inhabitants of the world's edge, are disciples
of Saints Peter and Paul . . . and we accept nothing outside
the evangelical and apostolic teaching.'

St Columbanus

The old stone ruin, standing in the cold Dingle drizzle, is not the
most hospitable place to start a journey into Ireland's Christian
past. A more obvious place would have been the Book of Kells in
Trinity College, Dublin. But like many native Dubliners, I avoided
what I felt was a tourist attraction and I was thirty-six when I finally
went. I stood in front of the massive panels showing illuminated
pages from the book on the walls of the visitor centre before shuffling
into a darkened room. And there it was, finally, in front of me in a
glass display case – a small, dull, brown book looking far less illuminated than I expected.

Muttering *Is that it?*' I wandered out again. I felt annoyed at having spent €14, disappointed for not feeling holier in its presence, and
amused at how the bright marketing images had hijacked my imagination. Without realizing it, I had already learned my first lesson about
how we remember our early Christian ancestors: brightened up and
idealized for modern consumption. But even the Book of Kells, I will
learn, has a shadowy side.

So if the Book of Kells is not the place to start my journey back to
Ireland's Christian roots, why not take a boat out to the rocky island
called Skellig Michael? It is an extraordinary place of beehive cells,
puffins and big, open questions. But its recent use as a location in the
Star Wars series has left me fearing the old monks have been displaced
by Jedi tourists.

Here in Dingle, many on a journey like mine would have settled for the Gallarus Oratory down the road. It has an interpretive centre and, more important as I feel a squeeze in my bladder, a visitor toilet. Gallarus is a corbelled★ stone clochán†: like a Skellig beehive cell crossed with an upturned stone boat. Almost five metres long with a low door at one end and a window at the other, the stones reach up to meet above. With no mortar, it is held together largely by the ingenuity of skilled stonemasons (and some discreet love from the Office of Public Works). Gallarus has weathered thousands of Atlantic storms, though no one is quite sure how many.

I was there years ago and it was an impressive and humbling experience entering what some claim is Ireland's oldest intact church. Entering Gallarus, Seamus Heaney once said, was like 'going into a turf-stack'.

Though completely dry inside, a welcome prospect on a day like today, Gallarus is wrong for my purposes. Like the Book of Kells and the Skelligs, Gallarus is now a tourist destination and an idealized part of our past, like the good front room reserved for the priest but otherwise ignored by the house-dwellers.

Though I know what I don't want, I'm not sure what I am looking for. Ahead of my journey, looking for an answer, I seek out Peter Harbison, one of Ireland's pre-eminent archaeologists. Sitting in the bright reading room of the Royal Irish Academy (RIA) on Dawson Street, in the heart of Dublin city centre, I tell him I'm looking for a place that captures the non-idealized essence of early Irish Catholicism.

Looking dapper in his greenish tweed jacket, Peter listens thoughtfully and, with a knowing sparkle in his eyes, he says, 'You want Kilmalkedar.'

In the RIA library, his second home, Peter pulls out original massive volumes of the Ordnance Survey. He flicks with confident fingers to the Dingle Peninsula map, studies a vast page for a moment and then points triumphantly to Kilmalkedar and St Brendan's Oratory.

Some suggest Dingle's oratories are from the fifth century and

★ A self-supporting style of building, often with stone or brick, most commonly seen in arches.
† A beehive hut, often a chapel, with a corbelled roof, often found on the southwestern coast of Ireland.

served as chapels, but Peter Harbison is not convinced. Drystone structures like these are almost impossible to date, he says, particularly when they have a building style that remained unchanged for long periods. Peter believes the Dingle clocháin were built somewhere between the ninth and twelfth centuries and derive their name from 'Gall Aras' meaning something like 'shelter for foreigners' – those visiting the peninsula, in particular pilgrims.

It may be just one of Ireland's oldest pilgrimage bed and breakfasts, I tell him, but Kilmalkedar sounds good enough to me. So here I am striding up from the road, taking a gravel path skirting a field, and there, hidden behind wind-crippled trees, is Gallarus's lesser known cousin: St Brendan's Oratory.

History has been less kind to this structure than Gallarus – and fewer tourists come as a result. Stoop low, step through the entrance with its lintel stone, and you enter a curious space. On all four sides, the walls are composed of flat, flinty stones, one stone resting on the next. Follow the line of the structure from the ground up, and something interesting happens. Almost imperceptibly, the stones in the side walls change direction. They rise and move inward, narrowing the space. Up and up, layer upon layer of stone until around row forty-four, without warning, the stones simply stop.

The upper wall and roof have collapsed long ago, the fallen stones have vanished. This was a structure its builder intended to remain, supported by its own contrary corbelled construction, but instead it has collapsed in on itself. These oratories with their elongated beehive design, Peter told me in Dublin, are prone to sagging. The corbelling technique eventually reaches its limits, then gravity wins.

And yet the missing roof here feels less a disappointment than a liberation: a clochán coupé, open to the world, weeping gently in the drizzle. In my mind I hear Leonard Cohen, crooning about the crack in everything that lets the light in.

What's gone is gone but just as interesting is what has endured: the narrow window still looks perfectly east, to catch the rising sun, for whoever once found themselves here. A place like this would have attracted all sorts of people, whether worshipping or resting from a long day's pilgrimage: believers, doubters and the many who embraced religion as a social outlet. The beliefs and struggles of this oratory's visitors were probably more similar to our own than we might imagine.

This oratory, half-hidden and forgotten by many, seems as fitting a tribute to our Christian heritage as more impressive sites, many now tourist attractions. Like them, this building was built to last, and went on and on until it simply stopped and collapsed – without fully disappearing.

Outside, it's hard to tell if the oratory just sits on the landscape or if, like even the enfeebled Catholic Church in today's Ireland, it has foundations that go far deeper than the eye can see.

Nearby a tree, its shape mangled by the wind, is growing out of an ancient stone wall. A robin sitting on the wall studies me and hops away again. The tree, the bird, the wall, the curious visitor – making up a scene today that could just as easily be part of the landscape any time in the previous 1,300 years. The oratory has been here a long time and will be here long after we are all gone. For now it seems a suitable metaphorical starting point I am seeking for the Church in Ireland: something built to last, collapsed under its inbuilt flaws, laid low and far from the mainstream of daily life. And deep foundations linger that, whether heeded or ignored, still make a mark.

If we're going to own our history, it means owning places like Kilmalkedar and all that the ruin represents. Standing in the isolation of the Dingle Peninsula, I wonder what was already going wrong with Christian Ireland when this oratory was built. A bad decision was taken with its roof, clearly, but perhaps with the best of intentions, the most advanced knowledge of the time. Maybe it was just careless builders. But if the roof hadn't collapsed, we might never have seen its flaws – or maybe chosen not to.

In the quickening gloom, I think of the far grander religious structures around Ireland, monuments to Christian grace and archaic endeavour – Cashel, Clonmacnoise, Glendalough – and the bridge they offer to older beliefs. Kilmalkedar is a more modest stone on a path stretching back thirteen centuries and beyond. This place lies on the Cosán na Naomh, an old pilgrimage road that begins in Ventry and ends at the foot of Mount Brandon and may well date back before Christianity to the pagan festival of Lughnasa, which marked the start of the harvest. A few fields over, Kilmalkedar has stones remembering a magical cow. A holy cow? I'm curious to know more but the drizzle and the approaching dark focus my mind.

The interplay of eras here is clear in an adjacent Romanesque church, part of the monastery founded by Maolcethair, a local saint who was martyred in 636 CE. The current steep-roofed building dates from the twelfth century. It has an engraved semicircular door lintel and is surrounded by weathered graves, an Ogham* stone dedicated to someone called 'Mael Inbir, son of Brocán', an alphabet stone,† a sundial and a stone cross. And in the middle of it all, looking a little incongruous, is a much later addition: a lichen-covered stone statue of the Blessed Virgin Mary.

Pilgrimages to places of soft drizzly rain like this are very much part of the Irish Catholic experience. Yet all I know about this early period is St Patrick, and I realize I don't know as much as I think.

A few days later, far from the Dingle drizzle, I'm loitering with intent in the shadows of St Patrick's Cathedral, Dublin. Like the Book of Kells this is another belated first for me: a 41-year-old Dubliner finally crossing the threshold of one of Ireland's finest Church of Ireland cathedrals, named after our patron saint. I learned in school that Patrick was the son of a British middle-class family, captured and brought to Ireland to herd sheep until he could flee. Studying a wall plaque, I fall into conversation with a French woman called Marianne from Montpellier. I tell her what I know about Patrick but, when my knowledge is soon exhausted, a nearby security guard steps in. Why, Marianne wants to know, did Patrick return to Ireland?

'Patrick more or less got a vision, you see, and he was more or less told to transform Ireland from paganism to Christianity,' says the guard, swiping furiously on a vast, unresponsive touch-screen display before him. Marianne listens politely but is struggling with the idiosyncratic narrative, and a Dublin accent that gets stronger as the guard builds to his key argument.

'People think Patrick was Catholic, but he was *no, such, thing*,' says

---

* An early medieval alphabet used primarily to write the early Irish language, known only from surviving inscriptions on stones.
† A standing stone displaying an alphabet dating from early Christian times.

the guard, his right index finger prodding the frozen touch screen to emphasize his point. 'There was no such thing as Catholicism then because it wasn't out at the time.'

Marianne is struggling now, as is the guard, with the history of schism: St Patrick predated by eleven centuries the Reformation that split the Christian Church. Ireland's Protestants and other Christians venerate him as much as its Catholics, and all sides try to co-opt his legacy to underpin their own legitimacy. St Patrick is arguably Ireland's longest-serving political prisoner.

But much of what we are taught about Patrick as the starting point of Christianity is a simplistic version of reality. Historians say Christianity seeped into our island gradually, before Patrick, perhaps brought by British traders or people fleeing for their lives from the Continent.

Ireland's relationship with Christianity can be traced back to around 431 CE. At the third ecumenical council in Ephesus, the Nicene Creed of Christian orthodoxy was pronounced final. Four centuries after the crucifixion, the rules were clear to all. As the ink was drying, 3,000km west from Ephesus, Prosper of Auxerre records in his Chronicon (Chronicle) that 'Palladius, ordained by Pope Celestine is sent . . . to the Irish believing in Christ as their first bishop'.

Patrick had yet to visit Ireland in the role that would make him famous, converting the Irish, but there were already enough Christians in Ireland to merit a papal visitation. Palladius, a deacon from a noble family and later a priest living in Rome, headed to what was called 'the barbarous island' or, in a seventh-century retelling, the 'island in the cold north' populated by 'wile and harsh men' disinclined to believe his teaching.

Perhaps anticipating a tough crowd, Palladius is said to have brought gifts: relics of Saints Peter and Paul. But not even such high-end souvenirs appear to have impressed the locals and Palladius vanishes after one mention (from admittedly patchy source material), most likely back to Rome, though he might have stayed on as late as 461 CE.

The second proselytizing visitor is Patrick who, for all our modern-day March 17th certainty, is also a man of mystery: a slave-shepherd turned missionary operating between 461 and 493 CE. He was a man of the Church, and he knew a lot about herding animals in Irish gales, but his British peers looked down on him because of an unnamed youthful indiscretion and workmanlike Latin that indicated a general lack of book learning. Even at fifteen centuries' remove, the wounded tone is clear from the opening of his Confession: 'I am a sinner . . . I am looked down upon by many.'

His memoir says he had no reason to return to the place from which he had earlier escaped 'except the gospel and God's promises'.

What makes him interesting is that, while Palladius was a papal envoy, Patrick may have been a rebel freelance preacher. Instead of a green-clad, shamrock-wielding saint, I like to think of him as an early Blues Brother.

Patrick's Confession gives a taste of what he was preaching to those who cared to listen.

There is no other God, nor will there ever be . . . one without a beginning . . . and his son, Jesus Christ, whom we testify has always been, since before the beginning of this age, with the father in a spiritual way.

It's impossible to know for sure how compelling a proposition this sounded to Irish Celt ears, given how little we know about their religion. Like the Greeks or Romans they worshipped dozens of gods. But unlike other polytheistic religions, the Irish gods had no clear hierarchy, and wore different hats at different times for over a hundred different Irish *tuatha* or clans living on the island.

The clan landscape into which early Christian missionaries arrived resembled a Celtic *Game of Thrones*. The locals' shifting alliances and double-dealing may have been inspired by their gods, who were prone to be 'ruthless, unpredictable and prone to take offence'. More likely, the gods created and venerated were reflective of the worshippers.

Early Christians appear to have decided not to fight the locals or challenge their beliefs in gods and other supernatural beings. Instead the blow-ins began interpolating their Christian beliefs and structures into what they found on the ground. The new arrivals heard stories of the band of warriors, the Fianna, encountering the sun warrior Lugh, who helped Ireland overcome the 'dark Fomors, who darken the earth with their shadows'. Lugh, in full battle dress, was repackaged as the Archangel Michael.

The same happened with local practices. Even today, Irish school-children learn of a throw-down that reportedly took place on the sacred Hill of Tara. The upstart Patrick challenged the druids' domin-ance, and their holy fire tradition, with a blaze of his own. Looking on warily, a druid told King Óengus of Munster that 'either he extin-guish that fire today or it would never go out in Ireland'. Or at least that's how a later hagiographer reported it, and how we learned it in school.

The arrival and spread of early Christians in Ireland was equal parts evolution, subversion and pragmatism. Getting new hooks into old beliefs was a process Pope Gregory called 'adaptation'; Seán Ó Faoláin prefers 'supernatural infusion'.

But one thing is clear: there is no evidence for the popular claim today that Christianity was forced on the Celts. It was embraced by locals, historians say, thanks to its intriguing new teachings, its early preachers' softly-softly approach and the new group's rapid consoli-dation of power and wealth. Whatever our contemporary views of Christianity, the new religion didn't close minds, it opened them. An isolated island was, thanks to Christianity, opened to a world of new languages and, with them, new ideas.

Given their previous often brutal beliefs, it's hard to imagine many Celtic Irish eyelids batting at the sometimes fierce, sometimes compassionate God of the Old Testament, or the idea of Jesus as God-made-man. Some mourn how the Celtic salmon of knowledge swallowed the forbidden biblical fruit, but others are less sentimental. Seán Ó Faoláin argues our 'imaginative dominance [was] not, at any rate, lessened by the arrival of Christianity'.

Modern historians agree. 'Christianity changed pagans but pagans also helped shape Christianity,' says Dr Elva Johnston, associate pro-fessor in the history department at University College Dublin. 'They ensured that the religion flourished through localization within a broad doctrinal unity.'

This point cannot be made often enough, modern historians say. When they talk of this period in medieval Western Europe, they speak of 'micro-christendoms'. These realms had a local accent, but any major doctrinal distinctions – such as the Irish way of calculating Easter, which conflicted with Rome – soon vanish. There is a persistent idea today that early Irish Christians knitted their own hippy Christianity, an idea with deep roots, against which modern Irish historians say they fight a valiant but often losing battle.

Any new ideology needs a base and Armagh was to be Ireland's Eternal City. But it had competition, if the author of a manuscript from around the year 800 CE is to be believed. This text describes 'thronged Glendaloch, the ruam of the western world' – where 'ruam' is a nod both to the Eternal City and an Old Irish word for graveyard. Despite the geographic gulf between them, early Christian Ireland's links to the seat of Peter are evident. Rome was important to the early Irish Christians, both as a point of reference and place of pilgrimage. Even St Patrick suggested, in a text ascribed to him: 'The Church of the Irish, or rather of the Romans; as Christians you should be like the Romans.'

So what are we supposed to think about Celtic Christianity? Prof Liam Breatnach's eyes bug out alarmingly when I use the term. One of Ireland's leading experts on early Irish language and texts, he meets me in his office at the Dublin Institute for Advanced Studies. By raising 'Celtic Christianity', I have struck a sore point.

'That's all wishful thinking,' he says. 'There was no such thing as Celtic Christianity, the Church was always utterly subservient to Rome.'

The Irish Christian tradition is steeped heavily in the Celtic traditions that went before, he concedes, but we're still waiting for a historical smoking gun to signify a clear Celtic Christian tradition. Such popular claims are part of Ireland's game of historical dominoes, he says: only when one era, and its people, fall to the next – Celts to Christians, to Vikings, to Normans – do we idealize what went immediately before. That's why he thinks the Celtic era is particularly robust in Irish memories. A lack of knowledge of the period leaves ample room for contemporary imagination and, as he terms it, wishful thinking.

Instead of knitting their own Christianity, what is more likely to have happened is that the new – Christian – druids, like Patrick, were absorbed into the ranks of the *áes dána* – men of learning – and fanned out to convert the willing, accommodating themselves with local rulers and, if need arose, paying them protection money. Some local rulers had it both ways – taking Patrick's money and imprisoning him as well – but he always got out again to push on with his mission. At least eighty churches have links to him. St Brigid matched that number in convents and institutions for women.

Regardless of the early Christian journey, the end point – even after a short time – is clear. The chieftains converted willingly to the new teachings, bringing with them their clans and their lands. By the mid-seventh century, the Church was handsomely endowed and the medieval era ended with a very different Ireland. Liam Breatnach produces a map showing how, by 1540, vast swathes of Co. Dublin – Lusk, Raheny, Kilmainham, Clondalkin – were in church hands. It indicates a massive buy-in from the landowning Irish that cannot have been accidental, Prof Breatnach thinks, given the legal effort required to transfer land ownership in those days. The result: an asset-rich early Irish Church even wealthier than its post-Famine successor, centuries later.

'Even then the Church was a corporation,' says Prof Breatnach, 'and once anything goes in it doesn't come out again.'

4. Saints, scholars . . . and slaves

'Let us know nothing more profitable for ourselves than to examine ourselves daily . . . reviewing that dubious life.'

St Columbanus

The road back to early Christian Ireland is a lively journey of false assumptions and dead ends. Our early Church was heavily influenced by Celtic culture but, historians say, was loyal to Rome from the outset. That doesn't mean early Irish Christians lacked rebel spirit. They largely rejected Patrick's proposed diocesan church structure – where Ireland was split into regions ruled by bishops who reported to Rome – in favour of a monastic model. These new monasteries were attractive because they could be family affairs, where newly educated clerical sons worked alongside the rest of their kin.

With rich lands and lay abbots, the monasteries grew into early urban settlements and attracted many more to the new belief with its organization of learning and power. Growth led in turn to diversity: some monasteries were known as places of learning, others attracted recruits to their austere practices of study, silence, poverty and simplicity.

Stringent medieval monks like Finnian challenge the idea that these early Irish believers were all holy people. He produced a 'penitential' – or code of penance – by filleting the Bible, early church council teachings, secular law and monastic practices in other countries. Other such 'penitential' writings followed, sold as spiritual medicine to cure sins and bring the sinner back to God. These directories of rules and punishments seem brutal to modern eyes, but historians disagree on whether they should be taken – or were applied – at face value.

A cleric who 'lusts after a virgin or any woman' is ordered seven days' bread-and-water penance, rising to a year for acting on the lust-ful thoughts and three years for killing the resulting child. A similar sentence awaits a cleric who 'falls to the depths of ruin' by returning to carnal desire 'and begets a son with his concubine'.

For many modern scholars they're a telling snapshot of the societal realities of the time, and a people deciding whether – and how – to accept Christianity, and on what terms. But as late as the mid-twentieth century there were historians – perhaps to avoid scandalizing their readers – who suggested such codified penances were more preventa-tive in nature: dealing with behaviour offensive to God based on how it disturbs the public order. For them, the civilizing aspect of the new religion is crucial.

Early accounts of Irish Christianity are heartening, hilarious and even chastening to read because they reveal a people just like us: cavorters, carousers and disapproving killjoys. Windows had yet to come in Ireland, but already people were squinting.

By 700 CE, Irish monasteries were populous, powerful centres of worldly wealth, with married clergy and gold and silver galore. This is the world that produced the sumptuous Derrynaflan Chalice, found in Tipperary in 1980 near the site of a local abbey. It is a prod-uct of staggering wealth and remarkable craftsmanship, an indication of how effectively Christianity inserted itself into hierarchical Irish life by tapping local wealth and power structures without disturbing either.

In the first 300 years of the Irish Church God was somewhere in the mix, but so too was a steady process of wealth accumulation and consolidation. Priests and monks became the new druids and local leaders, abbots and bishops the new kings, with wealth to match. As the years passed, some felt monasteries' pursuit of wealth and influ-ence was pushing religious concerns down the list of priorities. A reform or Culdee* movement against secularization and degener-ation of monastic life had some success but struggled to take root, particularly after the arrival in 795 CE of the Vikings from the north. The Norsemen plundered the monasteries not because they were

---

* A reform movement of clergy within the early Church with an austere, pious and solitarian style of religious worship.

curious about the Gospels, or had it in for Christians, but because they'd heard these new communities were fabulously wealthy.

Their smash and grab missions are not the only clue that our saints and scholars narrative is somewhat limited. The Book of Kells is celebrated, rightly, as an extraordinary artistic and spiritual accomplishment. But this illuminated volume of the Gospels is a product of monastic worldly power and wealth. For every monk toiling in a scriptorium, many more people were building, renovating and defending the monastery. Many were not there of their own volition: Patrick was not Ireland's only slave.

The artistic monks and extractive elite were at the top of the pile. Beneath them was a deeply unequal society of labourers and slaves. The early Irish Christians at the top of the heap didn't let the Bible's love-thy-neighbour message stop them enjoying privileges they denied to their inferiors. For them, their way of life was the natural order.

St Colmcille's Rule, a how-to for religious life, assumes the monks reading the text already have servants or even slaves and provides advice on choosing one who is 'discreet, religious, not [a] tale-telling man, who is to attend continually on you, with moderate labor of course, but always ready'.

That leaves the monk free to dedicate himself to a life of reflective luxury, as celebrated in a Celtic novena by St Colmcille: 'Delightful it is to live on a peaceful isle, in a quiet cell, serving the King of kings.'

Irish twentieth-century bishops, the princes of their churches, can trace their roots back to actual princes from royal dynasties who ruled over churches for generations – run on slave labour. It's a link that may be unpalatable, but such was the reality of how society was organized in a world immeasurably harsher than our own. But how many of us want to see this?

Seeing and not seeing has a long tradition in Catholic Ireland. Generations of historians have pushed back against the holy tapestry we've woven of early Christian Ireland, but to no avail. Set aside Irish Christianity's slave labour origins and turn instead to the hoariest trope of all: the hermit in splendid isolation, musing in verse on the wonders of God's creation. Collected in books of Celtic poetry, verses such as this one are too pretty to disregard.

> Blackbird, it is well for you
> Wherever in the thicket be your nest,
> Hermit that sounds no bell,
> Sweet, soft, fairylike is your note.

Study the original source material, as historian Donnchadh Ó Corráin did, and you realize that these lines were not penned by a dreamy hermit in an isolated lean-to of fern, ash and hazel branches. This and other poems were written by men in formal monastery settings, 'whose lives were lived out, as teachers and administrators, in the great monastic towns'.

Often, the point of the poems was as far from nature as you can get: written to drill monastic students on tricky points of grammar. One such early Irish poem, 'Writing out of Doors', filled with woodlands and trilling birds, was written to teach young Latin students the use of the first person singular pronoun.

We choose to celebrate marginal poems extolling nature but their original manuscripts yield a long and diverse list of themes, from 'miserly food' to 'the beheading of splendid dear John'. Other such poems reveal fears of going to 'torment-filled Hell' or offering 'good in return for evil'. None of these pop up in treasuries of early Irish verse.

The diversity in the early Irish Christian Church is remarkable – if you choose to see it, that is. All of human life is here on our island of saints and scholars – and slaves. The writings these early Irish believers left us show them as sex-obsessed or drill sergeants. In other words, modern Ireland's clerics – the extremes and the moderates in between – had their equivalents right back in the early days.

It's not the only parallel. Irish society back then was as class-conscious as what came later. Back then, as later, Irish people abused their children – often the offspring of incest or adultery – or handed them over into church care as a watch to a pawn shop. An early Irish cleric wrote: 'A child abandoned to the church is its slave unless he is redeemed. Nor, if he be violent, shall his evil conduct stain the church if it corrected him as far as possible.' It's likely these wretches – quite separate from young oblates in the monasteries, who later became clerics – were expected to do the monks' laundry and other menial tasks – or worse.

Accepting the many sinners alongside the saints and scholars does not negate the golden age that did exist in Ireland. There was no shortage of real achievement, staggering given the size of the population: Irish monks developed new scripts; invented a new layout that changed for ever how text was read; set new standards in European book making; added to Europe's biblical literature; developed Latin handbooks; and predicted eclipses before others in continental Europe.

'Early Christian Ireland was far more advanced than we give it credit for,' says Liam Breatnach, as he explains the links between the coming of Christianity and the shift away from the Celtic tradition. 'Would it be such a bad thing to admit it?'

Admitting that, though, would mean understanding just how much our view of early Christian Ireland is coloured by the writings of later centuries, in particular Church of Ireland figures like Archbishop James Ussher. Ussher was anxious to present the contemporary Church of Ireland, the minority Establishment church on the island, as the natural successor to the early Irish Church. The Catholic Church of the day, by implication, was run by authoritarian bishops who were too close to Rome. The belated irony is how his anti-Catholic efforts were, in time, absorbed into the patriotic fusion of Catholic belief and Irish nationhood. In the century since independence, this faith–identity link has weakened, yet many still defend the idealized view of our historical origins as a matter of faith.

In her dim office, between towering piles of books, Dr Elizabeth Boyle suggests our modern take on early Christian Ireland is even more slippery than St Patrick's non-existent snakes. The head of Maynooth University's Early Irish department observes a steady stream of students with 'weird psychological hang-ups' about the Irish Catholic Church. Particularly striking, she says, is their readiness to accept the scandals of the last twenty-five years as the work of a flawed institution, while embracing an unsullied vision of early Christianity as evidence of an 'uncontaminated past'.

'It's as if people want to think humans have gone from a state of moral purity to absolute sinfulness,' she says, 'but that's not how it works.'

In universities around the country, Irish historians of the early Christian period all tell stories of angry young students' shattered illusions. One tells me with delight of how an indignant millennial reported her to the faculty authorities for asserting that St Patrick had sinned. (Remember, Patrick's Confession begins: 'I am a sinner.')

Many other dogged beliefs plague early Irish historians' teaching lives. One is about the character of Celtic-era laws, seen by many as a progressive system squashed by regressive Catholic teaching. What few want to hear, says Dr Boyle, is how the Celts' Brehon Laws operated a sliding scale for punishing crime, depending on the social status of the victim. That makes it sound less noble. Meanwhile, the 'regressive' early Irish Christians were producing advanced legal texts about empire, kinship and hierarchy. This was more nuanced than what went before, she argues, and thus survived.

'Somehow that hasn't captured the public imagination,' says Dr Boyle, 'unlike monks and their cats.'

My friend Imogen Stuart says she is guilty as charged. She is one of Ireland's most prolific sculptors, in particular of religious art, and her works merge early Irish religious themes with a German expressionist style. Among her key works is *Pangur Bán*, based on the old Irish poem written in the margin of a manuscript of hymns and grammatical texts.

> I and Pangur Bán, my cat,
> 'Tis a like task we are at;
> Hunting mice is his delight,
> Hunting words I sit all night.

The playful aside – a moment's musing on a monk's cat – is a more pleasing way to remember old Ireland than the reality of the Latin grammarian.

Pangur Bán is the inspiration for one of Imogen's most impressive works, now on display in the visitor centre of Áras an Uachtaráin. Like many works, this had its origins in the well of her artistic inspiration since 1949: Glendalough, Co. Wicklow.

I am a little humbled that it has taken four decades – and an insistent blow-in from Berlin – for me to finally make it to the lake, the iconic round tower and the sixth-century monastic complex clustered beneath.

Imogen moved to nearby Laragh, home of Irish sculptor Ian Stuart, after meeting him in post-war Germany. She had survived wartime bombings in her native Berlin and was looking forward to a life as a sculptor and a more peaceful future in Ireland. Immigrating to mid-century Ireland, she says, was like taking a trip back in time to St Kevin's holy glade.

'Everything was magical. It still is a magical place here, in any weather,' she says as we stand in the monastery graveyard, her sky-blue rain jacket glistening in the misty rain. Though the historians' arguments are still ringing in my ear – *Don't swallow the Celtic Christian propaganda* – she's right: there is something special in the air of this green, glacial valley. But what?

Some fifteen centuries on, no contemporary material on Kevin survives, leaving all sorts of room for interpretation. Kevin is said to have been close to nature but, even if he wasn't before, he would have converted to the great outdoors after a short time in this stunning landscape of gentle, heathery slopes. Today's landscape still bears the ruins of his harmonious additions: a stone monastery ruins with round tower and lichen-covered Celtic cross gravestones.

Kevin is said to have been born into a noble family and been educated by monks. He moved to Glendalough to live as a hermit – eating little, praying, going barefoot – but his fame as a holy man grew. People came to seek his wisdom, thereby defeating the purpose of his self-imposed isolation; one legend has Kevin drowning a female admirer who tried to seduce him. Imogen hasn't heard that story but remembers hearing of Kevin praying, naked, in the icy lake. Or holding his hand out of his cell window in meditation, so still that a blackbird built a nest in it. A nature lover, he reportedly remained in the position until the eggs hatched. So many Kevins: saint, misogynist, murderer or nature lover.

'And since the whole thing's imagined anyhow,' wrote Seamus Heaney in 1996, 'Imagine being Kevin. Which is he?'

As with early Irish Christianity, which Kevin do we choose when we examine our past – and why? As we walk through the graveyard, Imogen brings Kevin and his contemporaries to life in a way my school religion books never did. Her curiosity about this early period is all the more remarkable given the musty Catholicism she encountered when she arrived in Ireland. Ian Stuart, later a drug-dealing artist but then a pious young man, insisted she convert to Catholicism before they married. He found a priest nearby who was delighted to teach a German Lutheran convert, but Imogen still remembers the tedium of catechesis: 'I had to bore my knuckles into my eyes to stay awake.'

The post-war, pre-Vatican II Irish Church she was baptized into wasn't all that interested in the early Christian period, she remembers, yet this era has provided her with a lifetime's inspiration as a working artist. Now over ninety, she has seen more of Irish life than most Irish people and continues to be inspired by this era. Her curiosity about religious questions, she thinks, stems from her liberal childhood in Berlin, as well as the many artistic and liberal priests in Ireland who commissioned her to brighten up their churches.

'When I came to Ireland there was only one commissioner of art and that was the Church,' she said.

Like generations of artists before her down through the centuries, Imogen insists it is not just pragmatism – and a steady stream of commissions – that allows her to see the beauty in the Bible, Christianity and the Church.

'Even if the Church messed up in other areas, we should remember everything we have to thank them for,' she said. 'People forget, or take for granted, that they owe their education to them. Yes, some got slaps and beatings, but it wasn't all bad.'

Some who experienced the rougher end of Irish Catholicism think differently to her, I suggest. How does she reconcile the contradictory components of the Irish Catholic experience – the beauty and the beatings? How does she fit it together? Looking at me as if it's a strange question to ask, she answers without skipping a beat, 'It doesn't fit together at all.'

Driving back to Dublin, Imogen and I talk more about the challenge of accepting the contradictions. The early Christian tradition is not 'either or', it's 'both and'. Our understanding of what came later will be skewed unless we can see majesty and shame in these early, 'golden age' centuries.

Christianity begins with a man left to die on a cross. The popular Christian story in Ireland began with a brutality all of its own: a young man was most likely kidnapped from his home and left on an exposed hill in Ireland, huddling with his sheep, with no way of knowing if he would ever see his home or family again. I wonder how benevolently he viewed his Irish captors and slave-owners. And what of the children abandoned by their parents, or circumstances, to the early Irish monks? Some became religious themselves, others became ancient forerunners of our institutional inmates. Structures of power, and their abuses, were in place long before Irish princes embraced the new order to survive.

Every society, and every generation, uses and abuses history for its own ends. Selective ideas of a pure, Celtic Christianity are the work of previous centuries' public relations. Pruned of troublesome historical detail, and varnished to suit contemporary nationalist or clerical narratives, the Celtic Christian story generated important political momentum and gave emotional comfort in hard times. This framing of our Christian past offered touchstones that no Penal Laws or occupying powers could take from us. And these same stories gave us something to build on when those powers retreated.

But even seventy years ago, alarmed by our idealized version of our early Christian past, writer Seán Ó Faoláin warned of 'piling on top of something already sufficiently embroidered by nature a lot of superfluous William Morris trappings'. And the contrast with our nostalgia for a golden past makes the painful reality of our more recent abuse past even worse than the depressing reality. Embracing a more critical approach to the past would, however, open the door to an uncomfortable thought: at all times in our history, millions of Irish people – with varying degrees of power, knowledge and agency – contributed to what became Catholic Ireland's leaning tower of piety.

5.   Holy victimhood

'What wonder if our step betrays
The freedman born in penal days!'

Thomas Davis, 'The Penal Days'

On the wall inside the door of my Berlin apartment hangs a bronze penal cross. Around 40cm long, it has stubby arms that are distinctive to the crucifixes dating from the era of the Irish Penal Laws, a time when Ireland's Catholic majority were subjugated by the London-backed Protestant minority. The cross was created by Imogen Stuart. Throughout her seven-decade career Imogen has designed penal crosses for churches around the country. She is intrigued by the form and, in time, I have grown to share her fascination, even though I felt awkward accepting the cross as a gift.

Visitors to my apartment eye it warily but, for me, it is as much crossroads as cross: an intersection of my Catholic and Irish identities, which makes for lively inner conflicts. For a grappling Catholic like me, the penal cross is the equivalent of a mezuzah for a secular Jew: a cultural touchstone with deep and solemn religious roots. The cross is also a reminder of how Ireland's Penal era lingers in my mind as a vague narrative of brutality towards previous generations who suffered for their Catholic faith. Slipped in alongside this was the religious-nationalist indoctrination: suffering makes you hardier, and holier, than others.

After learning how emotion has been deployed to colour the early Christian period, I look at the cross with new eyes. How much is it an artistic genuflection to real Irish history and faith, and how much does it recall a subsequent recreation – distortion, even – of that period? Give suffering a religious, exceptionalist framing, as Irish bishops did in the nineteenth century, and you can change the game.

Historian Liam Kennedy suggests such narratives of victimhood and suffering are sometimes empowering, but often sources of dysfunction, 'especially when laced with aggressive self-righteousness'.

I feel a flash of self-righteousness when, after a morning of heavy reading about the Penal period, I break for lunch with a Danish friend. He lived in Ireland for a time before I was born and I tell him of my research journey back to the Penal Laws.

'Which penal laws?' he asks. 'There were so many.'

In a quiet Greek restaurant in Berlin, far from Ireland, his remark triggers in me an unusual flash of Irish nationalist pique. I sense a brief awakening in me of a Most-Oppressed-People-Ever sense of victimhood, which I didn't even realize was in me.

'Where did that come from?' I wonder as I swallow the feeling again with a sip of water. After all, Michael is right: the history of organized religion is also a history of suppressing others' faith, often with brutal force. Almost every country in continental Europe has seen religious repression and warfare, often on a vast, staggering scale, from guillotined French priests in the Terror, to Germany's vicious anti-clerical *Kulturkampf*. Ireland's Penal Laws had uniquely cruel elements but Michael is Jewish and his family history in the twentieth century takes penal laws to another, far darker place.

As we continue our lunch, my mind is distracted. When we learned about the Penal Laws in school, I wonder if I was taught to think about the period or to emote? I need to know more, so it's back to Ireland again.

On a sunny Saturday afternoon, a crowd of sixty people are seated in a semicircle of large, oblong rocks dominating a hillside glade. The centre of attention is a large flat rock on higher ground that is serving as an altar. Behind the softly billowing white cloth that covers the altar is another rock, this one upright and in the shape of an irregular pentagon. Nailed to the stone face is an iron cross.

We're at a Mass rock in the Hollywood hills, not in California but outside the small Co. Wicklow town. All around are the rolling curves of the national park, carved out during the last Ice Age and, in mid-August, a harmonious patchwork of soft green fern and budding purple heather.

It was over these hills and through the Wicklow Gap that St Kevin is said to have wandered to nearby Glendalough, where he set up his monastery and died 1,400 years ago. From the early Irish monasteries, missionaries left these shores around 600 CE to bring Christianity back to Europe. The collapse of the Roman Empire triggered a dark age for European culture until it was lit once more from the pilot light in Ireland. Now, fourteen centuries later, the same faith, in a drastic reversal of fortune, faces existential pressures in Ireland.

Today's crowd has come to pray at this hillside Mass rock, one of dozens of such hidden places dotted around the country. Mostly forgotten places of worship, they came about during an era of colonial cruelty that, in the words of a nineteenth-century writer, saw the country 'deeply, horribly saturated in Irish blood'.

The Mass today, the first on the site in twenty years, was posted on Facebook by the organizing committee of Hollywood Tidy Towns. Maria Cullen, a committee member, says locals now see themselves as responsible not just for flowers and litter, but for the region's links to Irish Christianity.

'It's up to every individual to decide why they are here,' Maria says as we wait in the car park before heading up the hill. For her the last decades of revelation and horror in the institutional Church have created a need to have 'more nature and spiritualist values attended to. If you can't find that at ten thirty on a Sunday, this way you can at least get out and get some fresh air,' she says brightly. The local priest, she jokes, is encouraging of her group's efforts to 'drum up a bit of business' but he is too elderly to join. No replacement has shown up yet when we leave the main road and process down a beaten track. Past a tattered yellow-and-white Vatican flag, fluttering on a pylon, we cross a wooden bridge above a brook of brown, brackish water that feels like a portal to the past. Waiting again for the priest, an older woman pulls a handful of rushes and – in a spontaneous memory test – sees if she can still remember how to make a St Brigid's cross. She passes the test.

Gerry, the local deacon, eventually shows up, full of hectic apologies. The intended celebrant got sick and it's been a struggle to find a replacement at short notice, but thankfully he has one: Fr Micheál Comer from Eadstown parish near Naas. Today's priest shortage is like being back in Penal times again, he jokes, as we begin the march up the hill, performing as we go the Stations of the Cross.

Like the landscape around me, the popular memory of Penal times is irresistible. Visiting Ireland in 1979 a well-briefed Pope John Paul II recalled the 'Mass rocks in the glens and forests by "hunted priests"'.

The priests would have slipped through such glens as this past cottages, now ruined, that would have seen a hundred station Masses.* Today's crowd reflects Catholic Mass congregations around the country today: senior citizens, some with grandchildren, and just one couple in their forties with their two young children. The two teenage stewards who lead the way up the hill are physically and mentally disconnected from what's going on behind them. The procession is led not by an altar boy or priest but by a man carrying the crucifix head-high and wearing a Tidy Towns high-viz vest. I'm reminded again of how, in twenty-first-century Ireland, the doctrines of Health and Safety trump Catholicism every time.

As we climb up and up again, the black glistening soil becomes thinner, the lush green ferns give way to purple heather. We stop fourteen times for reflection and then round a bend to an idyllic, natural amphitheatre.

As the crowd makes itself comfortable on the rocks, upholstered only by a light coating of lichen, a bespectacled middle-aged man in a plaid shirt makes his way to the altar and introduces himself as Fr Norbert Fernandes, a visiting priest from the diocese of Westminster in London. He asks if he can concelebrate Mass. He doesn't have his vestments, he says, but has his ID.

'Well if you have that, we're in business,' says Fr Comer, handing him a green stole for his neck.

Before Mass starts, Fr Fernandes introduces himself to the surprised congregation. He was having drinks with friends in the pub

* These are Masses that were said in people's homes, after which the host family and neighbours would continue to socialize together. The custom originated in Penal times, as a way for communities to have secret Masses away from prying eyes, but it continued well into the twentieth century and still happens in some rural areas. Hosting a station Mass in your home every few years was considered an honour and a great occasion, and was usually treated as an opportunity to spruce the place up.

in Hollywood when they saw the signs for the Mass rock and decided to investigate. In possibly the first such accent ever to speak here, he jokes, 'Here you are protecting yourself from the English . . .'

Ice broken, the Mass begins in the summer sunshine. This week's Gospel is the Sermon on the Mount, perhaps the greatest collection of Christian teachings.

Blessed are the poor in spirit: for theirs is the kingdom of heaven.

Blessed are they that mourn: for they shall be comforted . . .

In that Gospel, Jesus tells the confused crowd before him that, unlike their ancestors who ate and still died, he is offering them the chance to eat his bread and live for ever.

Was that a comfort for my Irish ancestors as I imagine them, standing barefoot in places like this? Did it help them survive day to day, putting in perspective the persecution and violence of life around them? Or, back then, did they even bother going to Mass?

In his homily, Fr Comer says many in Ireland have given up on the 2,000-year-old message of Christianity. To those who haven't, and have just hiked up the hill, his message is encouraging but cautious. 'We cannot just do this to feel good about ourselves,' he says, 'but to associate with the people who ensured that future generations had the faith – that's us – and came up here to have Mass in secret.'

As the Mass concludes I wonder what our ancestors would make of the people gathered here for what seems like one of two reasons, sometimes both: spiritual need and silent protest. One woman in her sixties from nearby Ballymore-Eustace is here for the peace, she says: to reflect and to be thankful. Another man, in his early seventies and with agitated eyes, says he is here because he is looking for a respite from modern Ireland.

What, I ask, is modern Ireland for him?

A shallow place, he says, where one clergy has replaced another. Unprompted, and without knowing my day job, he denounces the archbishop of modern Ireland: my *Irish Times* colleague and one of Ireland's best-known cultural commentators since the 1980s, Fintan O'Toole.

'People will eventually realize he doesn't actually have anything to offer,' he says. 'I'm not sure who put the bishops up on their pedestal, nor how the liberals managed to get up there after.'

He is bewildered at how his one-time Catholic majority has, within the blink of an historical eye, been reduced to a modest, even mocked, minority. Liberals have 'fixed' public opinion in Ireland, securing backing for marriage equality and abortion, he says. Behind the wounded tone it's clear he preferred the older way, when his group was in the majority. Now things have flipped, and decades of conservative, clerical dominance of Ireland have ended, replaced among some by a new victim mentality.

This mentality – however much it is real and however much imagined – is key to understanding the Penal era. Leading historians of the era agree on little else. One, only half-joking, warns me: 'This era should come with a health warning.'

What was unique about the Penal era in Ireland was that it was a campaign by a Protestant minority against a Catholic majority. Following the Siege of Limerick in 1691, when Jacobite (Catholic) forces were beaten by the opposing Protestant Williamites, a treaty was agreed promising religious freedom for Catholics. The effect of subsequent new laws was the exact opposite. From then on Catholics were disenfranchised, banned from public office and holding firearms, and punitive laws applied to fundamentals of daily life, from land inheritance to owning a horse.

To 'prevent further growth of popery', laws demanded the registration of priests, allowing one per parish, and banished bishops. With no provision for training new priests in Ireland, some saw a planned extinction of Catholicism.

After 1709, Catholic clergy found themselves trapped between an obligation to register with civil authorities and a papal ban on doing so. In 1714 Bishop Hugh MacMahon of Clogher wrote to the Pope that 'priests have celebrated Mass with their faces veiled, lest they should be recognized by those present'. With a £100 bounty on his head the bishop said he 'frequently had to assume a fictitious name and travel in disguise'.

The laws prompted some priests to go underground or flee abroad. Of those who stayed, a number were killed. For example, a

Fr Timothy Ryan was arrested and executed in 1726 in Limerick on a charge of marrying a Protestant man and a Catholic wife. A Fr Nicholas Sheehy, parish priest of Clogheen in Tipperary, was hanged in Clonmel on 15 March 1766. Four years after his execution, his executioner was himself stoned to death by an angry Catholic mob.

Hearing stories like these reminds me of how the period was presented to me in school: as a plot against the native Irish and their faith, persecuting their priests to be rid of Catholicism in a generation. The suffering was real but somehow its scale seems skewed. Many historians say the focus of the Penal Laws lay elsewhere: preserving property and power in Protestant hands. This could, of course, be aided by disenfranchising the native Catholic majority and enticing them, including with force, to convert to Protestantism.

That a mass conversion from Catholicism failed to materialize has been championed by generations of Irish and their leaders as proof of our devotion to the 'one true faith'. But that logic is based on many assumptions, including the assumption that the punitive anti-Catholic laws that existed on paper were implemented in practice, which many historians say was rarely the case. A lot depended on the local Church of Ireland landlord, who rarely had an interest in upsetting his tenants. And many of the laws were kept *in terrorem*, as a legal threat. 'If someone gets too uppity, the law could be dusted off,' says Vincent Morley, a historian specializing in the era.

Even after the worst had passed by the mid-eighteenth century, and all the Catholic bishops' seats were once again occupied, the situation for the Church was by no means ideal. Apart from the still-existing laws, bishops were grappling with serious in-house problems among their clergy. After a 1753 diocesan visitation, Bishop Nicholas Sweetman of Ferns took issue with at least half of the priests he visited because of dirty vestments, careless Masses and indifference to their faithful.

One priest, the bishop wrote, 'minded dogs and hunting more than his flock' and declined to celebrate Mass on holy days. Another, the parish priest of St Munchin's in Limerick, continued to celebrate Mass after he was suspended in 1755 for allegedly fathering children by two women.

Just as the implementation of the laws differed widely, so too, it seems, did levels of religious observance. While some Irish Catholics walked miles to get to Mass on Sundays – the people we like to remember – in other regions up to 80 per cent of people stayed away.

Some stayed away for fear of reprisals, but others did not. And many who practised their faith did not creep around the countryside. In Ulster, for instance, plantation policies seized Catholic land and transferred it to the ownership of Protestant settlers. Though this squeezed the numbers of local Catholics, not even the Penal Laws brought about the end of public practice. Contemporary records of pilgrimages north to Lough Derg in Co. Donegal note how, then as now, 'religion is practised freely and openly'.

In 1714 Bishop MacMahon noted pilgrims arriving from all corners of Ireland for the three-month pilgrimage season, with continuous Masses from dawn till midday. 'An extraordinary feature of the pilgrimage,' he wrote, 'is that none of the Protestants in the locality ever interfere with the pilgrims, although people are forbidden by law of parliament to make it.'

The situation on the ground then appears far more pragmatic than the narrow persecution narrative I remember in school. Even the meaning of the era's distinctive penal cross design is contested. Generations have learned that its distinctive stubby shape and narrow crossbar made it easier to conceal the cross up a priest's sleeve. But it was also a more stable construction that maximized the use of material. In Lough Derg, far from being concealed, such crosses were sold openly to pilgrims.

City-dwelling Irish Catholics seem to have had a better Penal era than their country cousins. In 1731, during a search of six religious orders in Dublin, local sheriffs claimed they found no one to arrest; records of the Augustinians and Dominicans from that period record money set aside for 'claret to treat the sheriffs in their search'. In the capital, but also in Cork and Waterford, Catholic bookshops continued to do a brisk trade. It was in this period, historians say, that middle-class Irish Catholics, in their choice of reading material, began absorbing the 'anxious severity' of British Catholics.

It's disconcerting to reconcile the ringing tills of Catholic bookshops in cities with images of furtive, barefoot Mass-goers at a rural Mass rock. Both are part of the narrative: in a dark era for many

Catholics in Ireland, others got on with their lives with far less interference.

Concerns in London during Ireland's Penal era were quite different. While the Catholic Irish fumed over their oppression and the treatment of their clerics, Anglo-Irish Protestant members of the House of Lords were alarmed by reports of a resurgence of 'papists' around the island. A Jas. Hackett of Newry reported on 27 November 1731 that he knew of one Mass house, several altars and other places of worship in the region, as well as a school run by a 'papist'.

He told of a former Church of Ireland clergyman who 'on account of his extravagance and vice [was] forced to take refuge in the Church of Rome . . . and now goes around as a missionary, perverting as many as he can'.

Mr Hackett added: 'I believe there are many more such persons in ye country, and I am told that the number of young priests is daily increasing.'

In total, contemporary reports from around the country in 1731 show a Catholic Church that is bridled, but not decimated: 892 Mass houses; 54 private chapels; 1,445 priests and 549 schools.

The data on priests forced abroad to study for the priesthood tells its own tale. Even as times improved in Ireland, in the second half of the eighteenth century, half of all ordained Irish priests in Europe failed to return home. The need for priests varied, too: some parts of the country reported such a surplus that in 1742 the Holy See intervened to limit the number of ordinations. Throttling the number of priests from within – reducing the ratio of priests to people and level of pastoral care on offer – was a factor in this period, alongside ordinances from the Crown.

Finally, the narrow Catholic victim narrative overlooks Catholic perpetrators: the massacres and drownings of Protestants at the hands of Catholic mobs; and Irish Catholics who denounced others. The brother-in-law of Friar James Hegarty betrayed his whereabouts to Crown forces, resulting in the monk's beheading near Buncrana in 1711. The disgusted neighbours of a clerical bounty hunter in Limerick made sure they had the last word on his gravestone:

Mankind are pleased whene'er a villain dies
Now all are pleased for here Jack Cusack lies

Such narratives weren't restricted to rural Ireland. In June 1714, John Sweetman of Red Houses, Baldoyle – down the road from where I grew up in Dublin – testified that he attended a Mass celebrated 'by one Father Tracie a Popish Priest in the town of Hoath [Howth]'. Not only did he denounce the priest, but also four other Mass-goers: 'James Comon, Christopher Higley, Toby Tallant, Patrick Carr all of Hoath'.

Beyond payment, the circumstances of the denunciation are not recorded but the Baldoyle man merely anticipated some priests in embracing opportunities presented by the Penal Law. On 7 November 1714, Bishop Hugh MacMahon wrote from hiding to the Holy See, about how 'four magistrates armed with warrants were in search for me, instigated by an unworthy person to whom I had refused a parish'. A decade later, Bishop Sweetman of Ferns was imprisoned for a time after one of his own priests denounced him to the authorities as enlisting men for a foreign army.

Like the isle of saints, scholars and slaves, the Penal era of the Irish martyr is also the story of the Irish traitor. Like the early Christian era, this period is mythologized as a high point of religious fervour. But maybe it was just the usual group of people any society produced at any time, trying to get by in the circumstances life put their way. Three centuries on, modern Irish historians say it is important to examine whose agenda is served by accepting without question the Penal era as one of 'unexampled sufferings' or an 'ordeal of persecution unparalleled in the history of mankind'.

Trying to impose subsequently a historical narrative of grace under pressure, they argue, says less about the era in question and more about later generations' contemporary needs. In the 1850s, for instance, Ireland's first cardinal, Paul Cullen, with a mix of empathy and fatalistic hyperbole, suggested the 'cruel ingenuity' of Penal Laws was to persecute the religion of the people and see 'the Catholic priesthood sent into exile or dragged to the scaffold'.

His concern was not entirely selfless, channelling a popular understanding of the period while burnishing the image of his Church as defender and comforter of the oppressed Irish. Along with his reforms of church structure and faith practice, this nineteenth-century framing of the Penal era helped his Church secure the power it sought – with widespread popular consent.

Today's historians argue over how conscious or unconscious this push was and whether clerics – themselves Irish – were actively or passively exploiting or channelling emotional resentment for their institution's ends. Starting with Maureen Wall's *The Penal Laws* in 1961, Irish historians have worked to expand the narrative beyond Good Catholics and Evil Protestants. But, as with the early Christian period, university lecturers who teach the Penal era say they have their work cut out for them, given the firm ideas of each successive year of first-year history students.

Dr Charles Ivan McGrath, associate professor in University College Dublin's School of History, presents in lectures many facts that contradict the traditional narrative: that many Mass rocks predate the Penal period and were the sites of open-air Masses long after chapels and halls were available; or that the Penal Laws were enacted by parliament in Dublin – not Westminster – by politicians no less Irish than people we are happy to adopt as our own, such as Dean Jonathan Swift and Maria Edgeworth. Not all first years are happy, he says.

'They come in with the victim notion, and I don't know where to start because this traditional narrative is everywhere,' says Dr McGrath.

In his own work, Prof Sean Connolly presents the eighteenth-century Penal Laws less as an oppressive daily reality and rather more as window-dressing to appease anti-papal zealots and British politicians looking for a quick populist boost before elections.

'The Penal Laws did give insignificant local bullies the chance to throw their weight around at the expense of people, but it was not illegal to walk into a church nor was it to go to Mass,' he tells me. Even if the laws were designed to ensure Catholicism died out in one generation, Connolly says, it's 'very hard to say how many people really thought that'.

Historian Louis Cullen goes further, suggesting today's understanding rests on the retrospective narrative created by Cardinal Cullen and a Catholic political-clerical class in the nineteenth century. To secure and consolidate their grip on power, he argues, they had a 'vested interest in exaggerating the magnitude of the Catholic achievement of survival and the background of legal and political discrimination'.

Inevitably, challenging the traditional victimhood narrative has attracted its own pushback. In 1989 historian Brendan Bradshaw, a Marist priest, took issue with the zeal of modern, revisionist historians to play down the human trauma inherent in the Penal era. He argued they embraced a 'conception of professionalism which denies the historian access to value-judgments and, therefore, access to the kind of moral and emotional register necessary to respond to human tragedy'.

Dr Bradshaw criticized their reliance on official sources that excised pain from the record, instead of meditating on history, real and remembered. Bradshaw offered instead the idea of the historian as mediator who, besides studying sources, can acknowledge the burden of past tragedy that is 'both historically true and humanly responsive'. This approach, 'without diminishing the tragedy, pays due regard to the propensity of the historical process for turning the least promising human situations to constructive purpose'.

In a similar fashion historian Vincent Morley takes issue with those who frame the Penal era as more inconvenience than oppression. Casting the net wider to take in popular writing and literature, he says, reveals how Irish Catholics perceived themselves, and thus felt, at the time: resentful at, in their eyes, hordes of heretics oppressing them for their loyalty to the one true faith; furious at being tenants in their own country; unfailingly loyal to the deposed Jacobite house of Stuart against the Dutch interloper, the forces of the Protestant House of Orange. The Penal Laws wounded the Irish deeply, he suggests, but he steers away from the term victimhood.

'That has pejorative connotations, a sense of helplessness: "We cannot do anything for ourselves, we are always going to be at the bottom of the heap,"' he says. 'I don't get that sense at all from reading literature of the period, instead I see a resolve that things will get better.'

As an example of the wounding, he cites a verse attributed by some to Eoghan Rua Ó Súillebháin which, in English, reads:

'Tis not the poverty I most detest,
Nor being down for ever,
But the insult that follows it,
Which no leeches can cure.

Popular memory in the present has contributed considerably to the Most-Oppressed-People-Ever label we sometimes use for ourselves, variously in jest, self-mockery and self-loathing. But historian Oliver Raftery, a Jesuit priest, says this is for many Irish the 'touchstone of how Catholics have often read their past and interpreted their historical experience'.

The Cromwellian violence against the Catholic Irish in the late seventeenth century for supporting Charles I – and the violent retaliation by the Irish against the Protestants on their island – yielded to the legalized discrimination of the eighteenth, which in turn transitioned into the nineteenth-century horrors of hunger and emigration. Simply too much for anyone to bear, it is no surprise that Catholic clerics would fashion a coherent narrative of Christian suffering in this life that would be followed by eternal reward in the next.

Even Vincent Morley, who is more sympathetic to the Penal era suffering narrative, admits, 'It would be remarkable if the Church decided to leave such an important asset unused.'

Regardless of the motivations at the time, regardless of their severity, Prof Oliver Raftery suggests the Penal Laws left a community of people with a 'lingering sense of displacement . . . from its own place, its own land, its own environment'.

Persecution, displacement and bloodshed – in memory as much as reality – lent the Penal era Catholic Church an authentic legacy of suffering that opened Irish experience to a long tradition of Christian martyrdom and, argues Prof Raftery, gave rise to a narrative of victimhood.

The result: a new 'Faith of our Fathers' Catholicism,* teaching the nineteenth-century Irish about previous generations, 'chained in prisons dark . . . still in heart and conscience free'.

---

* Though, contrary to popular belief in Ireland, 'Faith of our Fathers' was not about our oppressed ancestors. It's a nineteenth-century English hymn celebrating Reformation-era English Catholic martyrs.

It's testament to the lingering historical trauma, and how it welded suffering to Irish Catholic identity, that this union has outlived clerical influence over our country. Until the recent decades of scandal, embracing the Irish Catholic framing of our history as a narrative of unquestioned, undifferentiated cleric-lead victimhood helped provide cover for abusing clerics. They were men of God who had suffered with us as victims so, for many, simply could not be perpetrators. That category did not compute.

Contemporary Irish historian Charles Ivan McGrath, associate professor of history at University College Dublin, sees an 'Irish gene' at work here, stubbornly resistant to any historical narrative that questions an exclusive victim role. This defensiveness towards looking in a differentiated way at the past makes for strange alliances in Ireland today, he says, even among his first-year students at UCD. They may have little connection to the Catholic Church yet rush to defend its framing of Irish history.

'People might be horrified by church teaching on homosexuality, for instance,' says Prof McGrath, 'but by clinging to the historical crutches of the Penal Laws people are, perhaps unknowingly, clinging to the church narrative [of our past].'

His concerns echo those of other Irish historian colleagues, confronted with idealized notions of Celtic Christianity not limited to their students. The source of their concern was flagged a century ago. Fr William Burke, a historian, argued in 1914 that Ireland's Penal and Famine tragedies did not result in mass conversions to Protestantism, but pauperized and degraded the people. Unsurprisingly, people clung to these disastrous experiences of the past and, by doing so, altered the Irish personality in the present.

It is hardly an exaggeration to say that most Irishmen are still haunted by a sub-conscious feeling of inferiority social or even intellectual. They have many virtues but amongst them can hardly be reckoned personal dignity, mental independence, and self-restraint. They shrink from initiative and are impressionable to a degree. Their subtlety, their indirectness of expression, their want of candour has often been remarked. They rejoice at recognition and welcome patronage, yet on the other hand their intemperateness of language and feeling often alienate those whose good will they would . . . conciliate. In short, the habits of slavery induced by the penal code have deprived us as a people of that sturdy individualism which respects oneself and respects others, and which is as widely removed from insolence as it is from servility.

In the heather of the Hollywood hills, no one is thinking too deeply about the legacy of the Penal Laws – even as they act on it. The local volunteers – who organized the Mass, set up the altar and now strip it again after the priest has departed – are, unknowingly, carrying on a key tradition of that time. Given priest shortages and banished bishops, it was the ordinary people who rose to the challenge in Penal times of keeping the Catholic faith alive.

I take one last look back at the Mass rock and the valley carved out by Ice Age glaciers. On the way down, leaning against a stone, local couple David and Mary drink tea from a flask and give snacks to their two young children, red-haired and milky skinned. 'The Mass rock is a piece of history in the area,' says David happily, 'so it's great to see Mass still taking place up here.'

The original worshippers here felt oppressed by the ruling class of their country and their descendants here feel the same sense of exclusion in a secular society. The Penal Laws are gone, but how we remember that period, and its after-effects, continues to inform – and limit – how we look at our present.

Days later, I return to Berlin and, closing the apartment door, I look again at the bronze penal cross gleaming warmly on the wall. Like the cross fixed to the Wicklow Mass rock, it could just be decoration. But its burnished brass is a contested object of Irish faith and memory, a reminder of how the latter became subservient to the former.

6.   The little green book

'We have just enough religion to make us hate,
but not enough to make us love one another.'

Jonathan Swift

I'm sitting with Lotta, a Swedish friend, on her balcony in Berlin. It's June and the blossoming linden trees have released their sweet scent into the balmy summer evening. Lotta and I have been close friends since realizing we each had more questions than answers about life, death – and religious belief. We sit on the balcony for hours – she a lingering Swedish Lutheran and me, a grappling Irish Catholic – drinking white wine and feeling our way forward in the dark.

This evening, Lotta is railing against her fellow Swedes' inability to read a metaphor. Her homeland is now so secular, she says, that people struggle to think beyond the literal. The Swedes may be world champions in interior design and pop music but, when it comes to the spiritual dimension, to considering something that exists beyond their immediate experience, she says the Swedes are lost at sea.

'Losing the ability to talk about religion is like losing a language. You're no longer aware of what you're no longer able to think about, or about what you can no longer express and, eventually, what you no longer feel.'

Everyone has an inner life and inner thoughts, she says, but what happens if a society questions your right to have them, or strips you of the language to express them?

Days later, I'm amused to hear our balcony conversation features in Lotta's latest weekly newspaper column. Later, I hear it was one of the year's most-shared articles on the *Svenska Dagbladet* website. Her polemic about modern life, stripped of a spiritual dimension, clearly hit a nerve.

Given how many Irish are intrigued by the Swedes, I wonder how many of us sympathize with their struggle. Of course, the two countries have vastly different experiences of religious institutions and faith. In Sweden, leading intellectuals are, these days, rebelling against the state Lutheran Church by declaring themselves Catholic. Irish intellectuals were among the first to walk out after revelations about Catholic institutions and clergy, if they hadn't already left, precipitating a wider public departure and exhausted silence on religion. Not that there was much said before. The silence that bothers me now may be any number of silences: anger, exhaustion, apathy, ignorance or bewilderment – or all of the above. Living for years in a country like Germany, where the Catholic Church is traditionally a minority faith, changes the perspective and assumptions about belief. Thanks to the cultural legacy of Martin Luther, there is a weaker tradition of institutions attempting to own religious faith. One of the rebellious monk's core principles, triggering the Reformation, was that anyone seeking a relationship with God could do so themselves, without clerical intermediaries. As a result, even Germans who despair or mock organized religion can, without difficulty, separate spirituality from institution, like they separate democracy from a corrupt political party.

Only when I moved to Germany did I realize the unusual and problematic nature of our set-up in Ireland. Inside a Catholic educational system, Catholic indoctrination was as much of a given as stuffy classroom air at day's end. But our experience was not normal, just common. And much of what happened – or didn't happen – in those Catholic school classrooms, above all in our religion classes, continues to colour my generation now. That much is clear when you mention religious belief in Ireland – thinking often automatically jumps to religion-as-institution and, in turn, to the Catholic Church.

That our formative experiences of Catholicism have colonized the space where we might reflect on the role of spirituality in our lives is also clear when people concede their spiritual needs but are too embarrassed to discuss them any further. There is a fear of appearing backward, as a hostage of supernatural thinking or, for Irish Catholics, of being beholden to a discredited institution. I'm struck, on visits to Ireland, by how defensive some people can get when challenged about the need for – and worth of – a belief system such as Catholicism. Some have a deep antipathy to faith systems, no doubt, but others lack the language to explore their inner feelings about spirituality and faith – and to do so in public – and thus push back.

As I make my own journey trying to understand Catholicism, independently of Ireland, the most interesting parts of the map are the grey zones. But these grey zones rarely feature in the Irish discussion of Catholicism, where the choice seems binary: you have to be either all in, or all out. Getting away from the institutional Catholic Church, many people with spiritual or reflective needs have found yoga and meditation. Others have embraced popular psychology or science. And still others, frozen with grief at funerals, find themselves returning, like prodigal sons and daughters, to the unreflected familiarity of ritual or the comfort of long-neglected Christian ideas about life, death, mercy and grace. Like returning to a spouse with a record of domestic violence, however, the return is often ambivalent and conditional.

A great source of ambivalence is the anger towards an institution in Ireland that failed badly, then tried to cover up its failure. After years taking literally the metaphor of their faithful as a 'flock', the institutional Church continued to treat people, outraged by revelations, as a lumpen woolly-brained herd simply needing to be calmed and corralled.

Another source of wariness, at least for me, is a painful realization of my own shortcomings when it comes to making an informed choice about faith, simply because I feel so uninformed. Exploring vestigial traces of religious or spiritual attachment should be easy, given how, until recently, most Irish spent their early years in Catholic schools, with half an hour of religion daily in primary and countless more hours in secondary. Yet many emerge with an understanding of Catholic faith and doctrine that is as rudimentary as their grasp of another compulsory subject in our schools: the Irish language. The resulting debates, more often than not, reflect these rudimentary levels of knowledge.

A crucial part of being Irish is coming to terms with a uniquely Irish model of education with in-built religious indoctrination. This

system's historical model arose from the economic need of an impoverished independent Irish state. Yet the effect of inviting in the
Catholic Church was to lock people into a tried, trusted pay-and-
pray model. Once they'd rejected this 'flock' and 'sheep' model of
religion, many in Ireland saw their exit from the Church as inevitable. My approach is slightly different: if I were to reject the Catholic
faith, then I'd prefer to do it in style – informed rather than angry –
rather than follow the flock to graze safely in more secular pastures.
And for that I need language, rather than silence, to collate my
thoughts. But I feel the language has been withheld, for reasons of
control.

In George Orwell's dystopian novel *1984*, written in 1949, a totalitarian party dominates every aspect of citizens' lives. A language
reform creates Newspeak and eliminates vast swatches of vocabulary
with the aim of preventing even the possibility of rebellious thoughts.
The Soviet Union banned *1984* because Stalin objected to Orwell's
warning against totalitarian regimes. Meanwhile, the authorities in
1950s Catholic Ireland, utterly reliable in their inability to read a
metaphor or spot satire, banned the same book as part of a campaign
against the imagined menace of godless Marxism.

Decades on from *1984*'s warnings on Newspeak, the language of
spiritual belief is so absent in Ireland, anathema to most, that even
young non-believers struggle with whether they are atheist or agnos-
tic. In a few short decades Ireland has gone from a country where you
couldn't escape religion – whether silent, pervasive devotion or rigid
doctrinal practice – to a place where faith dare not speak its name.
Someone summed up religion in twenty-first-century Ireland to
me as 'missing but not missed'. But if, for the sake of argument, someone felt something was missing, would they even be able to articulate
the feeling?

My generation was spared the worst excesses of Catholic doctrine,
yet what I remember from my religious education is a lingering feeling of being patronized. To trigger that feeling, all I have to do is
think of the name Zaccheus. Generations of Irish of a certain age will
remember how our religious syllabus turned a minor biblical figure,
mentioned in passing only in the Gospel of St Luke, into a leading

man.* Wondering why a minor tax collector still taxes me, I contact my first and all-time favourite teacher, Brid Verdon. She saw me through my first years at primary school and is now retired.

'Oh yes, Zaccheus,' she says over coffee, releasing a sigh as she explains what she remembers about the story's purpose in our religion books. It highlighted how Jesus forgave the sins of the ostracized tax collector and demonstrated reconciliation ahead of children's First Communion and Confession. But Mrs Verdon soon tired of teaching the story of Zaccheus.

'Year after year we had to trot it out, trying to embellish it or dramatize it,' says Mrs Verdon. 'He was up in a tree so you'd have to put some child up on a height and other children trotting around with Jesus.'

What was going on behind that story?

Our religion course, Mrs Verdon says, believed an anecdotal, experiential approach to religion was best. Anything to get children away from the rote learning that went before. That the new approach left me with little memory of my primary religion lessons – apart from poor Zaccheus – speaks for itself. In her kitchen we debate the merits of different education approaches for a while.

'The thing with rote learning is that it sticks in your head,' says Mrs Verdon, 'whether it's the times tables or the catechism.'

My first and last encounter with religious rote learning, and the catechism, came at the end of my first year in St Paul's College, a secondary school run by the Vincentian order on Dublin's northside. Our last class before the summer holidays was religion with our Armagh-born teacher Fr Tom Dougan. He was a salty figure who liked to burst into class shouting, 'Sit ye down and shut ye up.'

It was June 1990 and the air in our prefabricated classroom was heavy with anticipation of the looming holidays, now just minutes away. But Fr Dougan was making no concessions. His mind was on the photocopied page he handed us as he walked around, each side

---

* The story goes that because Zaccheus worked on behalf of the occupying Roman Empire, he was considered abhorrent amongst the Jewish community. So it was quite a shock to Jesus's followers that, when he was preaching in Jericho, Jesus made a point of summoning Zaccheus from his hiding spot up a tree and invited himself to the tax collector's house for supper.

containing two pages of dense, wobbly type. As he passed me, he muttered, 'I shouldn't be giving ye these.' If he wanted to pique my curiosity, he succeeded, and I began to read.

Question: Who made the world?

Answer: God made the world.

Q: Who is God?

A: God is the creator and Sovereign Lord of heaven and earth and of all things.

Q: How many gods are there?

A: There is but one God. Who will reward the good and punish the wicked.

Q: Where is God?

A: God is everywhere; but He manifests His glory in heaven, where He is enjoyed by the blessed.

As readers of a certain generation know, and will never forget, this is the opening of the green-covered *Catechism of the Catholic Church* which runs to nearly 3,000 questions and answers. The book is used as a manual in catechesis, the religious teaching of children and adult converts, setting out doctrine and introducing the sacraments.

The catechism as the basis of faith formation was popularized by renegade monk and Reformation leader Martin Luther in 1529; the Catholic Church played catch-up with its own version in 1566. Generations of Irish schoolchildren were drilled on its contents, expected to provide an answer by rote when the visiting bishop fired a random question their way. Failure to do so meant you might not make your Confirmation, and result in a – proverbial or literal – belt of the bishop's crozier.

If you're looking for an amusing after-dinner game, lob one of the questions above at an Irish pensioner without warning and chances are they'll rabbit back the answer. They may not know what the answer means, nor where in their mind it has been hiding, but that was their Catholic experience.

I am relieved I was spared that little green book but, three decades after encountering it, I still remember my fascination with its attempt to collate the knowledge and teachings of the Catholic Church in a way that was so at odds with the spirit of our religion books.

In St Paul's, the catechism disappeared along with Fr Dougan in June 1990. His last act of insubordination as a teacher suggests he was no fan of our religion course – which we viewed as a 'doss' class with no exams. I would like to understand more but when I head back to St Paul's I learn that Fr Dougan died just a year after his retirement. Another priest from that time, Fr Eugene Curran, is still there and is amused to see me back. I ask if he has a theory about why Fr Tom might have slipped us the catechism on his last day.

Fr Eugene says his late colleague was someone who believed teachers should provoke thought. In religion class, that meant making people think about what it meant to believe – or not.

'My approach, which would have come out of discussions with Tom, is that I'd rather you go out of religion class a convinced atheist than a lazy Catholic,' he says. 'It's important to know what you believe.'

So what do I believe? In school I remember only rare moments when I was truly stimulated. In fourth year, my brain was giddy after its first brush with philosophy in Plato's *Last Days of Socrates*. In history class, I couldn't get enough of the Reformation. I inhaled as much as I could about this real-life clash of ideas and battle for power, far more interesting to me than the fictional *Lord of the Rings* saga we read in English class. Even without delving into questions of faith, I could sense religion had far more to offer than our textbooks suggested.

But the spark lit briefly by Fr Tom was soon extinguished, and subsequent religion teachers failed to hold my interest. While my maths teacher would not have apologized for teaching algebra, my overwhelming memory of those obliged to ground us in religious education is their air of apologetic insecurity. And, sensing their lack of confidence or conviction as only schoolchildren can, I soon switched off. In hindsight, the low-level tension in these classes signalled a widening fault-line in the wider society. A decades-old entitlement of the Catholic Church to use its schools as a site for faith formation was facing growing resistance from younger generations who saw religion classes as an irrelevance, a waste of time, or both – and were not afraid to communicate this. But now that Zaccheus is back in my head, I am curious to have a reunion.

The Central Catholic Library is an antiquated but pleasant institution on Merrion Square that seems to exist outside the known space–time continuum. In the first-floor reading room, I shiver as, behind me, a gas fire loses its battle with single-paned sash windows that suck warmth from the air and send it out into the gloom.

It doesn't look like the library has many visitors, I think, as I study categories of dusty books and centuries of knowledge I will probably never grasp: Life of Christ; Church History; General History; Philosophy; Religious Life; Old and New Testament.

Perusing piles of theological and literary journals – anything to postpone starting work – I'm startled by how high-end the articles are. That takes me back to 2001 when I first heard the term 'Catholic intellectual' on a visit to Poland. My instinctive response – to laugh out loud: the words 'Catholic' and 'intellectual' seemed contradictory to me – left my Polish friend, a man of my own age, visibly shocked. He explained the importance of Poland's Catholic intellectual tradition throughout its history. During the communist era, Catholic intellectual clubs, where people could read and discuss books and issues outside the Marxist mainstream, were particularly important; they were what we might now term a 'safe space'.

Nearly two decades on, I realize now that my reaction back then was based on the assumption that my experience of my religion was universal and that Ireland's long, uninterrupted history of Catholicism gave it an original-of-the-species authenticity. So, if Irish Catholicism is the real deal, and I felt frustrated by what I experienced as low intellectual wattage, then surely Catholicism everywhere must be the same? Catholicism was a mental prison to be endured, then fled, not a belief system thinkers embraced or to which writers converted. How, then, to explain Catholic intellectual writers like Flannery O'Connor, Evelyn Waugh and Graham Greene?

Bringing my mind back from Poland to the icy reading room in Dublin, I feel intimidated and humbled by the thousands of books around me – testimony to just how intellectual the religion I grew up in can be, if its members are allowed to breathe and think. But Irish Catholicism has never thrived on intellectual breathing, and I'm not here today to look at any of those books.

I'm here to study the textbooks fanned out in front of me on the desk: the 'Children of God' course for primary schools and 'The Christian Way' series from my secondary school years. I stare at the books for some time, hesitating to touch them again. Then I reach for the first volume and flick through it quickly, as if to get it over with in a short blast of antique fonts and polyester sweaters. Soon the reading room of the Catholic Library melts away and I am a schoolchild again, feeling something between anger, despair and embarrassment. I start to scowl at the feeling of being patronized, but my scowl turns to a smile when I switch to the teacher's manual of 'The Christian Way', Book One, page 1.

'Invariably,' wrote author Raymond Brady in 1980, this course 'runs the risk of falling between two stools; it will not be sufficiently experiential for some nor adequately academic for others.'

You can say that again, Raymond.

As I read the pupil and teacher's course books in parallel, the more intrigued I become by what reads now like a slow-motion pedagogical car crash. Ireland of the 1970s and 1980s was modernizing at a rapid pace, but an unspoken conflict was building: how much Catholicism could this new Ireland handle, and how much authority was the Church prepared to share – or even sacrifice – to stay part of the new daily reality?

The 'hidden agenda' of the first-year course, according to the Christian Way teacher's manual, is 'the development of Christian community'.

Book One, Chapter One of the textbook asks students to explore the excitement and challenges of a new community by drawing a ground-plan of their new school. On page 4, students learn that 40,000 people were involved in building, and 140,000 involved in the flight of, the first spacecraft to the moon. This, we learn, is teamwork on a vast scale. After the flight into outer space, Jesus gets a first look-in on page 5, with His own reminder of community: 'Where two or three are gathered together in my name, there I am in the midst of them.'

He vanishes again on page 6, where we see instead the lyrics of 'Getting to Know You' from the musical *The King and I*. On page 9 students are told that 'school has a part to play in helping you to follow Jesus', but it doesn't explain how or why. Among many other gaps is the book's confident assumption that students are automatically interested in following Jesus: 'Here [in school] the study of your faith is organized so that you can understand better what you believe.' I'm not even ten pages in and already I feel a flash of familiar frustration that the book is raising more questions than it answers.

The rest of the religion book continues with the same structure: front-loading experiential components before getting, eventually, to the religion bit that sometimes seems an after-thought. The section on the Last Supper is preceded by a lengthy passage on how breaking bread remains a sign of friendship, even if it is 'no more than two straws in a bottle of Coke, the breaking of a toffee-bar or an open bag of chips'.

My mind wanders to the myriad wonderful German words I know now to explain what I am feeling. One is the pejorative verb *anbiedern*, the attempt to curry favour with someone. This can prompt a backlash in the other – even a feeling of *fremdschämen*, being embarrassed on someone else's approach. To my adult eyes this *anbiedern-fremdschämen* dynamic is what permeates the book. It conjures up in my mind an image of a middle-aged Fr Trendy,* trying hard to relate to unimpressed teens, who are too polite or too bored to say anything, but roll their eyes on the inside.

At the same time I don't envy any schoolbook author trying to explain transubstantiation in a few paragraphs to 1980s schoolchildren. One of the trickiest – and for some the most outlandish – aspects of Catholic faith is explained away here in short order: 'Jesus is really present in the Eucharist. This action of God is a great mystery and our minds are not capable of grasping it fully.' Perhaps it's no wonder the Irish performer and commentator Blindboy Boatclub felt he could refer to the Eucharist on national TV as 'haunted bread'.

My old religion books hop back and forth between religious education and instruction, with Book Two offering statements from a doctrinal black box: 'The person who believes in God is no wiser than the scientist about how the universe began'; the unborn child 'has all its human powers and features in miniature' . . . it is of priceless value because it is 'unique and unrepeatable'; 'there is an evil streak in us. This imperfect nature of ours causes us to sin.' No context, no discussion, and little assistance in the teachers' manuals. This

---

* A fictional character created by Dermot Morgan, who later played the lead role in the television comedy *Father Ted*.

Irish Catholicism is not open-source: it is proprietary software with locked-down source code.

What strikes me clearly now is a tension I sensed only vaguely, back in school. These books make a nod to liberal progress yet sag under the dead hand of controlling conservative habit. In many ways they reflect an increasing tension I felt growing up in 1980s Ireland, between two groups. One group assumed everyone should believe, or should want to believe, and still felt entitled or obliged to impose its views on the rest. The second group, seeing few ways to openly disagree, had lost interest and already mentally checked out, but in the interests of a quiet life, maintained an expression of mild interest.

In his introduction to the secondary school book series in July 1980, Cahal Daly, then Bishop of Down and Conor, wrote that he hoped 'teachers and pupils catch the author's enthusiasm'.

He added, 'Without it, there can be no credible transmission of the Good News . . . into our tired world.'

His hopeful words are understandable, written just months after Pope John Paul II visited Ireland. Many agree now that the 1979 papal visit was a tipping point in Catholic Ireland, the apogee of Catholic belief and self-confirming hubris that quickly triggered a slide into crisis and collapse. The Christian Way series is evidence of a conflicted organization struggling for the first time to make a case for itself, to convince an increasingly educated population of concepts previously accepted – if not always understood – without question.

Once rote learning became passé, and its unquestioned authority came under fire, these books read like a church leadership unsure of what to do next. The Christian Way books are the manual for a doomed sales pitch. Written by a salesperson hired to reformulate a traditional product for a liberalizing market, but undermined by managers who impose their final will, repackage the old product and insist on the last word in the marketing.

Closing the last book of the religion course books, I'm struck by the missed opportunity of it all, and wonder if this course contributed to, or merely catalysed, the drift from Catholicism in Ireland. If these volumes were the entry to spirituality and Catholic teaching in Ireland, is it any wonder generations ran for the exit? Among the anger or apathy felt by many of my Irish peers, how much is linked to being patronized in the 1980s? The salespeople didn't sound very convincing, the sales pitch was confused, and they wonder why no one was buying?

Maura Hyland is one of the Christian Way salespeople. She began working for Veritas – the publishing house of the Irish Bishops – in 1981 and was its director for sixteen years, until 2016. She says the authors of my religion books had the unenviable task of grappling with two new sets of thinking: the liberal reforming spirit of the Second Vatican Council and the experiential, pupil-centred methods of teaching that spread through 1970s education – including to the teaching of religion.

This was the starting point for her and the Veritas team. Complicating matters further, their clerical employers were divided – between liberals and conservatives – over whether greater openness was the chance of a new beginning – or the beginning of the end. Facing an increasingly secular world, something not outwardly apparent in Ireland at the time, Hyland and her authors tried to discard the stiff doctrinal language of old and explore the Vatican II idea of personal faith through language and experience in a way they felt was relevant to teenagers.

Did anyone, I ask, think of asking the teenage target market at the time if they found the approach adequate, or the language relevant?

The answer is no. The only criticism Maura Hyland remembers back then came from older conservative clerics who warned the books didn't provide enough foundation in doctrine. But this conservative camp was on the back foot in the late 1970s, Hyland remembers, with their attachment to a style of devotional Catholicism more at home in an era of passive conformity.

'People didn't wonder why they had breakfast, said prayers or went to Mass, it was the way things were, what you did,' says Maura Hyland.

As Mrs Verdon told me, the spirit of the new books was to embrace the progressive, pupil-centred approach to teaching that was popular at the time, says Maura. The programme operated on the assumption – largely mistaken, as it turned out – that children were being supported in their parish or experiencing religion in the home. What Veritas felt should have been a three-legged stool of faith transmission was, by the 1980s, effectively balanced on one leg – the school. Without church involvement and the family contribution, Hyland believes things were doomed, regardless of any schoolbooks.

While Maura thinks of 1980s Catholic Ireland as a stool with three wobbly legs, I see it more as an old car drifting along on stored momentum and fumes. I grew up in a country where some assumed – and others pretended to assume – that there was a need to keep alive Catholic Ireland, and its power structures. Bishops and the true believers hoped that Ireland was inherently, essentially, Catholic and would remain willingly so. But they confused others' silence with consent and agreement.

By the time I went to school in the 1980s, the introduction of free secondary schooling in 1967 was already making a huge contribution to creating a new Ireland, a modernizing, increasingly educated society of liberal pluralism. This collided with an institutional Church in Ireland that, historically, had little interest in encouraging people to think about the place of world religions in human civilization – and their continued relevance, or irrelevance, in contemporary times. Adults' understanding of religion remained stunted at secondary school level, if they even got that far, in part because Irish bishops guarded more complex theological teaching as their personal property. The study of the divine and of religious belief, a subject open to all at universities across Europe, was locked up behind Ireland's thick seminary walls, like Rapunzel in her tower. Religion, Irish-style, remained frozen in time, as simplistic as second level maths.

As education and prosperity opened new options in Ireland, religion was not on the menu for the wider public. People became increasingly confident about exploring the wider world, and their place in it, and old Catholic Ireland was primed for a crash. When the inevitable implosion came – the clerical sexual abuse revelations in the 1990s – the already loose wheels were not long coming off the Catholic cart. Irish faith – trapped in the arms of the Irish institution that had held it fast for centuries – crashed and burned spectacularly.

Implosion

PART TWO

Influence

7.   The pride of Laragh

'Not to speak is to speak. Not to act is to act.'

Dietrich Bonhoeffer

A framed photograph hangs in a display case at the back of St Brigid's Church in Laragh, Co. Cavan. Dated 19 February 1995, the photograph marks the return in glory of a local boy made good. Wearing red vestments, a white bishop's mitre and an open-mouthed smile, Seán Brady looks twelve and not fifty-five, somewhere between elated and embarrassed.

He's just been appointed Coadjutor Archbishop of Armagh – assistant to the archbishop and next man in line to the seat of Patrick. Here in Laragh – Proud Laragh, they call it – the locals couldn't be prouder. My mother grew up in Laragh. Her brother Gene, who played football with Seán when they were boys, used to joke that there was nothing holy about a Brady tackle.

It's more than twenty-five years since that proud Laragh man returned as an archbishop. Gene is gone and, after a memorial Mass for his older brother – another uncle who knew Seán Brady – I linger in the church to study the photograph of the man they knew. His life took a very different path to theirs: priest, archbishop, primate and cardinal. In 2013 he participated in the conclave that elected Pope Francis. Apart from actually becoming Pope, you can't rise much higher in the Roman Catholic hierarchy than Seán Brady did. Nor can your reputation fall much further.

In 1975 Seán Brady was part of a secret church investigation into one of Ireland's most notorious abusing priests, Brendan Smyth. Nothing happened as a result of the investigation and Smyth continued to abuse children for a further sixteen years. For thirteen of those years, until returning to Cavan to become a parish priest, Seán

Brady was 2,000km away in Rome, working as Vice-Rector and Rector of the Irish College. Not long after Brady's return to Cavan, Brendan Smyth handed himself in to police in Northern Ireland, who had sought his extradition on sexual abuse charges. In June 1994 a Belfast court sentenced him to four years in prison. That December, Seán Brady was announced as Coadjutor Archbishop of Armagh.*

Seán Brady may or may not have realized, but the day Brendan Smyth walked into that Belfast police station, a timer started ticking on the bomb under his prelacy and his reputation. Another thirteen years would pass before the role of Brady, by now a cardinal, became widely known, and he was sucked into the perfect storm of clerical sexual abuse and its cover-up.

Almost a decade on from that revelation – an unprecedented drama that tainted his reputation – Brady's name polarizes opinion in Ireland like few others. His defenders, particularly those who know him in Cavan and Armagh, insist he is a decent man who found himself in an impossible situation. Many in Cavan draw parallels to businessman Seán Quinn, another local man made good, whose huge contribution to the region, for them, counts more than his acrimonious downfall. What from Dublin looks like contrarian backwardness looks different from a Cavan perspective. And external attacks only solidify that support. In the way that locals appreciate that Quinn brought jobs to the area, they remember Brady's quiet kindnesses – his work as a teacher with his students, his comforting late-night visits to sickbeds and his presence at wakes.

Not that everyone in the area still supports him. During the 2007 ceremony in the Vatican when Brady got his cardinal's robes, a reporter in attendance from Cavan's local *Anglo-Celt* newspaper felt a lump in his throat when the Laragh banner was raised. 'The wonder of it all,' wrote Tom Kelly, 'how the sturdy half-back of years ago is now both the human face and optimistic leader of the Irish Church.'

Three years later, after revelations about his role in the Brendan Smyth affair, *The Anglo-Celt* shifted away: 'Cardinal Brady would best serve the future of the Church at this time by resigning. We

---

* Smyth would subsequently go on trial and be convicted for similar offences in the Republic. He died in August 1997, a month into a twelve-year prison sentence.

reach this conclusion as a matter of great regret.' Friends of the cardinal say that, of all the attacks, the negative verdict of his own people was the most wounding. For his many critics, Seán Brady symbolizes everything that is wrong with the Irish Catholic Church: clerical, legalistic and more concerned about institutional – and personal – reputation than children's welfare.

Then there are the many victims of Brendan Smyth who live their lives with the devastating legacy of abuse, compounded by the knowledge of how Catholic clerics like Seán Brady failed to stop one of their own. Seán Brady retired in 2014 and has never faced any criminal charges, though compensation payments in civil suits were made to some abuse victims. Even as the cases end, though, the legacy remains: this is a part of the history of Ireland and its Catholic Church. Seán Brady is also a part of that history and, as I explore that history, I find myself wondering: what is it like being, arguably, Ireland's most hated living cleric? I decide to contact him and, after a brief phone conversation, he agrees to meet. One meeting turns into four. Only during our fourth meeting will we turn to the events of 1975. As those events approach during our third conversation, sensing what is ahead, I ask him if he wonders whether the anger towards him will ever abate.

With a hollow laugh, he says, 'I said that to somebody recently and he said: "Not in our lifetime anyway . . ."'

Our first meeting is to take a tour of Ireland's ecclesiastical capital, Armagh. I take the train to Portadown station where, sitting in a black overcoat with his palms pressed together between his knees, Seán Brady is waiting for me.

Almost eighty but looking at least a decade younger, he eyes me up coolly and marches off ahead of me towards the car park. I fall in behind him, noticing his slight limp. No questions today, I decide.

The divisive power of religion is all around us as we drive through Drumcree, site of vicious and violent Orange Order march stand-offs in the late 1990s, and Loughgall, where in 1987 British SAS troops killed an eight-man IRA unit (and an innocent civilian) during an IRA raid on a police base.

First stop is the Church of Ireland cathedral, site of St Patrick's first stone church and burial place of High King Brian Boru. Then it's up another hill to the Catholic cathedral, begun before the Famine and dedicated twice: in 1873 and 1904. It's the brightest and cheeriest Gothic Revival cathedral I can remember visiting. Brady unhooks the velvet rope around the sanctuary and we step into what was his workplace from February 1995. Archbishop Brady told the congregation here, at his first Mass as coadjutor: 'The Lord says, "I alone know the plans I have for you . . . only our sins can frustrate those plans." '

It's too soon to ask him what plans he had for his time in Armagh, and whether he was able to realize them. As we look out at the empty cathedral, so familiar to him, I can't resist asking whether he feels he was an adequate successor to St Patrick.

'I wouldn't go so far as to say that,' he says.

In a voice I will get to know well – sing-song yet equivocal – he adds, 'I tried to do my best.'

We have a civilized pub lunch and a non-committal, getting-to-know-you chat about our family links, Cavan and my life in Germany. Behind Brady's easy country manner and fresh, unlined face, I sense the moving cogs of a canon lawyer's brain.

A few weeks later, he suggests we meet again near Dublin airport at the Emmaus retreat centre. It's named after the destination, in the Gospel of St Luke, of two disciples when they met the risen Jesus. A very different Seán Brady greets me, beaming and carrying a hefty black, leather-bound book: the breviary that has been at his side for fifty years.

'That's the wife,' he jokes, settling down to tell me about his life. When we get settled, I interrupt as little as possible. I'm trying not to be a journalist and, in return, I'm hoping he'll not be a cardinal. Though I notice he's not suggested that I dispense with his official title. It stays that way throughout all our meetings.

Seán Brady was raised in the rolling hills of Drumcalpin, Co. Cavan. Two weeks after he was born on 16 August 1939, the Nazis marched into Poland, starting the Second World War or, in Ireland, 'the Emergency'.

As elsewhere in Ireland, Cavan's farming families were issued with ration cards and compulsory tillage orders. The local church commenced devotions for peace. Milestones and signposts were painted over as a precautionary measure to confuse the non-existent enemy. Whenever it rained, as it does often in Cavan, amused locals watched the paint run off and the place names reappear.

As I watch, Brady begins his own journey, to Drumcalpin rather than Emmaus, lost in the memory of that time. His voice – sonorous tone, mournful Cavan vowels – is the sound of childhood Sunday afternoons on my uncle's farm, on a hill opposite the Bradys. Not for the last time I will wonder: will this connection help or hinder my endeavour?

Seán Brady, the eldest of three siblings, grew up in a post-war Ireland where the mode of transport was still the horse and cart and the rhythm of life was set by the farming and liturgical calendars. The rosary at home every evening was as obligatory as Mass – in Latin – on Sundays and the first Friday of the month.

The classic narrative of Ireland's past suggests rural, post-war Catholicism marked a holy high-water mark. It's something of a surprise, then, when the former head of the Church in Ireland, with no prompting from me, wonders aloud if the kind of religion he encountered as a boy was 'more mechanical than mature'.

Private Bible reading was discouraged at that time. Far better to examine one's conscience, so as to make a 'good' Confession. The thundering judgement of priests' sermons filtered into the community.

'Some would say we were saying prayers rather than praying,' he says.

Was it a world where people confused devout with deferential?

'Oh absolutely,' he says. 'The system was very secure and disciplined but there was not much reflection.'

As primary school ended, his mother recognized her eldest son was not a born farmer. So, in an era before free secondary school, he was handed the huge privilege of further education at St Patrick's in Cavan town, about 20km from the family home. The fee was £60 per annum for boarders like him. The school gave the family a £15 discount – and as for the balance, 'the Brady family paid, and paid handsomely'.

Founded in 1839 as a minor seminary or feeder school for the priesthood, the old St Pat's building has the look – and, past pupils say, the feel – of a traditional, tough seminary or monastery. Academic standards were high and culinary standards low. Life was regimented: rise at 7 a.m., Mass, meals, lessons and study, to bed after 10 p.m. Boys went in aged twelve in September and didn't emerge again until Christmas, by now immersed in a strict atmosphere where the cane was used liberally.

Today Brady can still remember the turning point in his life here. It was a school guidance counsellor's talk on how the priesthood combined the skills of the other three most respected professions at the time: doctor, teacher and lawyer. ' "A priest," he told us, was someone "who will teach the most important truths in this life, plead at the highest court and heal the greatest ills." '

Brady remembers no pressure from home to enter the priesthood, though news of his intention to enter the seminary brought approval from his father. 'He told me, "You couldn't have given me better news." He wasn't disappointed I wasn't to be the farmer.'

In 1957 he swapped one St Patrick's for another, this time St Patrick's seminary in Maynooth. Might he have gone down a different path?

'I thought I could do agriculture at university if I got that far,' he muses, his voice hanging for a moment before the reverie is broken. 'But, anyway, I got to Maynooth [and] that's as close as I got to visualizing another way of life.'

The institution changed but, as with the name, the drill remained the same. His first impressions of his second St Patrick's are seared into his memory: the smell of the chapel's oak seats and the high doors that, even passing through them decades later, 'gave me a little bit of a shiver'. He remembers a formal, impersonal place of discipline and routine, with an emphasis on academic learning.

He mentions a recent BBC Radio Ulster broadcast, to which I listen later, in which a priest of Brady's vintage recalls his seminary as a world of petty rules and penetrating bells. There were lessons in 'ontology, epistemology, cosmology, anthropology, Christology, eschatology and a whole lot more . . . but we never learned about human nature'.

Brady agrees with some of those memories but thinks other judgements are too harsh.

Does he agree with former Maynooth professor Patrick Corish's

view that Irish seminaries specialized in turning out 'docile and disciplined' priests – good labourers but not good thinkers?

'I would say that is quite true,' he says.

After three years, Brady was ordered by his bishop to complete his
studies at Rome's Lateran University. Compared to Maynooth's
stringency, the Eternal City offered liberation, though Brady still
remembers his sense of 'smug complacency' comparing Rome's many
empty churches to the full pews back home. 'We thought we were so
much superior.'

At Lateran University in 1962, his class of eleven were studying to
enter an institution that, down the road in St Peter's, was reinventing
itself in the Second Vatican Council.

In hindsight it sounds compelling to have been in Rome at such a
crucial time of reflection in Catholic history. After long days of lectures, however, Brady remembers hearing 'only dribs and drabs' in
the evenings from meek Irish bishops who made little impact on proceedings. By the time he was ordained in Rome, in February 1964,
Brady had a qualification in sacred theology; a doctorate in canon law
followed three years later.

In 1967 Seán Brady returned to his old school, St Pat's in Cavan,
this time as a teacher of Latin, French and religious doctrine. There
were twelve priests on the staff at the time; he was part of a younger
generation of teachers, and the machinery of Catholic Ireland was
purring nicely.

'If it's not broken don't fix it,' he says, 'that was the mentality.'

Liam McNiffe, later principal of the school, was a pupil then and
had Brady for Latin. He remembers a punctual and eager teacher, a
'thorough gentleman, and very unassuming by nature'.

'There was still corporal punishment but I never saw him slapping
anyone,' he remembers. 'He would appeal to your better instincts and
was nearly too nice to be a teacher, but you would respect him because
he was nice.'

Fr Brady also worked at this time as part-time secretary to Francis
MacKiernan, a former teacher and by then Bishop of Kilmore diocese. He drew Brady into the 1979 papal visit as a logistics man,
managing the bishops' bus and the Pope's helicopter. Brady returned
in 1980 to Rome and the Irish College. A highlight of his time there

was introducing Jack Charlton's Irish international football team to Pope John Paul II in 1990 during the World Cup tournament in Italy. The Pope wanted to meet Packie Bonner, Brady recalls with a smile, 'because he'd been a goalkeeper himself'.

By the time his homeland beckoned again in 1993, cracks were spreading through the Church. Galway's prominent and popular bishop Eamonn Casey had been outed as having had a long-standing affair in which he had fathered a child. As he packed his bags, Brady remembers hearing 'prophetic voices' that all was not well in Ireland.

On 6 October 1994 the real earthquake began. Northern Ireland's UTV reported how nine Northern Ireland extradition warrants had lain unprocessed for seven months in the office of the Republic's Attorney General. Among them was a warrant for Fr Brendan Smyth. It had been issued in 1991 after the priest from the Norbertine order was questioned by Northern Ireland police on five complaints of child abuse. He disappeared South before a second interview and refused to return.

On 15 November, the Republic's then leader Albert Reynolds told the Dáil how the Smyth failure had 'ghastly and specific consequences for the children of the country'. It also had grave consequences for his government. Two days later, after a row over the Smyth revelations and related judicial appointments, his junior coalition partner pulled the plug.

Watching all of this from Castletara, Ballyhaise, Co. Cavan was Seán Brady. He was just settling into his first-ever parish posting and now a figure from his past, Brendan Smyth, was staring at him from the newspaper front pages like an angry bull.

A month after the Smyth case brought down the Dublin government, Seán Brady learned he was Armagh's new archbishop adjunct – an appointment that put him in line for the All Ireland primacy after Cardinal Cahal Daly. Many in Ireland were surprised by the appointment. In Laragh, the surprise was matched by delight that a local lad would follow in the footsteps of St Patrick.

How did Seán Brady feel at the time, given the past was now lapping around his ankles?

'What do you do? You think about it and say, "Okay, this is what God wants me to be." The superiors and nuncio make these decisions; you make your best shot, knowing you'll want a lot of help along the way.'

The Smyth story could have ended when the serial paedophile died in prison in 1997. Francis MacKiernan, bishop of the local diocese of Kilmore from 1972 until 1998, told RTÉ around that time he had ordered a diocesan investigation in 1975 – but he did not mention Brady's role. A 1997 tabloid newspaper report linked Brady to the case for the first time – but attracted little attention. It was another story entirely, in January 2010 – two weeks after Brady had buried his predecessor, Cardinal Cahal Daly, in Armagh – that resulted in Brady's past being dragged into the present.

When we meet for the third time, I sense our conversation about Brendan Smyth drawing closer. But I hold off, noticing Seán Brady is circumspect again. We're in a hotel opposite Croke Park, scene of the evening spectacular for Pope Francis during his 2018 trip to Ireland. The retired cardinal's visible presence during the papal visit was a provocation for some. The father of a clerical abuse victim from Co. Down said he was 'horrified, stunned and sickened' to see Cardinal Brady in the welcoming line at Dublin airport.

Days before our meeting, the Cavan man got a very different reception when he was made a freeman of San Colombano al Lambro, near Milan. The town, population 7,300, is named after the Irish saint, also known as St Columban, who passed through here on his final journey to nearby Bobbio, where he died in 615 CE. Locals say the Irishman brought them the art of cultivating the vine.

'That assured a warm welcome for anyone who came in his name afterwards,' jokes Cardinal Brady.

Since we last met, not knowing how many more meetings we will have, I've been revisiting media coverage of the Smyth affair. Watching the television interviews after his role became public, I notice three main elements: serious allegations, aggressive questions and defensive answers from a flushed-faced cardinal, more used to deference than sustained attack.

In one interview he said he was 'deeply sorry that this has

happened' and stressed his determination to 'bring healing and closure and to ensure that such crimes are never, never committed again'.

But his apologies were drowned out by calls for him to resign – and
outrage over his refusal to go. A painful, four-year farewell began.
Things flared up again in that time with a 2012 BBC documentary that
included an interview with Brendan Boland, a victim of Smyth's abuse
who met Brady in 1975. A journalist door-stepped Brady, demanding
answers to questions about his role in the Smyth affair. The cardinal
was confronted with his own words from 2009, directed at a bishop
criticized in a recent report about clerical sexual abuse in the Dublin
Archdiocese: 'If I found myself in a situation where I was aware that
my failure to act had allowed or meant that other children were abused,
well then, I think I would resign.'

In a statement issued after the broadcast, Brady said he had provided written replies to BBC questions six weeks previously, but
noted they were not mentioned on-air. His 2009 words, he insisted,
had been taken out of context. He was referring to someone in church
management with authority to prevent child abuse, authority he said
he did not have as a regular priest in 1975. For critics it was a defensive
response and another example of clerical hair-splitting.

After a smooth and silent rise, Seán Brady's star was falling fast and
threatening to burn up entirely. The case made headlines around
Europe, with Germany's left-wing *Tageszeitung* daily joking: 'Once
they shot primates into space . . . they should revive this tradition in
Ireland for Seán Brady.'

At our third meeting, he's visibly agitated as we draw nearer to
the central drama of his life, so I decide to sit back and let him talk.
What's on his mind?

The cardinal mentions the previous day's Gospel: the stand-off in
Jerusalem between Jesus and Pilate.

'"Do you know me,"' he asks rhetorically, '"or are you just relying
on what everyone else, even my enemies, say?"'

Brady's not comparing himself to Jesus but throwing down a challenge. I sense the outcome of how well I know him depends largely
on how frank he plans to be with me.

After Cardinal Daly's retirement in 1996, Brady, as new Primate of
All Ireland, recalls how he threw himself into work alongside other

religious leaders in working towards what became the 1998 peace agreement. Barely had decades of sectarian violence slipped from the headlines and airwaves, though, before they were replaced by the convulsions in Ireland's Catholic Church.

Brady's arrival in Armagh dovetailed with a crisis that would eventually choke the Catholic Church in Ireland. What began as a drip of revelations about priests and bishops who had fathered children became a clerical sexual abuse scandal proper, in 1995. Former Dublin altar boy Andrew Madden went public about how Fr Ivan Payne had abused him – and later paid him compensation loaned from diocesan funds. In July 1997 came the conviction of Paul McGennis, from my parish in Dublin, for abuse three decades earlier. A dam of silence was breached and a cascade of abusers' names gushed forth: Seán Fortune, Gus Griffin, Daniel Curran, Thomas Naughton.

Setting aside his own involvement with the Smyth case for a moment, did Seán Brady feel he had inherited a poisoned chalice?

'We didn't have any . . .' he pauses, 'real estimation of the dimensions of the problem . . . that unfolded gradually, you know,' he said.

He is referring to the bishops' long, public scramble up what they called the 'learning curve' over paedophiles in the priesthood. They said they knew as little about the phenomenon of abusing priests as the wider public. This learning curve defence rings hollow for critics who point to insurance cover some Irish bishops had taken out a decade earlier to indemnify themselves against potential legal action by victims of sexual predator priests.

Guidelines for dealing with child sexual abuse cases were issued on Archbishop Brady's watch, but some bishops were dismissive and viewed the rules as advisory rather than binding. Behind closed doors, officials present at key meetings remember some bishops suggesting abuse survivors coming forward were compensation opportunists rather than victims. A siege mentality set in.

What does Seán Brady remember from this period?

A 'big long saga', he says, of consultations with experts and a church child protection officer.

Being head of the Irish Bishops' Conference requires many talents. One is cat herder, given Ireland has twenty-six autonomous dioceses with no hierarchy among bishops. These structures and strong personalities mean the Irish Bishops' Conference is prone to feuding, stand-offs and learned helplessness. Brady insists he kept nagging his fellow bishops until all agreed on the need for stringent child protection structures.

What I want to know, I tell him, is how Seán Brady felt in 1997 as he looked in the mirror each morning.

'Worried, I suppose,' he says.

'Suppose' is a word Seán Brady uses a lot. Sometimes he uses the word to draw a verbal and mental line between hindsight and original memory; at other times I sense him using the word to drag a potential runaway emotion back into safer waters.

He was worried, he supposes, but struggles to recall any emotion or feeling from the time.

Perhaps it's not surprising he went on to autopilot back in the late 1990s. After inheriting a dam breach – the legal and financial struggle to manage an escalating sexual abuse crisis – he witnessed first-hand how this in turn shattered a centuries-old Irish taboo on confronting or criticizing Catholic clergy. Countless generations of pent-up frustration now came roaring at him, all at once, in tsunami waves of rage. At his side through this period was Desmond Connell, the ponderously academic Archbishop of Dublin, who struggled to realize his world had changed for ever.

As we sit and talk in a Dublin hotel it strikes me how our situation – a cardinal trying to explain his life to a writer – shows how radically the world has changed around the Irish Church in just two decades. My eye is drawn to Brady's sizeable bishop's ring, the kind Catholics in decades gone by were expected to kiss. Old footage shows senior Irish politicians falling to their feet in front of bishops in a show of obedience.

Rather than kiss a bishop's ring – for my generation an arcane practice from another time – I'd prefer to know how Seán Brady, the Cavan-man, coped with the church meltdown. I ask him to go back to the late 1990s, and a daily drip of clerical sexual abuse revelations. How was he feeling in the eye of the storm?

'Of course it leaves one distraught,' he says.

Hearing him switching instinctively to the 'one' third person, I say, makes him sounds more like Queen Elizabeth – though, I think to myself, she is even more evasive on her feelings than he. When he starts talking about using prayer to face the problem, I interrupt—

'You're shaving in the morning and you're not really liking what's going on. Would you rather get back into bed?'

'That's right,' he says mildly, and I sense a discussion being closed down, an invitation to emotional reflection snuffed out.

As we pack our things and prepare to part company, I'm confused and conflicted. It's easy to see why Seán Brady has so many friends in Ulster and beyond: he is a pleasant, considered man who speaks in Cavan vowels familiar to my ear. His sister, he mentions in passing, says he can be judgemental and harsh. Priests who served under him say he doesn't suffer fools gladly.

Behind the easy country manner are other figures I recognize: the shrewd Cavan farmer; the Catholic clergyman who has internalized the Northern Ireland survival maxim (*Whatever you say, say nothing*); and behind all that is the shrewd mind of a canon lawyer. Is he really bewildered by my probing of his arid emotions, or expertly batting my questions on to safe grass verges?

Before we go our separate ways, we agree to meet again soon to finally address the elephant in the room: Brendan Smyth. As I watch him leave, I wonder: is there any of the original Seán Brady still left in there? After more than eighty years, mostly lived in institutions, and nearly six decades serving the Church – I'm not sure if he even knows himself.

8.   The fall of Seán Brady

'The scandal that somebody who was ordained to serve people should
so abuse the trust as for their own pleasure was appalling . . .
it was kept very secret, very, very secret.'

Cardinal Seán Brady

From his breast pocket, Seán Brady produces two battered black and
white photographs. We're sitting in a quiet room of the parochial
house of St Patrick's parish in Dundalk. I had asked to see a picture of
him as a young man. In the first photograph he's a teenager in football gear with a shock of black hair; in the other, looking scarcely any
older, he is now a bespectacled priest wearing a tight smile and a tai-
lored black soutane he brought back from Rome. That unusual model
earned him the affectionate nickname 'Wingless' from students he
taught in his native Co. Cavan.

We've met today to discuss what happened three years after that
picture was taken, when the young priest in the wingless soutane sat
down in Dundalk's Dominican priory a short distance from here. It
was spring 1975 when Bishop MacKiernan of Kilmore asked Brady,
his sometime assistant, to help with a canonical investigation into
allegations of sexual abuse against a priest. The priest was Brendan
Smyth, a member of the Norbertine order based in Kilnacrott, Co.
Cavan and Brady, who had studied church law in Rome, was to
interview Brendan Boland, the fourteen-year-old Dundalk boy who
had made the complaint.

Smyth and Boland had met as server and celebrant at a wedding
Mass and the priest had become a regular visitor and a close friend of
the Boland family. Boland remembers Smyth not as the pop-eyed
'monster' of the tabloids but as a handsome, tall, broad-shouldered
man who laughed a lot. Pictures from the time confirm that: Smyth

was a striking man with a winning smile. Boland said later his parents 'mightn't have admitted it to themselves, but I know they must have quietly revelled in his attentions, just like us children'.

After a year grooming the Boland family and winning their trust, Smyth took Brendan and three other children – average age eleven – to Cork where he abused him and another boy in a bed and breakfast. Later the abuse continued in the boy's own bedroom, on a trip to Dublin, in Smyth's car and even a private room at school. Brendan Boland learned to compartmentalize his fear of the preying priest: 'I was expressionless for I had no control, good, bad or indifferent, over what was going to happen next.'

After St Patrick's Day 1975 he confided in a local priest at the youth club, Fr Oliver McShane, who took him home to tell his parents. His father vomited at the news; his mother cried all night. Neither have ever spoken directly to Brendan about it. Fr McShane called Bishop MacKiernan, seeking information about Brendan Smyth, and six days later the bishop ordered a secret canonical investigation in Dundalk.

Brendan and his father cycled to the friary, where Fr McShane lived, for an interview with two priests. One was local, Fr Francis Donnelly, and the other was a stranger. The stranger, known then as Fr John Brady, remembers little about his meeting with Brendan Boland except that it was Easter Saturday.

Similarly, Brendan says any recollection of what happened once the door closed – his father outside – was 'lost to my memory for decades . . . except how I felt . . . I do remember being frightened. In my mind's eye they were old men in black. And if they made any effort to be non-threatening, they failed.'

With his father banished outside the door, Fr Donnelly began asking Brendan Boland scripted questions. Brady noted the answers and was focused – too focused, he says now – on getting a statement and writing up a 'strong' report. It was an intimidating situation, he agrees now, but the young boarding school teacher, in contact with boys every day, didn't consider that at the time.

'Hauled into a room with three fellows there, his father wasn't there, it was horrendous really,' says Brady to me now. 'That is only dawning on me now, really . . . his double victimization.'

An hour earlier, walking past the austere, red-brick Dominican priory, I almost tripped over a chalkboard outside the adjacent Big House advertising a pub quiz. Punters can win €160: 'Just answer 20 questions.' In 1975 there was no prize from the priests for the fourteen-year-old, bamboozled with an extraordinary litany of questions that read like a warped catechism. None of the questions were concerned with his emotional welfare.

Would you know the meaning of the word erection?
You never got to like it?
Why did you do it with Fr Smith [sic]?
Had you any worry it was wrong?
You did not go to Confession for some time after?
Has this led to any actions with yourself?
Would seed come from your body as a result?

Looking back, Brendan Boland is furious at the line of questioning: clearly designed to make him confirm that he committed the 'sin' of masturbation. 'And if I enjoyed that, well, then I must have enjoyed being assaulted by Fr Smyth. Follow the logic.'

Seán Brady says now the interview failed on four fronts: taking a legal approach intimidating to Brendan; separating him from his father; putting to him questions 'not respectful of the boy's dignity'; and shrouding proceedings in secrecy.

When, six days later, Brady interviewed another Smyth victim – a fifteen-year-old boy – alone, in Ballyjamesduff, he recalls he left out a number of the questions he deemed insensitive. But, again, he swore this boy to secrecy and never thought of telling his parents about the interview.

Ask why secrecy was paramount and Brady pulls out a well-thumbed Holy See document on solicitation by priests – 'the foulest crime' – where investigators are instructed that they must 'observe inviolably the strictest confidentiality . . . under pain of incurring automatic excommunication, ipso facto'. It dates back to 1962.

Was he aware of that document in 1975?

'No,' he says.

So why is he showing me?

Because, he says, it demonstrates the culture of confidentiality that was all-powerful at the time, primarily concerned with protecting the reputation of the Church.

When I ask if he ever considered going to the police with the information, he says it would have been 'conflicting'.

I let the word hang in the air.

Someone who worked with Brady told me, weeks previously, he is 'unshakably loyal'. Another old friend of Brady has no doubt the young priest was 'horrified' by what he heard. But even more horrifying for him, this friend suggested, was the idea of disobedience for someone 'moulded by the church institution and canon law'.

The friend adds, 'He would always do what he had promised: obey the Church, do exactly what he was supposed to do, not speak up and undercut his bishop.'

Back in our Dundalk conversation, Cardinal Brady breaks the silence over the word 'conflicting'. He floats the idea of what he didn't do in 1975 – go to the police, trust secular over clerical authority – in the conditional case. It would never have happened. Even now, his loyalty is clear in his mind.

'How would I reconcile that [going to the police] with my view? That the good of the Church would be important in my eyes, that this was something the Pope thought sufficiently serious to have excommunication.'

Back in 1975, Brady typed up a report of the interviews with Brendan Boland and the second boy, signed '*Bene concordant Cum orig[inalibus]* (agrees with originals) *John B. Brady*'. He believed the boys were telling the truth, he says. But after handing over the report, he locked away what they had told him in a compartment in his mind.

After reading the report, Bishop MacKiernan stripped Smyth of his right to say Confession but the priest's direct superior, Kilnacrott's abbot, did nothing. Fr Brady went back to teaching Virgil and Latin prose composition at St Pat's. His only subsequent trips to Dundalk involved hospitalizing school football players with broken legs. Brady says now he assumed the issue would be followed up, but he didn't know that nothing happened. It's possible he decided it was not his place to know.

If Brendan Boland had been one of his nephews, I ask, would he have been more diligent in following up the case?

'I probably would, yes, eh, sure. But eh, yeah, I don't . . .' He laughs nervously.

'The big question,' I suggest to him, 'is whether you let Brendan Boland's suffering touch you.'

'That's it. I'd say not sufficiently. No,' he said. 'It didn't sink in how heinous it was, how premeditated . . . it wasn't treated in any of the textbooks except "the worst sin of all" . . . [there were] no details of what effect it was having on children.'

We know now that Irish priests of Seán Brady's generation were trained in institutions that were hothouses of theology and freezers for emotion and sexuality. For decades the formation process took young men in their teens and early twenties away from the world for at least six years. Achieving clerical status was to join an Irish elite where sexual desire was something to be sublimated and overcome, while sexual activity was something to be eliminated. Canon law describes celibacy as a 'special gift of God by which sacred ministers can adhere more easily to Christ with an undivided heart and can more freely dedicate themselves to the service of God and human kind'.

Some priests say they find the vow of celibacy liberating, freeing them from the strictures of family life; others view it as a burden that compounds pre-existing emotional isolation.

'Male sexual identity is a primary requirement for priesthood of the Roman Catholic Church,' notes Dr Marie Keenan, a psychotherapist, social policy academic and global expert on child sexual abuse, 'yet male sexual identity cannot be evident in actual experience, as seminarians and clerical men learn to live in a "no-man's land", a place where gendered male sexual expression is prohibited.'

Many Irish priests say their formation process left them in a state of total innocence and ignorance on sexual matters and shocked at the revelations of paedophilia and sexual abuse of children. The shock – at the idea, and the reality – of sexually abusing priests may have been widespread, but such shock was unlikely to have been universal among the priesthood – or the wider Irish population. A Dundalk friend remembers a work colleague in the early 1990s referring to the town's friary, where Seán Brady questioned Brendan Boland, as 'where they send the child molesters'. A Cavan acquaintance of Seán Brady recalls a conversation in 1994 with a health board official from Killeshandra, Co. Cavan. 'The guy told me, the parents

of the seven parishes around Kilnacrott [abbey] warned their children, "Don't go near Fr Smyth." '

Seán Brady's home county of Cavan was torn when his link to
Brendan Smyth was revealed. 'There were clergy who knew, there
were doctors who knew, there were nurses who knew, there were
gardaí who knew, there were parents who knew,' said one caller on
the issue to Northern Sound Radio on 3 May 2012. 'The one thing
they had in common is that they followed not a written law but an
unwritten policy that nobody talked about.'

On the other side of the argument, Brady's critics are just as firm:
as a priest, a teacher, an educated man and, primarily, as a human
being, he failed in 1975 – and again as a cardinal, in 2010, when confronted with that failure.

Abuse survivor Marie Collins met him several times during his battle
over the Smyth revelations and remembers him as 'belligerent', getting
red in the face and refusing to resign, because he had been doing what
the Church expected of him. That loyalty and trust, she sensed, left him
feeling he could not have done wrong. 'Someone like that won't turn
around and say, "The Church shouldn't have expected me to do that,"'
she says. 'Canon lawyers see everything [in] black and white; I've never
met a canon lawyer who had a rounded view of things.'

This is the wall I face in Dundalk. Presented with arguments from
his critics, Brady sees them as blinded by hindsight: applying today's
child protection and reporting standards to 1975, and viewing him as
the primate he became, with the power to get things done, and not
the ordinary priest he was then. And, as he agreed in an earlier meeting, Ireland specialized in a unique kind of docile priest.

Even accepting all that, for the sake of argument, did he feel no
additional moral obligation – beyond his legal duty – towards
Brendan Boland in 1975? An anonymous letter to the police didn't
occur to him, either, as a way to solve the problem?

He hesitates, considering his answer.

'It's strange that it didn't cross my mind that I had the moral obligation to report it to the guards, you know,' he says, while still
insisting there was no legal obligation to do any more than he did
then. 'Even today, if the same case arose, you'd still have to go to the
diocesan rep to go to the police, you know,' he says.

A leading child protection officer I consult after my conversation with Brady says current legislation would classify a priest today, finding himself in a situation similar to the one that arose for Seán Brady in the Brendan Boland case, as a mandated professional. That would give him a legal responsibility to report the case to Tusla, the child protection agency. The official concedes that back in 1975 there was no legal obligation on Brady to do anything.

The Brendan Smyth case was investigated in detail as part of the Northern Ireland Inquiry into Historical Institutional Abuse, which sat for two and a half years. The inquiry was chaired by Sir Anthony Hart and had a mandate to examine sexual and other forms of child abuse in the province's care institutions between 1922 and 1995.

Concerns over Smyth began before his ordination in 1951, while the first explicit concerns of a sexual nature surfaced in 1973. The HIA report on the disgraced priest's life can be summarized in numbers: 43 years a priest; 117 convictions for offences against 41 children on both sides of the border; possibly hundreds more victims; at least 29 people besides Seán Brady aware of Smyth's abusing, including 12 Norbertine priests, at least 3 bishops, other priests and members of religious orders, several detectives and 2 sets of parents who complained to the police in Kilnaleck (1952) and Finglas (1973).

The report's 52-page chapter on Smyth finds systemic failings in the responses of his order, the Norbertines, in two other religious orders, and in two dioceses. Seán Brady's home diocese of Kilmore is found wanting on ten points – including failure to notify either civil or ecclesiastical authorities or warn other dioceses about Brendan Smyth, and Bishop MacKiernan's lack of vigour in dealing with the Norbertine order. Though outside his direct control, the report found the bishop had not exhausted his means for acting to stop Smyth – had he wanted to.

The report is critical of the manner in which the two interviews with boys in which Seán Brady was involved were conducted. However, it says it '[does] not consider that the conduct of the two interviews could be said to be relevant to the abuse committed by Fr Smyth, and therefore we do not consider it appropriate to make findings of systemic failings in relation to the conduct of the two interviews'.

The inquiry found that the only time canon law procedures were invoked to bring Smyth's crimes to an end – the investigations initiated by Bishop MacKiernan, headed by Seán Brady – no follow-up resulted. This subsequent inaction regarding the abusing Norbertine priest ignored provisions in canon law from 1922 and 1962 for just such cases.

So, after embracing canon law to conduct a secret investigation, church authorities failed to follow through on canon law and act on a report from Seán Brady which accepted the truth of the complaints made against Smyth.

This selective and incomplete use of internal church law had devastating long-term effects. Smyth travelled the world – serving in parishes on three continents – but only Ireland tolerated his behaviour. Jurisdictions outside Ireland were more rigorous: he was sent home from Wales, Scotland and the US. In Fargo, North Dakota, parishioners signed a petition to have him removed. Files suggest the priest's reputation as a predator had spread as far as a school in Australia.

Excluding Irish religious, the number of those aware of Smyth's abuse here is likely to be far higher than thirty. There was no significant intervention here though so many people in Irish society – including senior members of the hierarchy – knew about Smyth, only Brady has become a lightning rod for public outrage. When I ask the child protection officer why this might be, the reply comes back quickly: 'It's because he is so prominent.'

But is prominence a crime?

'That is a good question,' the official concedes, without answering.

Listening to Seán Brady in Dundalk, it's clear that the years of sustained criticism have wounded him – but also firmed up and hardened his defence arguments. He has given the events of 1975 some thought since his involvement became public, but he is wary of saying anything in public in case he is accused of special pleading or viewing himself as a victim.

All through our conversations, in the back of my mind, there is frustration with an argument put forward regularly by church figures. It hangs over my final conversation with Seán Brady in Dundalk, too: the assertion that mistakes were made because clerics are not perfect people.

When I ask him about the church motivation to conceal, Cardinal Brady concedes that secrecy provisions were motivated by preserving church reputation. Then he adds, 'The Lord didn't entrust the Church to angels.'

Something in me snaps. I point out that he's offering a hindsight argument, because the Church into which he was ordained had a very high opinion of itself. It was a church led by people who did not consider themselves angels but most definitely princes – and Seán Brady became one.

'Deep down, behind the modesty,' I hear myself say, 'I think part of you wanted to be a prince.'

Brady's eyes, previously hooded, now flash with interest.

'I didn't put my head above the parapet; was that a way to become a prince?' he says, laughing mildly as the temperature in the room plummets.

I say nothing and watch.

'I don't know. Maybe. You always have to consider it,' he says. 'The temptation to pride is always around.'

Everyone who knows him cites his gentle air and his modesty, but I wonder aloud if Fr John Brady in 1975 felt unable to do more for Brendan Boland for two reasons: loyalty, but also ambition. After all, he stayed quiet twice: after the original 1975 investigation, obeying the rules of the canonical investigation, but also in the 1990s and 2000s just as he became, in turn, archbishop, primate and, finally, cardinal.

'It didn't strike me then, the enormity of this. We're looking at it forty-four years later,' he says hotly. 'I didn't think, "I could do this but, hell, I haven't time." I felt I had done everything and beyond, getting the second witness, to make sure the case [would be] brought to his superiors and would be sufficient to withstand challenge.'

When I talk to Brendan Boland, the Smyth survivor says that some of Brady's words now sound like the cardinal's thinking has evolved on the case.

'I just don't know if it's genuine,' he says. 'I was a fourteen-year-old boy and I knew it was wrong; he was a thirty-six-year-old teacher, a canon lawyer, a man of substance.'

With no prompting from me, he suggests Brady's motive for his action and inaction was ambition.

'The only way you could get on in the Church was to keep scandal secret,' he says. 'If you rock the boat you are going nowhere.'

I make contact, through an intermediary, with a former pupil of St Pat's who was abused by Brendan Smyth. 'Michael' says he had huge respect for Fr Brady during his time as a boarder, from 1977 to 1982. He doesn't blame his former teacher for the abuse, but he questions the cardinal's insistence he knew nothing about the abuse or the abuser.

Michael remembers Brendan Smyth as a regular visitor to St Pat's. Smyth drove a distinctive Renault 4 car up the avenue where priests took their post-lunch walks, and parked in front of the main entrance. Smyth had two strategies for coming into contact with boys, says Michael. On Friday afternoon he would wait to give boarders a lift home for the weekend. Or he would march into the school, have boys called out of evening study, bring them to the visitors' room and abuse them there.

'The priests knew each other and priests would know the comings and goings of other priests, it was a topic of conversation,' says Michael. He is sure Bishop MacKiernan and the school principal, Fr Colm Hurley, would have been aware of the priest's presence.

'I think Fr Brady knew,' he adds.

Michael told me that therapy had helped him to recognize the abuse he endured as 'a fragment of my identity . . . but I'm not in its spell any more'. He is less sure about the spell surrounding Seán Brady.

Another former pupil of St Pat's, a boarder from 1972 to 1974, who remains fond of Seán Brady, says the layout of the school makes it unlikely a priest from outside could visit the school – go in the little-used front door and take pupils into the visitors' room – without other priests knowing.

'The priests' refectory was directly opposite the visitor room, it would be difficult for somebody to park and go in without being seen,' he says. 'The windows are to the front.'

When I put the two men's observations to Cardinal Brady in a follow-up phone call, he sounds surprised and shocked by the claims – and denies them strenuously.

'Absolutely not, I didn't know, I didn't even know about Fr Smyth being there,' he says. 'You know the way people think you know more than you know. This fella is expecting me to step up but I have no idea really. I was never aware of any of that.' Brady insists, 'It would have been possible for anyone to go into the college unnoticed. The front door was open and unattended.'

Michael isn't surprised to hear Brady's denials. He's long since learned to deal with two Seán Bradys: the gentle priest he knew and the man he sees today, whose position in the Church, he says, hinges on Cardinal Brady maintaining what he calls an 'entrenched position'.

'Therapy helped me take him down from the pedestal I had him on,' said Michael. 'I think now he was given a position of power that he didn't want, didn't deserve, and has to live now with the consequences of abiding by rules he didn't write.'

These questions around power – sought and deserved – figure in my final contact with the cardinal. After we discuss Michael's abuse at St Pat's, Brady circles back to the idea I raised in Dundalk that he was driven – and compromised – by ambition. He says he is surprised that 'some people' – I think he means me – could jump to that conclusion. I'm intrigued my suggestion is still preoccupying him.

'St Pat's College in Cavan didn't seem very ambitious,' he says. 'When I was in Rome I wouldn't have been noticed for hanging around the Vatican.'

I suggest that ambition can take many forms: 'some people', I say (because two can play at that game), think strategically, to be in the right place at the right time to meet the right people; others achieve professional progress with a reputation as a loyal, safe pair of hands.

The tense atmosphere on the phone reminds me of the end of our talk in Dundalk. As we prepare to head our separate ways, Seán Brady's face is flushed. I am feeling on edge at the charged atmosphere. To defuse things, I ask him how he feels now about what happened then.

'There's a sadness, I suppose, a great sadness, a pain about the situation about Brendan Boland,' says Seán Brady. 'That we weren't more enlightened at the time, that it didn't occur to me to go to the police, or suggest someone else go to the police.'

He would consider meeting Brendan Boland, but that is unlikely to happen. In an email Boland writes he fears the cardinal would 'control everything . . . I don't want him to be in control any more'.

Nearly half a century after Seán Brady first heard of Brendan Smyth, how does Ireland's only cardinal view a man portrayed as a monster in the media, a man he says he never met? Sitting in the Dundalk parochial house, he thinks for a long time.

'He was a product of the system too. He abused the trust of the children and the trust parents of children placed in him.'

A 'product of the system too' – like himself? Sometime later, rereading that remark, I ask him in an email whether, in hindsight, he is ever annoyed that the Church put him in the position in which he found himself?

'Of course, I was annoyed, and I welcome the abolition of the pontifical secrecy for cases of sexual abuse,' he wrote. 'I know well that the pain of annoyance is very slight when compared with the enormous suffering of those who have been abused.'

Many people in Ireland have strong, firm opinions on Seán Brady and few seem interested in shifting. Some see him as a modest figure who knew what boats not to rock as he rose through church ranks; others view him as a product of clerical conditioning that began when he was twelve; others see him as a coward and an accomplice, witting or unwitting, to a predatory paedophile priest. Conflicted between loyalty to the Church and the needs of an injured child, he chose the former but insists he was trying to act for the latter, too.

The institution he helped defend from reputational damage in 1975 had set itself up as the nation's moral conscience – yet failed its most vulnerable members. The Church, and its former primate, played a unique role in maintaining an Ireland of secrets and lies. Anxious to avoid scandal, they created a far bigger one. They failed Brendan Boland, 'Michael' and all of Brendan Smyth's abuse victims.

In the eyes of Smyth's victims, Seán Brady's continued uncritical loyalty today to the institutional Church undermines his contrition. What's clear is that, beneath the placid exterior, he is nursing conflict over the Smyth case. A conflict over how best to do the right thing, and how best to live with the consequences. The closest I ever got to this inner conflict came when we discussed what he did and didn't do after the 1975 interview. It was a single, unguarded, revealing sentence: 'I wasn't free to talk about the earlier thing.'

Seán Brady's time as primate was coloured by the joy of the Good Friday Agreement, the double scandal of clerical sexual abuse and its cover-up, and an extended phase where clerical instincts to maintain secrecy trumped the need for child protection. Was the Smyth affair, I ask Seán Brady, the most significant event in his time as a clergyman?

'Probably.'

As that realization hangs between us, the only thing I can still think of asking is why he agreed to talk to me.

'I feel there is another side, my side of the story, that hasn't got much of an airing,' he says. 'You expressed an interest. You take your chance. I don't know.'

Outside, we take our leave of each other with cool goodbyes. I walk through Dundalk, past the Dominican Friary, and think of the drama that played out there in 1975. I think of Brendan Boland, already traumatized by the abuse, retraumatized by a secret canonical investigation. No one can ever really feel the betrayal experienced by a sexual abuse victim, but we can keep listening and learning. Thanks to the bravery of countless abuse survivors, no thinking adult can now claim to be ignorant of how predators make children suffer.

Would we have dealt differently with Brendan Smyth's toxic legacy, I wonder, if he had served more of his sentence instead of dying suddenly? Would that have left open another channel for our anger over the betrayal and the feeling of justice denied?

The man tasked with investigating entered his first church institution aged twelve. From then on he was set apart from his community. I think of the man in the mitre with the twelve-year-old's smile – the Pride of Laragh. And, after the pride, the fall.

The Smyth-Brady case remains so difficult because it crash-lands into a great moral and legal dilemma: how does someone decide what to do, when they encounter a conflict between law and what they perceive as just? Seán Brady insists he believed Smyth's victims and said so in his report to his bishop. His critics, pointing to the non-outcome of the canonical investigation, say Brady didn't have the courage to press his convictions. Irish bishops and the Norbertine order failed to apply canon law, let alone criminal law, and fell well short of the Church's own legal and moral standards.

For survivors of abuse by Brendan Smyth and other religious, still angry at the blight on their lives, an attempt like mine to try and understand Seán Brady's thinking and (in)actions may seem like a provocation. They have very good reason to feel that. Permitting myself at least the possibility of trying to understand Brady may be risky, but it is not the same as condoning his actions and inaction.

What about those not abused by religious? What about the wider population in Ireland? Following the debate over Seán Brady in the last years, I sense a longing for clarity. *Guilty. Not guilty.* No court has ever found him guilty of any crime – and the Northern Ireland inquiry did not name him in its findings – but there are many, many angry people out there who feel he is morally culpable.

I envy those who see the Smyth-Brady episode as an open-and-shut case. As a man of the Church we, rightly, hold him to a higher standard that the clergy have always demanded for themselves. But, behind the anger, I detect a lingering sense of shame over our passivity or sense of powerlessness towards abuse victims that is very difficult to explain today.

Erich Fromm, the great German humanist and therapist said, 'There is nothing of which any of us are not capable, given the right circumstances.' Our historic, economic and social circumstances made us subjects of a very particular type of Catholicism in Ireland. While the man who rose to head the Church remains a provocation for many, for others he is a source of ambivalence – perhaps because we sense that in his reactions and behaviour, he was like many of us, only more so. This is something I am struggling with in my conversations for this book – a realization that evaluating our Catholic past is far from a clear-cut matter. It is easy now to identify and condemn the terrible and cynical behaviour of the hierarchy at the centre of this narrative. But it is more difficult to acknowledge the full picture if that means considering and accepting wider, complex and more challenging factors in the narrative of our past – including ourselves.

Waiting on the platform in Dundalk for my train to Dublin, I feel no sense of relief. Has my Cavan connection to Seán Brady blinded me, made me unable to judge him impartially? Or has that link given me a get-out from passing judgement on an impossible situation and a complex man? I don't know.

As I board the train, I notice a sentence emblazoned on the white wooden guardhouse. It appears to be station art but, in my current frame of mind, reads like a taunt.

'*You'll never see the man again who sat across from you. Better to look away.*'

9.   Sex in a cold climate

'The parish could deem them a Jezebel and they could be incarcerated . . .
the women were obviously overworked and underpaid, if they
were paid at all, and no one seemed to retrieve them.'

Joni Mitchell on writing 'The Magdalene Laundries'

It's a beautiful sunny day in June 2018 for the garden party hosted by the Irish President, Michael D. Higgins. On the back lawn of his official residence, Áras an Uachtaráin, a vast marquee has been erected. Dotted around inside are big round tables covered in crisp white tablecloths. This could be a wedding reception or an anniversary celebration. The tea and coffee are flowing but silver trays of sandwiches have just been cleared – and a group of women, mainly in their sixties and seventies, settle down to watch what's happening at the top of the marquee.

Irish television host Mary Kennedy takes to the stage to welcome the women, assuring them they can expect 'lovely recognition' today. It's been 'lovely hearing stories' from the guests, she says, on this 'day of celebration'. Lovely?

The garden party is to honour the women who survived Ireland's Magdalene Laundries. Once Irish society discarded these women from its sight. Now they are guests in the highest house in the land, living testimony to another Ireland. *The last shall be first.*

As Mary Kennedy continues to talk she hints at, but never mentions explicitly, why we are here: 'When you were all, I suppose, in the situation that you were, there was no time to be teenagers and to dress up and to go to dances and that kind of thing.' Today is to make up for that, she says, promising the crowd a 'girlie afternoon'.

Cheers go up from the tables towards the front. Further back, many of the grey-haired guests look on impassively. It becomes apparent when I circulate later that many, having lived outside Ireland for much of their lives, had no idea who Kennedy was and didn't know what to make of her remarks.

Two hours earlier I had stood in front of the Áras with a cluster of journalists, unsure of what to expect. Coaches began to arrive with the women inside waving furiously through the windows. Like a bag of marbles, they spilled out and scattered in all directions. They were every kind of woman, from twin-set granny to cat-suited beauty queen. Some ducked inside the Áras immediately, others dashed over to the journalists.

'We were all slaves to the nuns and the Church,' said one, Jenny, to the delighted journalists. 'Ye were amazing you kept it going, so thanks.'

The garden party is one event in a landmark, two-day celebration organized by the 'Dublin Honours Magdalenes' volunteer group with the financial support of the government and Dublin City Council. Businesswoman Norah Casey, another driving force behind the gathering, emerged from a bus, took two women in hand and marched them over to the cameras. 'This is about dignity and respect,' she said. 'This country is great at honouring heroes – and these women are heroes.'

'Magdalene Women' is a blanket term for a heterogeneous group of at least 10,000 women: single mothers, victims of rape and abuse, orphans and many more. In the Ireland that they knew as young women, the Catholic Church and Catholic state encouraged their own families and wider society to view them as dirt: a homogeneous group of dregs, easy women and prostitutes. Their sin, such as it was, was to flag the gap between the ideal and the reality of our Catholic country. Rather than acknowledge or address the gap, the inconvenient reminders were locked away in laundries, run by religious orders, where they worked for no pay. Their labour helped cover their room and board as a symbolic act of 'penitence' for their sins. Residents' testimonies make them sound more like inmates serving open-ended sentences in prison, with no sentence and no rules on parole.

A puzzling, uncomfortable fact about Ireland's Magdalene Laundries is not why they were set up but how we made them our own, and why they persisted for so long here. Countries from Sweden to

Australia had similar institutions in the Victorian era but began winding them down in the early part of the twentieth century, just as Ireland's laundries were gearing up for another extended spin cycle. Those countries realized that this old residential reform model was broken and open to abuse. Not Ireland. It repurposed halfway houses for women with nowhere else to go into what researchers describe as punitive places of indefinite incarceration and ceaseless unpaid labour.

For Ireland's first decades of self-rule, when Catholic and national identities coalesced, some ten laundries were operated in Ireland by four religious orders: the Sisters of Mercy, the Sisters of Our Lady of Charity, the Sisters of Charity, and the Good Shepherd Sisters.

There were many routes into a laundry: court committal; transfers from industrial schools and mother and baby homes; social worker, clergy and garda intervention; release from hospitals or psychiatric facilities. Some women and girls were committed directly to laundries by their families or church groups, including the Legion of Mary.

US academic James Smith says today's heated discussion on the laundries represents a huge shift in Irish willingness to confront its past. Before the 1990s, he says, Ireland was 'traditionally silent when challenged with controversial social problems'. The laundries acted as a 'bulwark to the state's emerging national identity', penalizing women who deviated from an ideal of pure maidenhood.

'In a still-decolonizing state, those citizens guilty of such "crimes" contradicted the prescribed national narrative that emphasized conformity, valued community over the individual and esteemed conservative Catholic moral values,' he writes in a study of the laundries.

This brutal approach to women lives on today. Some conservative Arab, Turkish and Kurdish families disappear daughters out of Germany, the country of their birth, to marry cousins they have never met, in a 'homeland' that is alien to them. Young women who refuse, or who live what their families perceive as Western lifestyles, may be murdered by their own brothers in so-called 'honour' killings, often ordered by the siblings' own parents. Ireland's approach was to disappear such troublesome women and deposit them – often permanently – in a laundry, part of what Prof Smith calls our 'architecture of containment'. Women contained meant shame contained.

★

Now 230 women who spent time in these institutions in the eras of Presidents Hyde, O'Kelly and de Valera are guests of honour of their successor, President Higgins. Lingering on the lawn outside the marquee before the event begins, there is an air of expectation when the President appears. He glides over to our group and a woman beside me grabs his hand, shakes it vigorously and then remarks, delighted: 'I never met a celebrity before.'

When he takes to the podium, a sombre Mr Higgins soon makes clear he is not here for a 'lovely celebration', but for a serious reckoning with Ireland's past.

'The treatment of vulnerable citizens in our industrial and reformatory schools, in the Magdalene Laundries and in mother and baby homes represents a deep stain on Ireland's past, a stain we can only regard today with great shame, profound regret and horror,' says President Higgins in a quiet, dignified and difficult speech.

'Ireland failed you . . . its institutions, its authorities did not cherish you, protect you, respect your dignity or meet your needs and so many in the wider society colluded with their silence. As a society, those with responsibility pretended not to know or chose not to know.'

There is little clapping, just intense listening.

The road to today's meeting began in the Dáil five years previously when the then Taoiseach Enda Kenny delivered another striking speech of apology to the women listening in the public gallery and tuned in across Ireland and the UK. He said they 'might have been told that they were washing away a wrong or a sin but we know now, and to our shame, they were only ever scrubbing away our nation's shadow'.

His speech, and a subsequent investigation, generated much public debate and outrage at the role of religious orders, acting hand in glove with the state, and comparatively little debate about 'our shame'. Sitting in the Áras tent, I wonder will today be any different?

Many of the women around me were in the Dáil's visitors' gallery for the Taoiseach's speech in 2013 and remember a day of emotional and cathartic release. But, years later, there is still much to be resolved. Many promises made in 2013 have not yet been fulfilled – the files of religious orders and the state remain closed, and plans for coordinated reconciliation work, as well as a memorial, are vague.

★

Once the official part of the Áras event is over, a buzz of conversation returns. As a journalist, but not reporting on the event, I don't envy my colleagues working the tent in a rush. It looks like inter-generational speed dating, as women tell stories that will never be anything less than shocking. It's always a huge challenge at events like this to gather the stories that need to be told: the pace of daily journalism is often at odds with the storyteller's own pace. Working to deadline, it can be difficult to avoid reducing complex stories to easily digestible clichés.

I drift around talking to the women who signal they want to talk. Sixty-six-year-old Mary Smyth never knew her mother. Both – mother and daughter – were put away in laundries in Cork: Mary's mother in Peacock Lane and Mary in Sunday's Well. Pre-emptively put away, she says, 'in case I got pregnant by a boy'.

Jenny, the lively woman who talked to the journalists confidently when she arrived, is almost forty and is one of the youngest women at the event. She lived in three institutions, the last one being the Gloucester Street laundry on today's Sean McDermott Street. A nun told her she had 'the Devil' in her. 'I never saw a nun hit anyone,' Jenny says. 'But their day-to-day life was kind of abuse.'

As Jenny speaks, memories of seeing *The Magdalene Sisters* in a Berlin cinema flood back. It's a compelling film about life in a laundry that raises some shocking questions about Church and societal responsibility – or lack of it – in Ireland. In the final frame we read how the final Irish laundry – Gloucester Street where Jenny was incarcerated – closed in 1996. Watching the film in Berlin just six years later, the shell-shocked cinema audience is unable to move as the lights come up. As the cover of darkness lifts, I feel my face is hot and flushed. I want to crawl under the seat as my German friends – no strangers to such feelings of shame – swivel to stare at me.

'*How is that possible?*'

'*Did people know?*'

'*Why didn't somebody do something?*'

The questions have a ring of familiarity in this country, given its terrible twentieth-century past. No one among my friends is comparing Ireland to Nazi Germany, I know, because they know how unique and terrible the dictatorship's concentration and death camps were. But their shock is real at what they have seen on the screen and, practised in dealing with interrogating their own past, they move quickly to the kind of probing that is less common in Ireland's public debates: *what kind of society, people, allowed – wanted – this?*

I was a teenager when the last laundry closed and, like many others, carry no sense of guilt for what happened then. But living in Germany has been an education in concepts such as moral responsibility. Even if today's Germans have no guilt for Nazi crimes, decades of post-war self-examination have created a consensus that everyone in their society should feel a responsibility – with no expiry date – to inform themselves about what made the unthinkable possible. Keeping that knowledge alive is their responsibility to the memory of the millions of victims. Knowing and understanding the Nazi past is part of what defines being German today, and has made the idea of moral responsibility part of citizenship. No one here fears another Hitler but many fear that being ignorant of the dynamics and circumstances that made Hitler possible could see new crimes, in new guises. The past is a process worked through in the present, probed and tested by each new generation.

Sitting in the Áras marquee, listening to the women's stories, I can't banish the hot flush of shame from that night in the Berlin cinema, many years previously. And I find myself wondering about the appetite in Ireland for moral responsibility, to understand how this past was possible in our society. How many of those collecting stories here, zipping from table to table, feel the same? I wonder. And how many newspaper readers? Struggling to get in the party mood, I sit down at a random table. The older woman sitting beside me leans in. As if she's read my thoughts, she waves at the crowd around her and shouts, 'Who is this all for? Them or us?'

Margaret McCrellis has lived in Birmingham for forty-two years. She is originally from Kilrush, Co. Clare, the youngest of six children – five girls and a boy. She was thirteen when their father died. When their mother headed to England to find work, Margaret ended up in St Mary's Good Shepherd laundry in Cork.

'The priest thought he was doing me good but I still have marks on my back from one Sister who took the rail off the curtain and battered me with it,' she says. Her hair was cut; she survived on porridge, bread and water for breakfast which, if she didn't eat it, came back as dinner. She was released after two years, in 1964, when an aunt made Margaret's mother return to Ireland to sign her out. Many women's families never signed out their relatives.

How was her family life after that?

'I didn't bother with my mother after that. And when she died, I couldn't care less, because it was families that was part of this,' she says. 'Without them, there would have been no laundries.'

As I talk to Margaret, I look around the marquee and consider her question: *who is this for?* I realize that, just as the women were not one homogeneous group in the past, they are divided today in their experience of this event. One group of women are enjoying every minute – the music, the chocolates, the sandwiches, the President, the rolling lawns, the VIP treatment. They feel empowered, legitimized, and are overjoyed at seeing long-lost friends. For now, or perhaps from now on, they have found a way to live with the anger at the religious orders and society that locked them away. It's a wonderful sight and they are the ones who make the evening news and the next day's papers, dancing with joy as musician Liam Ó Maonlaí hammers a grand piano onstage and keeps time in his bare feet.

The music is so loud, and the dancers such a wonderful sight, that it's easy not to see or listen to the other side of the party. While some women dance, others have fled the din in the marquee. Still others sit down at the back, motionless and in silence, letting the 'girlie afternoon' pass them by. They wear purple stickers meaning they don't want to be approached for comments or to be filmed.

When Margaret got her invitation she was ambivalent because she rarely visits Ireland, but decided to come with an open mind. I ask her how she feels about her homeland on a day like today.

'I'm not at peace with Ireland, never will be, because I don't think people'll ever really be sorry,' she says. 'They're sorry they've been shown up for what they did to us.' Waving her hand, she says, 'This all here is about them, not us.'

Margaret's lingering distance – and anger – towards Ireland will not feature in the media coverage of the event. Wondering if there are others like her, I venture outside the tent where I meet Mary-Clare, another woman watching impassively from the sidelines. I get us cups of tea and we sit surveying the comings and goings, not talking for a time. Eventually, she's ready to speak, less about her past than this present. As she does, her deeply lined face is a moving tapestry of pain.

'I still don't think Ireland is really ready for us,' she says, 'and as long as that's the case, this is all nice but pointless.'

It's hard to know what to say about her anger towards Ireland, as much a part of the narrative as others' anger towards the Church. The complexity of the Magdalene past still creates complex feelings in the present.

The Áras tea party came two decades after the Magdalene Laundries went from local knowledge to international scandal. In March 1998, three million people tuned in to watch *Sex in a Cold Climate* on Channel 4. In the documentary, British – and Irish – viewers heard from women locked up in institutions in an Ireland where, as one woman put it, 'the Catholic Church ruled the roost'.

Watching the documentary today, it's striking how it tells two stories: about institutions and about the Ireland that created them. Watching other documentaries made subsequently in Ireland, that second narrative seems to have been lost along the way. Phyllis Valentine grew up in an orphanage in Clare and was committed to a laundry in Galway by nuns and a priest at the age of fifteen. Later, a nun in the laundry told her she was there because she was considered 'pretty' and the orphanage nuns were afraid she'd 'fall away'.

'"Falling away" meant you'd get pregnant and that would be another mouth for them to feed,' said Phyllis. Others in the documentary spoke of the complicated interplay between Church, state and their families.

Martha Cooney was fourteen when she told a cousin how another cousin had assaulted her. 'And they got rid of me very quickly. The biggest sin in Ireland – well, apart from having a baby, in them days, without being married – was to talk. You never let the neighbours know. And to get rid of you, there's no talk, there's no scandal. So that was the safest bet.' Martha was taken to a Magdalene Asylum in Dublin.

Christina Mulcahy, from Carrigan, Co. Galway, told how she got pregnant the second time her soldier boyfriend convinced her to have sex with him. After giving birth and her baby son was taken from her, she was driven home where she was met at the gate by her father with some of her younger siblings.

'What do you think you want?' he said.

'I want to come home.'

'You're not coming into this house. You've disgraced us. You're not right in the head. You can't be right in the head to bring a child into this world. And you deserve punishment.'

Christina spent three years in a laundry until she escaped. She was reunited with her first son shortly before she died of a terminal illness, in February 1997.

Today, more than twenty years on, the documentary stands up as a solid piece of work that shows a compassionate calm for the women, letting them tell their stories. What's also interesting is how the British film-makers don't pin everything on the Church but pull back the gaze to cast an unflattering light on to the society that existed around the laundries.

Reading the media reception after the broadcast, the shock of television critics is underpinned less by surprise than inevitability. As the *Irish Times* said, in March 1998:

The story of the Magdalene laundries is not new to us, but the stark and moving testimonies of the women in Steve Humphries's Channel 4 film bring home powerfully the bleakness of life for some women in 1940s Ireland and the film illustrates the degree and intensity of the searing misogyny which existed then in Irish society.

A few hours after the garden party, a crowd is building at the Mansion House on Dawson Street, in Dublin city centre. The people were attracted by Norah Casey's social media and radio invitation to honour the women who had worked in the Magdalene Laundries. While I wait, I've arranged to meet former journalist Gary Culliton. He wrote an *Irish Times* article about Gloucester Street laundry a month before it closed, after receiving a tip-off it was closing from a friend who ran a B&B on Gardiner Street and sent laundry there.

Over twenty years later, he still remembers his surprise that such places still existed, and that the last nun inside it, Sr Lucy, was happy to talk. He recalls the laundry room as a dark, loud 'satanic mill' with a deafening clank of rotating, ancient metal drums that made it impossible to speak. Not that any of the forty women, mostly old and grey, were talking.

'Sr Lucy's main concern wasn't the laundry but that the women didn't get the visits they should have from their families, and that many would not survive outside.'

Gary says it's important to remember what closed the laundries: the arrival of the domestic washing machine and new economic realities – not public pressure from Irish people. Social attitudes were a factor, he suggests, but only after decades where the laundries, in addition to clean bedsheets, 'tidied up and put a moral shape' on the country. These institutions existed for people that the wider Irish populace, conditioned by rigorous church teaching, didn't want to touch. Many were institutionalized, after decades in laundries, and the last Magdalene women Gary Culliton saw were, he says, 'less in a physical than a mental jail. Were the women unable to leave, or was society not able to let them leave?'

We finish our drinks and join the crowd on Dawson Street, outside the official residence of Dublin's first citizen, its Lord Mayor. People are passing the time by singing 'Molly Malone', a song about a woman who – in another era or under different circumstances – might have ended up in a laundry for selling her body on the street, rather than cockles and mussels.

The crowd is so large now that the Luas tram has been halted and gardaí move in to hold people back as the first coach pulls up directly before me. Sitting up front, Norah Casey is filming the arrival on her mobile phone with a broad smile of triumph.

The door hisses open and women descend the steps warily. Some are delighted and pose for the crowd. Others are weeping openly – it's hard to know whether it's joy or distress. They pass by quickly so it's impossible to ask. Of the well-wishers, around two-thirds are women. They hold signs reading 'Mná ♥ Mná' ('Women ♥ Women') and 'The Women of Ireland Salute You.'

As the crowd claps, all eyes are glued on the arrivals. Not since the days of the Corpus Christi parades has there been a chance to see real, live Magdalene women. Decades ago, Irish children were told by their parents to have nothing to do with those women with the strange clothes and haircuts. Today onlookers stretch their hands through the railings to touch them. There is no fear of contact now. For some watchers, all that is missing is a red carpet.

'It's like the Oscars,' says one onlooker happily.

An American woman caught up in the crowd wants to know what's going on.

'It's a sad history,' says a young, smiling man, 'that started with Strongbow★ . . .'

His timeline implies this sad history is in the distant past, yet the story of the Magdalene Laundries keeps washing back up with regularity because it isn't over.

The coaches keep coming, unloading women into the crowd. I don't see Margaret from the Áras among the arrivals. Many of the women, I hear, have gone into the Mansion House via a back door.

After almost an hour of applause, the last of the women vanish inside and the crowd disperses within minutes. Dawson Street is back to its post-work emptiness, the sunny day stretching into long shadows.

For days afterwards I struggle with feelings of ambivalence about the Dublin Honours Magdalenes event. There was so much positive about it: it brought their campaign into public view, forced politicians to listen at private events. The media coverage was positive, Norah Casey and the other organizers seemed happy – as were many of the women attending. Several hundreds of Irish people turned out to applaud them. Everything went well, looked well.

Then I remember a young woman leaning against the Mansion House railing after the crowd cleared, lost in thought. 'It was remarkable to see the women's faces lift when they saw us, the polar opposite of how they were treated all their lives, they didn't need to be ashamed any more,' she said. 'But I wonder how much resonates with the wider population, not just those here today?'

The young woman put her finger on the source of my ambivalence. For the organizers, this was about raising awareness; but how

★ Nickname for Richard de Clare, a leader of the Anglo-Norman invasion of Ireland in the twelfth century.

many looking on perceived the event – mistakenly – as drawing a line under this difficult past? In thirty years we've moved from hiding these women to being shocked by their stories (or pretending to be), to state apologies, to gestures of reconciliation and a Hollywood ending of public applause.

But aren't we getting ahead of ourselves?

The last two decades have created a new twist on an old legacy: huge mistrust between survivors and the state. The former point to unfinished business – from a full investigation to compensation questions and a memorial – while state officials and representatives of religious orders say it is difficult, if not impossible, to deal with various survivor and related groups. Many contain traumatized members, they say, who can be highly sensitive and easily upset by proposals. Beyond the immediately interested parties is a wider population with varying levels of interest and knowledge about the period, to say nothing of ownership.

When I asked people on Dawson Street how they felt about this part of our past, most struggled to articulate anything. If I probed gently, asking about responsibility to explore and remember this period in our history, the most common reaction was a look of blank bewilderment. Though these people were motivated enough to leave their homes and travel to the city centre to show solidarity with the women, many seemed unsure that anything more might be required.

Two days later, I am in Geneva and waiting in a dark alcove of Palais Wilson. Somewhere in this complex in the last years, the UN committee charged with monitoring implementation of the United Nations Convention against Torture (UNCAT) has noted repeated concerns at Ireland's failure to prosecute perpetrators and protect those 'involuntarily confined' in laundries operated by religious orders.

I am here for the *Irish Times*: to report on President Higgins's speech to a gathering of the International Labour Organization. Our interview on his speech over, I tell him I attended the Magdalenes garden party and ask how he felt after it was over.

The President's face crumbles. When the guests left, he sat with his wife Sabina and tried to process what they'd seen: the 'worn faces

that came before us' and their stories of 'incredible, incredible depri-
vations in relation to freedom'.

Does he think recent debate and events have helped integrate them
into our history, or are they still boxed away like clean, unclaimed
laundry? He hesitates, then talks of a chain of responsibility, then
as now.

'We didn't want to face up to it,' he says. 'You cannot say people
didn't know what was going on. There was a colluding silence. And
that colluding silence supported a state that didn't want to intervene,
and assisted this institutional regime.'

10.   The necessary lie

'They're tearing down the laundries
Where cruelty prevailed
In gardens with forbidden trees
Whose walls we never scaled.'

John Buckley McQuaid, 'Girls who Lived in Hell'

I'm running late for my meeting with Mary Magdalene. Two millennia after she lived in Jesus' inner circle, her name still conjures up the notion of a 'fallen woman'. Historians say this is a lie that they can track back through centuries of distortion. But this lie has very long legs. I pass the stone pillars and head inside Berlin's Neues Museum to meet my friend Verena. Days after we have talked on my balcony about Ireland's Magdalene Laundry legacy, she has a surprise for me here, in the priceless papyri collection she curates. In a shadowy room she produces a small series of tanned, crosshatched papyrus pages. In brown-black ink, the compressed Coptic script begins: 'The Gospel of Mary'.

This is part of a 144-page leather-bound codex from the fifth century, believed to have been originally written during the second, found in Egypt in 1898 in a niche covered with feathers. The surviving pages have Mary Magdalene describing several post-Resurrection appearances of Jesus to the Apostles.

It's a remarkable text that fills in blanks in the four Gospels of the New Testament – and continues on where they conclude. In parting words Jesus, in Mary's Gospel, says: 'Do not lay down any rules beyond what I appointed you, and do not give a law like the lawgiver lest you be constrained by it.'

Such documents must be viewed with caution, within the early Christian Gnostic or 'belief' tradition of the time. And yet as Verena explains the papyrus origins and contents, I wonder how different the Catholic Church might have been with this in the official biblical canon. The Gospel itself offers a clue as to why that didn't happen: it would have meant men accepting a woman as their equal.

The text relates how, when Mary told the group of disciples of her encounters with the risen Jesus, Peter moved in quickly to close her down, without even addressing her directly: 'Did He really speak privately with a woman and not openly to us? Are we to turn about and all listen to her? Did He prefer her to us?'

Standing in the cool shade of Berlin's Neues Museum, hunched over the ancient text viewed as 'apocryphal' and excluded from the canon, there's something depressingly familiar about the phenomenon of an 'uppity' woman being chastised by a short-tempered mansplainer 2,000 years ago.

Another Apostle, Levi, challenges Peter and suggests it is not up to them to question someone chosen as 'worthy' by Jesus. 'No doubt the Saviour knows her very well, that's why He loved her more than all of us,' he said to Peter. After all, Jesus appeared to Mary first after the Resurrection. In the end, though, the Peter camp won out. First, Mary Magdalene was banished from the Bible. Then later generations sowed rumours about her reputation. Pope Gregory, in his Easter sermons of 581 CE, was a huge influence in smearing Mary Magdalene as a repentant prostitute or a promiscuous woman.

That tainted 'Magdalene' label was attached to women judged harshly by the Irish Church, state and people. After decades of shame, the spell was finally broken over those two days in June 2018. At the Dublin Honours Magdalenes event, many former laundry residents walked tall through the crowds, no longer feeling ashamed for their past. The applause of fellow women on Dawson Street reflected their real, deeply felt need to lift from these women a burden of shame.

But whose is the shame now?

Two apologies – from our Taoiseach in 2013 and our President in 2018 – have hinted that this shame is now ours to own collectively. But does the wider population agree?

Considering the estimated 10,000 women who were detained in Magdalene Laundries between 1922 and 1996, it is a struggle to comprehend the scale, complexity and longevity of the horror. The state had many layers of involvement, from supplying over a quarter of the total number of inmates to awarding laundries lucrative contracts.

Many people in Ireland, still alive today, felt then that the containment approach was for the best or, if not, they had no power to change things. Some who saw inside the laundries were not aware of the institutions' underlying dynamic of duress and violence. The decades-long narrative that allowed for the existence of the laundries – that they performed a vital role in providing a shame containment facility for 'fallen' and troubled women – was finally unpicked by various investigations into church–state collusion. But even the understanding that emerged in the investigations phase, into where blame should lie, is not the final word. It could yet be superseded by a deeper reckoning, if voices that remain silent ever speak up.

Through an article in the *Irish Times* and a series of regional radio interviews, I put out a call for the 'Magdalene Men' behind the women in these institutions. No men came forward to talk. They are keeping their secrets. Instead I got many responses from women, many of whom knew men who fitted the description. One woman told me she was the daughter of one such man who, she said, wanted to raise her but was refused permission as he and her mother were not married and his name was missing from the birth certificate.

'I was adopted against his wishes and against the wishes of his family,' she wrote. 'Further, I have no right to access his full name without my birth mother's permission, she won't give it and so I cannot search for him. It may well be too late as he would be nearly eighty now.'

As we saw in the previous chapter, beyond the silent men are the silent families. For decades, ordinary people accepted, or were bystanders to, a church–state complex of shame and control. They became passive parts of the narrative by acting – wittingly or unwittingly – as shame multipliers.

And beyond those directly involved, I have met many ordinary people on this journey who have a nagging feeling about their small pieces of the complex jigsaw of Catholic Ireland. Some are plagued by questions of the significance of what they saw or did, didn't see or didn't do. Could they have done more, said more?

Take the taxi driver who brought me to Áras an Uachtaráin for the

Magdalene gathering. When he heard why I was heading to the Áras, he told me a story from his past.

St Patrick's Home on the Navan Road. I used to work for a taxi company [with] the Eastern Health Board Contract doing the work ambulances would do now. You'd pick up four girls and you'd bring them to James's [hospital].

I said to one of the older taxi drivers, 'What's going on with those girls on the Navan Road?'

He said, 'Do you not know? They're pregnant. That's where their parents hide them.'

Some of the girls would say, 'Will you stop and buy us a packet of cigarettes?' I always said yes and went in. I bumped into another driver once in a shop. When he asked who I was buying the cigarettes for and I told him, he said, 'I wouldn't be doing that, stopping with that low-life.'

I felt sorry for them, thinking, 'Jesus, what is going on?' It's only after, when it all came out that I realized I was too busy trying to pay the bills to pay attention. I hate hearing myself making allowances but what options did you really have? I do sometimes wonder whether we're trained early not to look too closely. Or was it easier not to look at what was going on? Was it the Church – my dad was demented with religion – or was it the rigidity?

As we glided through Dublin, I wanted to point out the important differences between Magdalene Laundries and mother and baby homes. But in the anonymous intimacy of a taxi ride, I chose not to interrupt. He felt a need to share something that was burdening him and I felt privileged he was sharing with me his conflicted feelings about another Ireland: deference, powerlessness, conformity, passive participation. He wasn't struggling with responsibility – he had personal experience of the power held by the Irish church–state complex back then – but he was struggling with forgiveness, and with himself.

When we arrived at the Áras I wanted to keep listening, or at least tell him where he could continue the conversation. A place where he could bring his tiny, truthful pieces of our complex, conflicted past and sort through them with others. Something was stirring in him, but I got out of the car realizing there is nowhere for people like him to go.

★

My taxi driver is not the only one adrift with his feelings. Sometime after the Dublin Magdalenes event, I contact one of its organizers to talk about the ambivalence I felt about it – and still feel. Norah Casey said she worried the event would trigger old traumas in the women, but was relieved by the good it did. Meeting and talking gave many of the women a huge boost, she said, lifting the lingering stains of shame some still feel towards their lives in the laundries. *It might not be possible to erase your terrible memories*, Norah Casey told them in June 2018, *but we can add new, positive ones.*

Afterwards, she received over 200 letters of thanks from participants, she says, many saying it was the most important day of their lives.

But Norah Casey remains ambivalent about the laundries – and our approach to the legacy. As an adult she learned that the building that housed her secondary school, St Joseph's, Stanhope Street, in Dublin's Stoneybatter, run by the Religious Sisters of Charity, also housed a Magdalene Laundry. And among those in the laundry was a girl who got pregnant during Casey's time there and vanished from classes.

'The hairs on my neck stood up when I realized she'd been moved from one end of the building to the other,' she said. 'I did not see those people disappearing from my classroom. Did I miss it, did I consciously never notice people disappearing from the class?'

Rather than mull over seeing and not seeing, Casey, a pragmatic businesswoman, has thrown her energy instead into efforts to build on the 2018 Dublin gathering: to document women's stories and create a space where they can be retold so future generations of Irish people can learn about what happened in their past. The real struggle, she says, is encouraging people to own this past. That is something she notices even among younger people who volunteered for the Dublin Honours Magdalenes event. People like her son.

'My boy is twenty, he studies history at UCD and doesn't spend any time thinking about the Catholic Church and the debates. He is more interested in climate change, more focused on the future than the past, and doesn't feel any moral responsibility over what happened to someone in another lifetime in a world away from him.'

★

Months after the Magdalenes event, I'm back in Dublin again and sitting with a group of women friends. With no effort on my part, the talk turns to the Magdalene Laundries. A friend's twelve-year-old daughter hasn't heard the term before so the group – the oldest ninety-one – explain to her how Ireland used to 'lock up its women'. The girl is shocked and intrigued, making me wonder if this past is part of the Irish school curriculum.

Then one of the women, the artist Róisín de Buitléar, has something to share. As a young mother she was a regular customer of the Donnybrook Laundry on Dublin's southside in its final years, before it was sold by the Sisters of Charity in 1992. She remembers bringing bedsheets, terrycloth nappies and tablecloths to and from the laundry, its workings hidden from view.

'They would open a slot and take stuff in. It was quite weird but you never questioned,' she says.

She felt 'horrendous' after learning of the working conditions, says she had no way of knowing more at the time but struggles today with the memory of her ignorance then.

Today the laundry complex stands derelict in Donnybrook. Slip inside the main laundry hall and you can see rubbish and dozens of pipes lining the walls around a riveted copper boiler from another age. A dusty, framed Sacred Heart picture leans against a table leg; abandoned bed linen lies about in piles. It's a strange place that, now as then, exists outside space and time. Eventually it will vanish, given the prime site it occupies in one of Dublin's most expensive areas. But what memory will remain, and who feels responsible for that memory?

Like my Áras taxi driver, Róisín is struggling with her memory – or lack of it – of the unseen women who were, indirectly, part of her life yet somehow just out of view. She is not to blame for the laundry itself, nor can she change it now, but she describes a low-level feeling of shame and is anxious to channel that feeling about then into action today – but is unsure what to do.

These mixed feelings – of shame, confusion and impotence – are familiar terrain for Dr Maeve O'Rourke. The human rights lawyer and lecturer at NUI Galway is one of Ireland's most visible and eloquent advocates for the survivors of the Magdalene Laundries. With other tireless volunteers in the Justice for Magdalenes group, she pushed for the 2013 state apology and helped bring about the 2018 Dublin gathering.

Moments like these generate a groundswell of public support, she says, but that rarely translates into real public backing to progress the campaign's outstanding demands. 'Many people think this has been dealt with or, if not, they can't say what hasn't been done or why.'

There is a long list of promises Ireland made to the women that have yet to be met, from a memorial to provision of healthcare. Working with other support groups, Magdalene campaigners want women granted full access to their own files via a state-funded archive, as well as an advocacy system to assist women instead of relying on volunteers to fill gaps.

Years of campaigning to address this past has opened Dr O'Rourke's eyes to two Irelands: the Ireland where politicians apologize and the public makes sympathetic noises and gestures; and the Ireland where civil servants push back against Magdalene survivors and their allies.

A common argument campaigners encounter is that the abuses happened in 'different times'. Even in these different times, however, these women were deprived of their rights under the Irish Constitution and the United Nations' 1948 Universal Declaration of Human Rights, including the right to liberty and a right not to be detained unfairly or tortured.

In his 2013 state apology Taoiseach Enda Kenny spoke of 'direct State involvement' in the laundry system and, five years later, President Higgins apologized for the 'forced labour' and 'humiliation'. At the same time the Irish state refuses to accept its responsibility for violations of constitutional and human rights – violations in institutions it insists were run privately. The Irish Human Rights and Equality Commission disagrees, finding the state is responsible for violations of constitutional rights. Far from the applause of Dawson Street, government officials told the committee responsible for the United Nations Convention against Torture (UNCAT) in Geneva that 'no factual evidence' exists to 'support allegations of systematic torture or ill treatment of a criminal nature' in the laundries.

The UNCAT probe of Ireland recommended a full investigation

into human rights abuses in the laundries. Any Irish probes to date have not done this and instead have had a narrow legal focus and an obsession with secrecy, says Dr O'Rourke. Public hearings have been either limited or non-existent; there have been no subsequent prosecutions, and records are sealed when inquiries are completed.

Why does she see the state acting this way?

Dr O'Rourke sees a red thread of impunity. Once the Catholic Church, in collaboration with the state, was so powerful it knew it would not be called to account for the consequences of its actions. Today she sees a similar attitude in the Irish state which, she says, has changed its language but not its attitude. The women once viewed as 'fallen' are now labelled 'vulnerable'. Once they were an 'other' trapped in laundries, and now they are an 'other' in a custom-built legal limbo where, largely powerless, an all-powerful state continues to control the narrative.

Rather than civil servants behaving with care towards these women and the great wrongs done to them, many women speak of officials acting as if these matters from the past are exasperating administrative loose ends. Indeed, behind the polite language, many women believe these civil servants regard many of them as whingers or trouble-makers out to take advantage of the state. So they treat complaints as issues to control, steer and, if they want, lock away. And they do it, the women and their allies say, because they can.

Officials sometimes suggest the survivors of laundries could take legal action. But, in practice, the state has several deterrents to this happening. It refuses survivors access to their files; its short statute of limitations window makes no provision for historic claims; it forces women receiving any payments to sign a legal waiver abandoning any claims against the state; and its energetic pursuit of huge legal costs in the past serves as a warning to anyone who still wants to go to court.

'The state presents itself as a benefactor handing out charity while blocking survivor access to basic rights,' says Dr O'Rourke. 'The women are presented as charity cases needing something from the state, in some quarters they are despised and shunted around to be dealt with according to how the state decides to deal with them.'

This paternalistic approach to 'vulnerable' Irish people has worrying echoes of another Ireland that many assume has vanished, she suggests, as do the 'weird silence' and passivity she encounters often when she discusses her work with ordinary Irish people.

'The more we know about what happened, the more we know it is no way in the past,' she said. 'For victims and our society, the hallmarks of what allowed abuses to happen in the past are still there.'

Talk to survivors of Catholic Ireland's excesses, and their allies, and you soon hear a common and consistent refrain: the real risk of today's attempted remedies repeating, or echoing, the historic abuses they're supposed to address. Ruling out deliberate malice, as most survivors and campaigners do, one explanation is that unquestioned, inherited bias, combined with the sheer volume of horrors revealed, have impaired the ability to reflect on what it was in Irish society that made these horrors possible.

Look beyond the details of abuse and, alongside the phenomenon of silence, there is often a common denominator of confusion. The legacy of the laundries often triggers a wrestling match in minds between guilt and shame. Mastering this past requires that we define our terms.

The simplest way I have found for differentiating guilt and shame is this: people feel guilt for what they have done but feel shame for who they are, or how they are made to feel. A religious Sister who bullied a girl in a laundry infringed the girl's human rights and may feel guilty. The girl who spent years there being told she was filth may feel shame.

Guilt is a wrong that can be righted by the wrongdoer – pay a parking ticket, serve a prison term – while shame is what philosopher Jean-Paul Sartre called a 'haemorrhage of the soul'.

People often feel guilty about involvement in a negative, controllable event and shame about a negative, uncontrollable event. It is possible to feel guilt and shame for one's own misdeeds but also for others'.

The idea of collective guilt comes into play, researchers say, when a negative event is perceived as relevant to the group and thus individuals within the group. But any feelings of collective guilt depend on one's own perception of control over the system.

Many in Catholic Ireland, for instance, had no control over structures and events and thus feelings of guilt are correspondingly low. Things are more complicated with collective shame, however: this can be experienced irrespective of control over events, when the negative event or behaviour of others in the group threatens the image of the group as a whole, and you as a member of the group.

I can still remember my flush of shame in a Berlin cinema almost two decades ago as the credits of *The Magdalene Sisters* rolled. The laundries were not my fault, my responsibility, but I felt strongly that it was my shame, as an Irishman, facing the dumbfounded stares of my German friends.

No one in Ireland wants to be made to feel guilty for abuses in Catholic Ireland if they had no means to change things, nor should they. But it is normal to feel collective shame at the ongoing negative effects of the negative events beyond their control or before their time.

Many years of life in Germany have taught me to separate things: the laundries are not my responsibility. But understanding what made these institutions possible, and the consequences of such systemic oppression in the past, consequences that are still palpable now, *is* my responsibility – and the responsibility of every Irish citizen.

Catholic Ireland – in particular the Irish citizens working on behalf of its Catholic Church and state – labelled women in crisis as 'fallen' and encouraged ordinary people to view them as being guilty of having violated God's commandments. They had turned from God, thus society must turn from them.

This court of public opinion made the women feel shame for their 'guilt'; their families were aware of the risks of being shamed too, unless the bringer of shame was banished from view and set to work – for their keep and their reputation. Shame as a stain, to be scrubbed in perpetuity: that was the church–state laundry narrative.

Nudged on by a steady stream of revelations, documentaries and films, the last years have been about changing that narrative and freeing women of their 'shame'. In his 2013 Dáil state apology to the Magdalene women, former Taoiseach Enda Kenny said Irish people put these women away because they were not in step with 'proper behaviour'. This hinged on a 'damaging idea that what was desirable and acceptable in the eyes of the Church and the State was the same and interchangeable'.

Ireland's treatment of women who worked in laundries was a 'national shame', he said, caused by 'profound and studied indifference'.

But his speech fell short on one important point. Rather than naming causes of this mass incarceration of women, he dodged the issue instead with a rhetorical question: 'Is it this mindset, then, this moral subservience . . . that welcomed the compliant, obedient and lucky "us" and banished the more problematic, spirited or unlucky "them"?'

It was a landmark address by a Taoiseach, and his reflection on national shame and responsibility was greatly appreciated by the survivors. But disappointment has followed. Many victims and survivors are impatient at the state's outstanding promises. Others wonder whether the state considers shame and guilt the same and interchangeable. Conceding national shame but denying national guilt does not, to many survivors, sound like a sincere approach to addressing the past.

The state's confusion is perhaps not surprising. Many of us raised in Catholic Ireland joke grimly at the Church force-feeding us the manual on guilt and shame. Avoiding these complicated feelings is normal and common. So common, in fact, that Donald Nathanson, a US psychiatrist and international expert on the emotion of shame, devised a 'Compass of Shame' that suggests four routes that we use to avoid thinking about the things we would rather not face about ourselves: we either withdraw, attack others, attack ourselves or avoid.

Those who withdraw adopt a classic shame pose – slumped and distant – to avoid giving others what they fear are further reasons to hold them in contempt. At the opposite pole are people who avoid the bad feeling shame creates – through addictive behaviour, over-compensation or so-called 'shameless' conduct. A third group of people respond to shame by attacking themselves, accepting a reduced status in life to have any life at all. Finally, when the other three options seem neither appropriate nor effective, people will attack others. 'Here the object is to reduce the self-esteem of someone else, to turn the tables and make the other guy feel awful,' says Dr Nathanson.

By coincidence, Nathanson first presented his model in 1992, just as Ireland was slipping into shock over clerical abuse. And the four responses he describes cover almost every stage of Ireland's engagement with those it institutionalized, and the decades of fallout since.

Of all four options, the attack response seems particularly familiar in the modern Irish context. Angry attacks on religious, attacks on the state, even attacks on 'ungrateful' survivors. Many of these attacks have a shame component and, after reading the Murphy or Ryan Reports* or meeting former institutional survivors, it is difficult not to feel shame and anger. But where do we go with these feelings, presuming we admit they are there? Those who speak about the legacy of our Catholic past have deep ambivalence; others resort to Maeve O'Rourke's 'weird silence', perhaps the contemporary successor to President Higgins's historical 'colluding silence'.

Everyone has their own response, even if it appears to be a non-response. Given the sheer breadth of the revelations on Catholic Ireland, everyone is somewhere on the compass of shame – if they are open to looking.

Many responses, or non-responses, to this legacy could be filed under the German term *Notlüge*. It's a compound word based on the words *Lüge*, lie, and *Not*, necessity. A *Notlüge* is the necessary lie you tell yourself to hold something together. Some lied to themselves to keep intact the image of the young Catholic republic; some lied to themselves that they didn't know the institutions existed. Some lie to themselves today – out of convenience, necessity, or a confusion over shame and guilt – that these institutions were operated by religious orders in a vacuum, operated by the few against the will of the many. Suggesting this past has no effect on our present is, perhaps, the greatest *Notlüge* of all.

The applause of well-wishers on Dawson Street was deeply felt but

* The Murphy and Ryan Reports were government reports both issued in 2009. The Ryan Report was the report of the Commission to Inquire into Child Abuse chaired by Judge Seán Ryan which dealt with abuses in industrial schools, reformatories and other institutions controlled by Catholic religious orders. The Murphy Report was the report of the Commission of Investigation into clerical sexual abuse in the Archdiocese of Dublin chaired by Judge Yvonne Murphy. In Chapters 12 and 13 of this book there is more detail about the work of both commissions.

it cannot end this problematic chapter of our past, nor can a 'lovely' afternoon in Áras an Uachtaráin. That day President Higgins said the lesson of the Magdalene Laundries is the 'great harm that can be done when publics are not vigilant, when publics are cowed into not having the courage to question the status quo'.

Applying his warning about the past to the present: what harm is being done today by an Irish public not vigilant, or cowed into not having the courage to question the status quo of the state's interaction with survivors? If we still do not view them as us, deserving our ongoing support, what have we really learned from this past?

In the cool hall of Berlin's Neues Museum, gazing at the fragile papyrus of the Gospel of Mary, the threads become clear linking this Magdalene and our Magdalenes. Mary's legitimacy as a disciple was challenged by one man, her reputation tarnished by another. Both men – Peter and Gregory – were Popes, while Mary's true authority and reputation were buried for centuries in disgrace.

Religious historian Karen King says the Gospel of Mary asks us to rethink the basis of church authority and 'provides the most straightforward and convincing argument in any early Christian writing for the legitimacy of women's leadership'.

What's more, she suggests it 'exposes the erroneous view that Mary of Magdala was a prostitute for what it is – a piece of theological fiction'. The Mary of this second-century text was a holy woman; her name is not a badge of shame, but of honour – though that may be cold comfort for the thousands of Irish women punished in her name for following in her allegedly 'sinful' footsteps.

As her ancient papyrus Gospel disappears into its dark storage cabinet, Ireland's Gospel of the Magdalene Women is still a work in progress.

11. Marie and Paddy

'If these sad facts teach us anything, it is that we must listen to those who cannot and have not in the past been heard.'

Judge Joseph Mathews

Two men damaged Marie Collins; both were priests and both served as priests in my parish, St Monica's. In the early days of this project, trying to understand my niggles about Ireland and its Catholic past, I realize I need to meet Marie. In a fancy Dublin hotel bar, after a bit of talking around the issue, I get straight to the point.

After nearly thirty years, I say, we've had three rounds with Ireland's clerical sexual abuse scandal: first, the initial revelations and criminal cases against abusing priests; second, the exposure of the cover-up by church hierarchy; third, the scandals over church-run institutions and state collusion.

'When do you think we'll get to round four?' I ask Marie.

'What's round four?'

'Us.'

'Derek, I've been waiting twenty years to be asked that question.'

Since then, Marie and I have met several times for conversations that are thoughtful, considered and probing, just like the woman herself. With a precise demeanour, somewhere between a kindly judge and a worldly nun, she listens closely and respectfully. She doesn't offer pre-cooked answers. She is watchful and warm, yet behind the fierce intelligence, dry humour, searching eyes and pale complexion is a woman hurt deeply by clerical sexual abuse and her subsequent campaign for justice.

Marie's story is familiar to many in Ireland, yet never loses its shock value. Born and raised in Dublin, in 1960 she was left by her parents in the care of a friendly young chaplain in Our Lady's

Hospital for Sick Children in Crumlin. She entered the hospital a happy thirteen-year-old, despite a broken arm, and emerged an anxious teen with a broken mind.

That her abuser was a priest, Paul McGennis, only added to her teenage confusion; the same fingers that abused her at night, and took photographs of her exposed body, offered her Holy Communion the next morning.

It wasn't until 1985 – after mental breakdown, medication, repeated hospital stays and four years of agoraphobia, none of which she linked to McGennis – that Marie sought out a therapist. An idle thought she'd had at a recent Sunday Mass, repeated casually in therapy, brought the memory of her abuser back to the surface.

She was anxious that her abuser was still abusing and sought out Fr Eddie Griffin, a priest in her parish, whom she considered a good friend. After realizing where she was going with the story she was starting to tell him, she says he interrupted her to say he didn't want to hear any more, or the priest's name.

Two of his sentences stayed with her. First: 'If you tell me his name I'll have to do something about it.' Second: 'You needn't worry, you are forgiven, you probably tempted the poor man, you are forgiven.'

Walking out, her mind was again flooded with waves of self-doubt and self-blame. The steel safety curtain came down in her mind. Lying to her therapist, she said everything was sorted and she shut down for another decade. During this decade Paul McGennis was a curate in my parish, his car and house filled with children. In the early 1990s she took up her fight against her abuser again and, in June 1997, her testimony helped secure a conviction – one of the first in Ireland.

Marie's case ticks almost every depressing box in Ireland's familiar clerical sexual abuse narrative: a devious perpetrator; authorities anxious to avoid scandal; and a traumatized victim plagued for decades by feelings of guilt and shame.

Marie Collins didn't know it but when she first tried to speak about her abuse to Fr Griffin the gardaí had failed her once already, a quarter of a century earlier. Back in 1960, McGennis had sent negatives to a UK lab to be developed. The lab went straight to the UK authorities, who passed the material to their Irish colleagues. Instead of investigating a crime, the then Garda commissioner made a personal call on Archbishop John Charles McQuaid and handed over to him the evidence, which was never to be seen again.

Jump forward three decades to the 1990s, when Marie Collins filed a complaint against her abuser. The gardaí, who had made evidence of abuse disappear three decades earlier, conceded they were unlikely to proceed with Marie's case. Then a second woman from Co. Wicklow came forward independently around the same time with similar claims against McGennis. Given the gardaí track record, it is likely that, had Marie approached them in 1985, when the McGennis trauma resurfaced, she would have been wasting her time. But she didn't do so then, and we'll get to that.

McGennis received a nine-month sentence for the Wicklow abuse to run concurrently with the sentence for abusing Marie Collins. Subsequent court cases and convictions followed, yet the initial McGennis case had very different outcomes for the first two women. While Collins was supported by her friends and neighbours, the other McGennis abuse victim had a very different experience in her more rural parish.

'She said half of the town sent her to Coventry for reporting McGennis, and this in 1997,' says Marie. 'It wasn't because they thought she was lying, but because they felt she had brought disgrace on the town.'

Others groomed by McGennis subsequently made contact with Collins. Two sisters told her how, aged eight and ten, they were invited by McGennis to tea at his house. The housekeeper in that Dublin parish declined to let them in, saying the priest was not home and that 'this is not a house you want to come to'.

When the girls insisted on coming in – the priest had promised them a book – the housekeeper agreed to look for it in McGennis's room, even though 'Father doesn't like me going in there'.

The girls followed her in and told Collins that, decades later, they remembered a 'spooky' dark and dusty room with a large, white screen. Perfect for viewing the kind of lewd slides Paul McGennis took of Marie Collins and others.

'The girls never went back after the housekeeper's warning. She must have known and seen something,' says Marie. 'She may have been powerless to do anything, perhaps from a Magdalene Laundry who thought saying something would see her put out on the street.'

After going public following McGennis's conviction Marie Collins became a leading figure in the campaign for justice by clerical sexual abuse survivors. She is largely complimentary about Archbishop Diarmuid Martin, but has no time for his predecessor, the late Desmond Connell, who was in office at the time of McGennis's trial and conviction. She remembers Connell as being less interested in helping survivors like her than in preserving the reputation of his institution and the priests facing often decades-old claims.

She had many tense meetings with Connell and, during one, she says he agreed to her demand to send counsellors out to St Monica's in Edenmore, to sort through the damage left by McGennis in the wake of his mysterious departure and the devastating story that emerged.

This is heart-breaking to hear, I tell her, because it never happened. Instead of clarity and counsellors, St Monica's got a new parish priest. Fr Eddie Griffin, the man who dismissed Marie Collins in 1985 – setting her back ten years and, indirectly, allowing McGennis to remain in our parish – became our new pastor.

'By putting Eddie Griffin of all people into Edenmore, I felt they were giving the two fingers to me,' says Marie Collins. 'He was the last man who was going to facilitate victims coming forward. He shut all that down.'

Over the years, Fr Griffin has refused to meet Marie Collins. She says he responded through an intermediary that such a meeting would be 'too distressing' for her. His patronizing response angered Marie but motivated her to keep going.

In the last two decades Marie has had cross words with two Popes (Benedict and Francis), attended innumerable meetings with Vatican and Irish Church officials, collaborated with constructive clerics and battled other clerics' doublespeak. She tried to work with the Church at its highest level by, in 2014, accepting an invitation from Pope Francis to join a pontifical commission to protect minors. Three years in, tired of curia political games and what she saw as the Holy See's hypocrisy, she resigned from the commission. She has heard every excuse, witnessed every obfuscation. Meanwhile, speaking engagements come in on a conveyor belt, as do interview requests from all over the world.

Being Marie Collins sounds physically and emotionally draining. Almost a quarter of a century after she came forward, she polarizes public opinion in Ireland. For many she is a heroine but in some Catholic circles she is regarded with irritation, or worse. When her name comes up in conversation with a prominent, elderly Irish senior cleric, no stranger to abuse cases in Ireland, he says of her suffering at the hands of Paul McGennis and his camera, 'She must have had a photogenic fanny.'

I sit in stunned silence. The comment leaves me winded, and still does. It's a glimpse of the level of rage, misogyny and contempt – open and masked – that Marie Collins faces on a regular basis.

During one of my conversations with Marie, I ask what keeps her going. She credits her persistence to an independent-spirited mother. Marie describes her mother as a 'devout Catholic but not the meek, silent kind'. She married a Protestant against huge clerical resistance and later, when a priest showed up to cleanse or 'church' her after giving birth to baby Marie,* she shooed him away. (Marie's mother was in her eighties when her daughter told her of the abuse she suffered. She was devastated to hear what Marie went through, and for not noticing anything at the time.)

Marie was a child of 1950s Ireland but her mother tried to cultivate her independent spirit by sending her to a private school, Miss Meredith's in Ballsbridge, where her teachers included Maeve Binchy.†

---

* In Christian tradition, the 'churching' ceremony blesses mothers after recovery from childbirth. With roots in Jewish practice, many Irish women felt the practice, presented to them as a post-natal 'cleansing', was demeaning.

† Another remarkable past pupil of Miss Meredith's was the late journalist Mary Raftery, whose work was so pivotal in revealing the story of institutional abuse in Ireland. Her three-part documentary series, *States of Fear*, about Ireland's industrial schools and reformatories was broadcast in 1999. *Cardinal Secrets*, her film about clerical sexual abuse in the Dublin Archdiocese, was broadcast in 2002. The public outcry resulting from Raftery's work prompted the establishment of the two commissions of investigation that led to the publication of the Ryan and Murphy Reports.

'When the priest came in every two weeks on a visit, we'd ask the most challenging questions. The teacher used to say, "You know they're all heretics, Father!"'

Neither a strong-willed mother as role model nor a more liberal education than most prevented Collins becoming an obedient Catholic who, she said, 'just drifted along . . . and didn't question or think about it'. She was a young woman who covered her head at Mass, ate fish on Fridays and knew her venial from her mortal sins.

And in 1985, I remind her gently, she followed her therapist's advice and sought out a priest about McGennis. Worried it might sound like an accusation, I ask gently why she didn't go to the gardaí.

'I don't know . . .' she says, her voice trailing off. 'I don't know why my thinking never turned in that direction.'

Usually Marie is a robust, certain person. But now her voice and gaze take on an ambivalent air, remembering an Ireland very different to today, with no access to other modes of thinking. This was an isolated island where a common experience of religion was limited and strict, she says. Vocal criticism of arrogant priests was as out of the question as wondering aloud why women were being locked up and babies vanishing.

Instead of the articulate Marie Collins, a staple of television appearances, another Marie Collins before me remembers the strictures of another Ireland. At a previous meeting, she insisted that women 'didn't get into Magdalene Laundries by magic [but] because they were ostracized by their community and thrown out by their families'.

Now she is questioning her own certainty. She wonders aloud whether remaining silent in times past can be excused – or at least explained. 'If everyone around you in society – family, friends, authority figures – tell you something is right – *This is for the best* – can you really be blamed for not looking outside that or not challenging it?'

And yet there is a point where she draws a clear line. Even if circumstances were difficult for ordinary people, their agency limited, she believes everyone has a responsibility to own their own past actions – or inactions – and to reflect on their effect now.

The inexhaustible well of clerical horrors, and the deep-rooted anger it generated, may hinder such reflection for some time to come. But Marie Collins has not given up hope of a broader discussion in Ireland. A discussion focused less on the clerics who yielded a firm grip on Irish society, and more on the grip itself and those who yielded to it.

Seriously examining why clerical power gripped people for so long cannot now change the situations it created, she says, but it can provide insights into the present. And the present is where she devotes her greatest energy today, in particular the issue of child safety.

Marie says she wonders if the attitudes that enabled Catholic Ireland – the importance of not giving rise to scandal and of minding one's own business – live on in a very changed twenty-first-century country. She has a term for her fear – 'deference addiction'. Ireland may have moved past the Catholic Church but she thinks the country has retained its 'deference addiction'.

Where?

In, for example, the regular scandals over dysfunction in our health service. There is a litany of them – problems with blood trans-fusions, breast screenings, smear tests – and they follow a familiar pattern: outrage over the failings of people in authority that inevit-ably evolves into a sense of helplessness, thanks in part to our deeply ingrained deference to those in authority. Yesterday: bishops. Today: health officials and hospital consultants.

Catholic Ireland's 'national blinker syndrome' lives on today, Marie argues, in what she calls our 'self-inflicted blindness'. Then, people struggled with the idea of abusing priests, an idea that simply did not accord with their expectations of religious. Today the incon-ceivable thing that is not being seen is familial abuse, an epidemic of modern Irish life.

'People don't want to look at that because it's themselves they are looking at really,' says Marie Collins. 'We all feel much more com-fortable to be able to point the finger at someone else rather than [our] selves.'

It's just after lunchtime in a west Dublin hotel bar. As a group of women nearby sup tea and swap gossip, Paddy Doyle and I sip spirits and trade jokes. He is on his second vodka – hold the tonic – while I am on gin.

Paddy Doyle's body is a wreck, thanks to an inherited medical condition and staggering negligence in his early years at the hands of Irish surgeons. Confined to a motorized wheelchair, he is kept going by pharmaceuticals, an air pipe under his nose, various beeping gadgets and a sense of humour that lies somewhere beyond black.

A few minutes after meeting, he says cheerily: 'My consultant asked me recently, "Paddy, why are you still alive?" I replied, "Out of spite." '

When we meet first it's exactly thirty years since the release of his ground-breaking memoir, *The God Squad*. Early on, I make clear I've not sought him out to revisit the horrors of his childhood. His book stands for itself, has lost none of its power, and remains essential reading for anyone trying to understand Ireland's recent past. What interests me, and why I am sitting with him drinking gin instead of eating lunch, is how Ireland has treated his book since its explosive debut in 1988.

The God Squad begins with the death of his mother from cancer in 1955 and his only memory of his father, long suppressed: seeing him hanging dead from a tree. Aged four years and three months, Doyle was brought before a district court judge, charged with 'not being in possession of a proper guardian' and sentenced to be detained in religious-run institutions for eleven years. That was how Ireland did things back then.

The book covers his hellish experience of institutional 'care', where physical and sexual abuse was piled on top of a damaged psyche already struggling to process his father's death. He is one of the children Austin Clarke wrote about in his 1963 poem 'Corporal Punishment', about children disappeared into institutions for the purposes of public order.

Ireland didn't want to hear about it in the 1950s and 1960s and, though Paddy says the book pretty much wrote itself, Ireland didn't want to hear about it in 1988 either. Refused by one Irish publisher, it was saved by another owned by the writer Dermot Bolger. Then a British publisher picked it up. A UK tour followed, culminating with a BBC television appearance with Terry Wogan. Ireland, shamed abroad, could no longer ignore the book. Exposed and forced to move, like a chess player in zugzwang, Paddy Doyle was no longer someone to be ignored.

The most extreme reaction, he remembers, came from his own people in Wexford. Doyle returned to step up his search for information about his parents and where they were buried. The thin-lipped locals in his home place of Killinick were even less in the mood to talk to him now that he was the author of a revealing book. One man said he knew about Doyle's dead mother and father but would stay quiet because, 'You'll only write it down and disgrace us all.'

Taking a sip of vodka, Doyle can quote verbatim, from memory, an anonymous letter he received around the same time: 'Don't forget that on the day your dad hanged himself, he left a loaf of bread on the window, and you were found gnawing through it like a rat.'

He lets the sentence hang in the air. Then, his matter-of-fact manner resumes as he recalls his visit to Killinick hunting for information on his parents. When he and a friend entered The Merry Elf, the less-than-merry locals walked out.

'One guy stood in front of me, as close as you are now, and said, "I knew your mother well, she was a great fuckin' ride." I am not often stuck for words but I was flummoxed. It didn't bother him at all.'

Instead of compassion for one of their own, a victim of terrible circumstance and Catholic Ireland's institutional horrors, he was attacked as a traitor. The brave, best-selling author was simultaneously a victim to be blamed for his own misfortune – and for, even worse, exposing it in public.

The question that has brought me here today is this: has the purpose of *The God Squad* been misinterpreted or oversimplified?

Paddy smiles. For three decades, he says, Ireland has been reading the book it wanted to read rather than the one he wrote. He has lost count of the number of Irish readers who have approached him to rail against 'those bloody nuns'. But in the book's introduction, as if anticipating how many readers will devour it as a sensationalist misery memoir, Paddy writes that his motivation is not 'to point the finger, to blame or even to criticize any individual or group of people'.

'It is about a society's abdication of responsibility to a child,' he writes. 'The probability is that there were, and still are, thousands of "mes".'

Three decades on, what does he think Irish society has learned about abdication of responsibility?

'We've learned nothing,' he says.

Why not?

Because, he says, Irish people continue to struggle with their part of responsibility for a system that mangled him and tens of thousands of others.

'We are great at hearing people talk – that is progress – but that doesn't force people to reflect on themselves.'

The challenge thrown down by *The God Squad*, ignored by many, was spotted by one reviewer, the late Labour Party minister Justin Keating. In his review Keating argued that the people who nearly destroyed Paddy Doyle's body and mind – and those of innumerable anonymous others in their care – were not subject to meaningful scrutiny by our society.

'How did we so lose our wits and our common sense,' wrote Keating, 'as to make such a monstrous mistake?'

Doyle's life today revolves around two searches, for answers and for justice, surrounded by people who want to shake his hand and others who refuse to talk to him. Neither search is making much headway because, he fears, decades of abuse revelations have not shaken public opinion as much as they have influenced published opinion. Another shock headline does not necessarily bring about any societal change.

When he tells his story today, he often hears he should leave his past in the past. Others tell him some nuns or priests were good and should be allowed to live out the rest of their days in peace. Such remarks are familiar to all survivors of clerical sexual abuse, made to feel by society as a provocation. But many who talk to, or take issue with, Paddy fail to notice, let alone pick up, the gauntlet he threw down at their feet thirty years ago, spotted by Justin Keating. *How did we lose our wits to allow this to happen?*

'You could still ask Keating's question today about Irish society and its failings, but nobody is really interested,' Paddy Doyle says. 'What you might get is, "I don't go to church any more." That is someone's contribution. That's it.'

A new challenge today, he says, is growing apathy among those who think the abuse issue has been addressed and 'solved'. His book broke new ground, afterwards broadcasters Louis Lentin* and Mary Raftery dragged what lay beneath to the surface and put it on television. The level of outrage after the transmission of Raftery's series *States of Fear* forced the government of the day, led by Taoiseach Bertie Ahern, to apologize and present a redress scheme to make 'fair and reasonable awards to persons who, as children, were abused while resident in industrial schools, reformatories and other institutions subject to state regulation or inspection'.

The state insists the arrangement was the best available in the circumstances of the time, but survivors like Paddy Doyle say the set-up of the redress scheme merely compounded the abuse it was supposed to ameliorate.

For Paddy, redress was an invitation to a 'fancy room somewhere in Dundrum'. After hearing four hours of evidence, facing aggressive solicitors he feels conducted themselves as if in a courtroom, a judge offered him €300,000 – the highest award to date. He had a month to think it over and, like everyone who went through the redress process, he was told that accepting the award came with a requirement to sign a non-disclosure agreement. Breaching the confidentiality agreement like this in our conversation could result in a fine or a jail term of up to two years. Many who had found the courage to speak for the first time, he said, were to be silenced again by the state.

Paddy Doyle is different: his past is in the public domain, the subject of a best-selling book written long before the redress scheme, and its author is of the bloody-minded variety. Even now, sipping vodka thoughtfully, he is clearly intrigued by what will happen now that, technically, he's broken the gag order with me.

'To be honest with you, I'd love to be sent to jail for telling people what went on. Can you imagine?'

Our conversation about his abuse keeps returning to the redress process and what he perceives as the fresh abuse at its heart: a mean-spirited attitude on the part of politicians, civil servants and, he thinks, public opinion.

'The real block for people abused in institutions is the general

* Louis Lentin's drama-documentary *Dear Daughter*, the story of Christine Buckley, an inmate of the Goldenbridge industrial school, was broadcast in 1996.

public feeling, "We let them talk, they got money, they got fixed up and that's it, what more do they want?" That's the saddest part for me: that the only way we think we can fix up things is with a cheque.'

He is speaking from bitter experience. When Paddy returned from Dundrum, his youngest son asked his father how much he had been awarded. Hearing the figure, his son started to cry: 'He said, "Jesus, that's all my da is worth."'

Paddy says the money is sitting in a bank account, untouched.

Many survivors like Paddy Doyle don't want money – they never did – they wanted real remorse, based on real self-reflection. But after thirty years of talking, Paddy fears Ireland is no closer to reconciliation with its past, because people don't want to – or feel they can't – go there. Public avowals of the importance of listening to abuse survivors' testimony say one thing; private hearings, courtroom tactics and gagging orders say another.

A memorial for survivors of all the institutions of containment, planned for erection at Dublin's Garden of Remembrance, is on indefinite hold, he says.

Paddy Doyle's broken body is living proof of the damage done by the young Irish republic to its most vulnerable. He is a witness to the flaws of that system, and to our own flaws. He set us a challenge in 1988, to reflect on our abdication of our responsibility to a child. Instead of an invitation to reflection, readers seized it as the opening shot in a finger-pointing campaign.

If this is all history, if Ireland is no longer in the thrall of the Catholic Church it blames for the abuse, Paddy Doyle wants to know why he still sees thousands of young Paddy Doyles in today's Ireland. He was hidden by a court in an abusive institution, an approach society then felt was for the best. Today's young Paddy Doyles, he says, may face a life of homelessness in bed and breakfasts, and all the emotional anxiety this brings.

Listening to Paddy is a learning, chastening experience. Like Marie Collins, chance put him outside the pale of yesterday's Ireland. He was 'only an orphan'. The lasting physical damage from being only an orphan means he is still on the outside. And even today's Ireland struggles with owning him and his past.

In the west Dublin hotel, our glasses are nearly empty and we are getting ready to part company. On a hunch, I draw three Venn diagrams, two circles in each, in my notebook. I ask Paddy to pick the one that best captures his view of the relationship between the Irish people and the Church plus the various institutions it ran. Is our past best represented as one circle of Church-plus-institutions adjacent but separate to the circle of Irish society? Did the Church-plus-institutions and Irish society circles overlap somewhat? Or was the Church-plus-institutions circle inside the Irish society circle?

Without hesitation, Paddy points to the third diagram. 'They are in there inside the rest of Irish society. We have to stop putting them outside with our stories.'

It's clear Paddy is anxious not to be portrayed as bitter about his experiences. His humour is proof that he is bigger than that. But between the hilarious jokes, he is angry, disillusioned and mistrustful of many people in Irish society. And if he remains alive 'out of spite', it's less to be a memorial to a past cruel Ireland than it is to be a provocation and challenge to today's apparently more tolerant Ireland.

What would restore his faith in today's Ireland?

'That's a hard question to answer. I think [it would help] if people were more honest, if Irish society was more open about the abuse that is still happening today, that is still being covered up.'*

---

* As work on this book was being completed, I received the news of Paddy Doyle's death in 2020. This section stands, exactly as originally written, by way of tribute to an extraordinary man.

12.   One in four

'Everyone knew, but no one said . . . I have heard no one address the question of what it means, in this context, to *know*.'

John Banville

Nine hours into the New Year and I'm loitering with intent outside the National Maternity Hospital on Dublin's Holles Street. Beside the entrance and the 'no smoking' sign, two wan-faced women in pyjamas and towelling dressing gowns stand with cigarettes raised in their right hands.

Young fathers push past with pristine prams for their newborn babies. John from Cork is now father to Molly and the owner of a pram that cost nearly €1,000. 'For fifty euros more they offer you some sort of "be safe" feature,' says John, tired eyes laughing. 'They really know how to get you.'

Hurrying after him is another father who hasn't had a wink of sleep but at least has a son to show for it: Hugo, weighing 3.4kg.

During a lull in comings and goings I study the plaque on the facade dedicated to the 'Oxen of the Sun' episode in James Joyce's *Ulysses*, set in the original maternity hospital that stood here.

A third glassy-eyed young father appears beside me, smoking and texting simultaneously, saying his son Patrick took all night to come. Better than poor Mrs Purefoy in *Ulysses*, who was in labour in Holles Street for three days.

The last, and most collected, father I encounter can't wait to see his partner and young son, Leo. I hazard a guess why.

'After *Ulysses*?'

'No,' he says with a grin. '*The Producers*.' He vanishes before I remember that Gene Wilder's hysterical accountant, Leo Bloom, in the Mel Brooks movie was the director's own sly nod to Joyce.

With one, two, three, four New Year babies on my mind, I cross the street and enter a narrow modern brown-brick building opposite. Up a steep staircase, I wait in a room of brown carpet, yellow walls and black leather seats. The window beside where I'm sitting is blocked by a large sheet of plain white paper, but when I stand up again I have a perfect view of the entrance to the hospital. In years to come, I wonder, which of the four New Year babies – Molly, Hugo, Patrick or Leo – will need the services on offer here? Which of them will return to the place of their birth, Holles Street, to visit One in Four, the organization that works with survivors of sexual abuse?

One in Four was founded by a survivor of clerical sexual abuse, Colm O'Gorman, and commenced operations in Ireland in 2003. In her office the current executive director, Maeve Lewis, tells me the organization's name is both a blessing and a curse. It captures a simple truth about the reality of childhood sexual abuse in Ireland – one in four people experience it – but the name also prompts disbelieving pushback.

Often Lewis finds herself in taxis explaining to an inquisitive driver where she works and the origin of the One in Four name: the 2002 Sexual Abuse and Violence in Ireland (SAVI) survey of 3,000 adults, which revealed the levels of contact sexual abuse experienced by both men and women, in childhood and in adulthood.

When the taxi drivers hear this the shutters invariably come down, says Lewis: 'They say, "That can't be right, I don't believe it . . ."'

Even more confounding for our taxi driver, if Lewis were to continue, would be hearing that the vast majority of One in Four's clients today are not survivors of clerical or institutional abuse. But we will come back to that.

To date, investigations into historical abuse in Ireland – sexual and otherwise – have focused on institutions with links to Church and state. Over a decade ago, when the monumental Ryan Report was published, the Irish public might well have concluded that the Church had a monopoly on most historical abuse of children in Ireland – sexual and otherwise. Mr Justice Seán Ryan's five-volume report on the sixty reformatory and industrial schools run by Catholic orders was dubbed by the *Irish Times* a 'map of an Irish hell', on the tenth anniversary of its publication. It was presented in May 2009, after ten years' work by the Commission to Inquire into Child Abuse. The inquiry's task had been to investigate the schools which were in receipt of state funding and were, theoretically at least, subject to state supervision.

Its trawl back to 1936 revealed a numbing netherworld of endemic physical, emotional and sexual abuse of children by institutional religious and lay workers, with ineffective or absent state supervision. It documented a system that ran Ireland, based on clerical coercion and social snobbery, which treated children more like 'prison inmates and slaves' than people with legal rights and human potential.

One in Four's Maeve Lewis remembers clearly the day the Ryan Report was published – and the day after, when she visited her rural family home near Nenagh, Co. Tipperary.

'In the kitchen I found my mother weeping over the *Irish Times*,' she says. Lewis's mother was weeping because she and Maeve's father, a local Labour Party figure, had known about the boys from the Artane Industrial School sent down to work on local farms. Some were treated well, her mother said, and others 'worse than the dogs'.

'The boys would turn up at Mass, hungry, dirty and bruised,' says Lewis. 'I said, "Did nobody do anything?" "No," she said. That was why she was weeping.'

Lewis's mother was one of many in Ireland who wept in May 2009, confronted with the full horrors of something about which they had some, if not full, knowledge. Alongside the old memories were old feelings of helplessness, silencing, fear of rocking the boat, afraid of being targeted.

'Just afraid,' said Maeve Lewis. 'If my parents and my grandmother, who was a formidable woman, felt like it wasn't their business, I can only imagine what people who were less feisty might have felt.'

Before her death in 2012, Mary Raftery, the maker of *States of Fear*, suggested there 'wasn't an absolute knowledge but a well-rounded suspicion' of abuses in the Goldenbridge industrial school and other such institutions. Some sixty residential facilities operated by the Catholic religious orders under state supervision were the focus of the Ryan inquiry. Setting the abusive tone in these institutions were religious personnel, cloaked by a 'culture of self-serving secrecy'.

The investigation's public and private hearings, and its final report, were a watershed. A decade on, it made a staggering revision of its estimate of the number of children in such care, down from 170,000 to around 42,000.* In addition many limitations were placed on its truth-telling abilities. Legal challenges from religious prevented it attributing exact blame and naming abusers publicly. Despite the scale of abuse uncovered and documented, no prosecutions followed.

In recent years Justice Ryan has been invited to speak in other countries engaged in similar work. We met first when he was in Berlin to address a German state child abuse commission.

'The work of a commission itself concludes with the report,' he told his Berlin audience, 'but the actual work for the people involved, if they want to do it, is the reconciliation.'

Exactly a decade after his report appeared, I seek him out again to ask about that big 'if'. Does he think Ireland is closer to reconciliation with its past?

His short answer is no. His longer answer: it's complicated.

'I think there is horror and dismay but I don't see an appetite for more,' he tells me.

Why not?

Diving into Ireland's institutional past is an onerous task requiring an understanding of the context of the era, he says, in particular an attitude to children shocking by contemporary standards; the rigid reality of children's institutions; the closed, hierarchical nature of congregations running them; and their complex relationship with the state. Grasping that is a complex task, a long journey which itself is shaped by the choice of starting point.

That talk of starting points makes me think of the Venn diagrams I drew for Paddy Doyle and other interviewees. Inside, overlapping or external – where does Ryan place the circle representing the Catholic Church in Ireland and its institutions in relation to the circle representing the state? His answer differs from Paddy's.

'They were overlapping with the Irish state, were paid for by the

---

* In a statement in November 2019, Justice Ryan explained that 'the total given in the report was derived by adding the yearly figures for the population in the institutions, but that did not take account of the fact that children were counted in each year of detention'.

state,' he says. 'The people with the formal power were in the Department of Education, the state; the people with the actual power to implement or resist change were the congregations.'

He points out how Catholic doctrine and lobbying ensured a state ban on contraception, producing children for which the young Irish state had zero or negligible state welfare payments or facilities. In many cases this resulted in people handing over minors to religious orders and their young, inexperienced members. This child-welfare role overwhelmed untrained religious order members, part of a Church whose moral doctrine drove up the birth rate. As he tells it, Ireland was trapped in a vicious circle. The country was producing too many children to support, many of whom were pushed into religious life; too many religious needed to be found work, and were left supervising the next generation of too many children. The only logic Seán Ryan sees in the system is that it gave congregations work for their members and a source of income from state funding, not all of which he believes was spent on children in their care. In hindsight, Judge Ryan says he still doesn't understand how anyone thought abuse could be avoided in this 'mad, crazy system.'

It was a cosy division of labour between Church and state – populated on all sides with members of ordinary Irish families, it's worth remembering – where each stuck to their own and didn't call out the other. The Ryan commission documented how religious orders resisted anything viewed as external interference – requests for accounts, institutional reforms – and how they were not pressed by state officials to comply.

With a few honourable exceptions during the hearings, Justice Ryan remembers the religious orders' obsessive attempts to contain scandal and portray abusers as 'bad apples', rather than a product of systemic problems in flawed institutions.

More than a decade on, I ask if he thinks some Irish people adopt a similar strategy today: frame religious orders as an alien 'other', isolated bad apples rather than an integral part – and failure – of Irish society?

'I hadn't seen that but now that you say it . . .' he says, voice trailing off as he considers this idea.

For Seán Ryan the institutions operated by employing a 'tunnel vision' that existed in Ireland. As a self-critical example he tells me of a day in 1971, a year before he was called to the bar, when he watched a court case involving a woman seeking a judicial separation. The case was held in public, reported on in all the papers and decided by a jury of twelve men.

'When I look back on that, why didn't one of us call it out and say "this is monstrous"? You did have a sense it was unfair but it was the system.'

If Seán Ryan – a young law student, future judge and part of the system – felt powerless in the face of this system, what chance was there in that Ireland for someone with less education and fewer opportunities?

Reflecting today on the country he probed in his report, Seán Ryan compares Ireland to Eastern Bloc countries in the communist era. 'We were a closed society, if people did speak out they did tend to be ostracized. It was a bit like a communist regime, you kept your head down.' And, he says, like many people in post-communist countries, it is only natural for people who lived through it to feel 'relief that it's passed'. As time passes, though, he suggests this relief is shot through with 'a sense of guilt that the general population did nothing about it, that we allowed ourselves to be so cowed'.

Reading the Ryan Report remains a deeply shocking experience. Even more than a decade on, the mind struggles to grasp the scale of cruelty, physical and sexual abuse. At the time of publication the focus was, rightly, on the survivors of a horrific system. But there is a whole other narrative in the report that is rarely discussed. This alternative narrative is about the ordinary people, the bystanders to abuse. Countless people like Maeve Lewis's family, or the district court clerk cited in the report who heard in the 1960s about sexual abuse in industrial schools from a garda who drove committed children there.

'In today's climate I'd have protested to the Department of Justice,' the clerk told the Ryan investigation, 'but in those times, at best my protest would have been ignored, at worst I'd have been disciplined.'

Those with a well-rounded suspicion or even knowledge that something was wrong chose not to act, felt they couldn't, or doubted their intervention would change anything. They were the bystand-ers, the passive onlookers to events they felt were beyond their control. This is a textbook example of the 'bystander effect' – the term given to the phenomenon whereby the greater the number of witnesses to something, the less likely people are to help a person in distress. There are many theories offered as to why this happens. One is that, the more people around, the greater the feeling of a diffusion of responsibility. Another is social control: when someone else fails to react, individuals take this as a signal not to react either, sensing a response is either not needed or not appropriate. The more ambigu-ous the situation, or unfamiliar the environment, the less likely a bystander is to intervene.

Like Paddy Doyle before him, Judge Seán Ryan hoped his report would 'give rise to debate and reflection'. But neither his inquiry nor those that went before or have been conducted since have had a remit to look at the largest population group from the era under investigation: the bystanders. Two decades have passed since the first revelations of the abused, and perpetrators, have emerged. But for millions of people in between, no truth-telling forum exists.

The in-betweeners, the bystanders, live with conflicted mem-ories in what Italian concentration camp survivor Primo Levi called the 'grey zone' – a place of trauma and blurred distinctions. Ireland's grey zone is filled with millions of people who, decades ago, felt that allowing religious orders to run hospitals, schools and institutions was not only acceptable but the right thing to do. Others alongside them in the grey zone had doubts about this system but knew instinctively that such doubts or contrary views were unwelcome. Some saw it as none of their business, while still other bystanders are ordinary people – from bus drivers to politicians – who remain silent about the physical and sexual abuse one in four of them experienced themselves as children, a silence that reduces both their own emotional resilience and the capacity to take on others' abuse.

Given the high social cost of challenging the status quo in Catholic Ireland, many people who had vague or well-rounded suspicions could not afford to care more. For many survivors, the cost of speaking out now has dropped and is now lower than the cost of remaining silent. But for the many ordinary Irish bystanders, their ongoing, deep silence is the silence of people with nowhere to go with their memories and their conflicted feelings.

In the wake of the Ryan Report's publication John Banville asked rhetorically whether 'the systematic cruelty visited upon hundreds of thousands of children incarcerated in state institutions in this country . . . would have been prevented if enough right-thinking people had been aware of what was going on?'

'Well, no,' he answered himself. 'Because everyone knew.'

Saying that 'everyone knew' is a rhetorically satisfying line. But it disables more than it enables. Instead of encouraging engagement, it elicits pushback and brings down the mental shutters. Not everyone in Ireland agrees that 'everyone knew'.

After all, who is this 'everyone'?

And what, for that matter, is 'knowing'?

Can we even agree on what one could have known?

There is no one Catholic Ireland in the recent past, but millions of individual Irelands, all experienced differently. Letting in feelings about this past, acknowledging the emotional or personal cost of knowing, may have been too great to bear. It may still be. Admitting anything – now as then – is a cause of shame, confusion or something in between. Realizing that others may share a similar shame, how-ever, is one step towards ending silence.

Ask leading Irish therapists about child sexual abuse in Ireland – clerical and otherwise – and many agree that there is much unfinished business. The word that comes up often is 'trauma'. Trauma describes a sort of survival mode a person enters when they encounter distress-ing or disturbing events that overwhelm their ability to cope. The mind, to protect itself, can suppress extreme distress so it cannot be accessed immediately. It's a protective and adaptive response – a sort of emotional circuit breaker. The trouble is that the very action of shutting things down can cause the original source of the distress to be so effectively suppressed that it disappears from consciousness. However, even suppressed, trauma continues to influence how we act and react.

'The truth, in its delayed appearance and its belated address, cannot be linked only to what is known,' writes trauma specialist Cathy Carruth, 'but also to what remains unknown in our very actions and our language.'

Long before the Catholic Church moved into its dominant position in Ireland, our country was a site of multiple traumas: colonialization and land theft, religious repression and mass starvation. Buried traumas like these can cause feelings of helplessness and a diminished sense of self, just as they can hinder someone's ability to experience a full range of emotions and experiences. People's capacity for reflection – essential for dealing with trauma – is blocked. And on this series of blocked traumas, in the mid-1800s, is where the modern Irish Catholic Church pitched its tent.

The metaphor of a large tent is how US psychiatrist Vamik D. Volkan explains societal trauma in a large group identity. Such a tent gives a group a sense of shared belonging and individuals a sense of core personal identity within the confines of the tent. According to Volkan's model, any such group is inclusive to a point, but will punish anyone or anything seen to contradict or threaten the collective good. He argues that stressed groups, facing strain on the canvas skin of the tent 'feel entitled to do anything, sadistic or masochistic, to protect their large group identity against a threat'.

During the nationalist campaign preceding independence, Irish people organized themselves into a cohesive group within a metaphorical Catholic tent that provided social comfort, solidarity and protection. Applying Volkan's theory, the harshness of Catholicism in Ireland may have been a desperate, trauma-based struggle to defend this fragile 'Irish' group identity. The prudish morality adopted in Ireland, a stringent Catholic retooling of Victorian English views, was drummed in through social conditioning to produce a people cowed into living outside their emotions and unable to address the trauma or the wounds beneath.

Our trinity of Church, state and people created institutional structures governed by what French philosopher Michel Foucault dubs the 'triple edict of taboo, nonexistence and silence'. He provides an analysis of this phenomenon that could have been written about Catholic Ireland: a 'Victorian shutdown' of human experience and sexuality, a place where the unordered and abnormal is 'driven out, denied and reduced to silence. Not only did it not exist, it had no right to exist and would be made to disappear upon its least manifestation – whether in acts or in words'.

A woman who became pregnant out of wedlock, or the resulting child, were challenges to the system – and had to be hidden. Today, the refusal of those who were a source of scandal in old Ireland to remain hidden any longer is a provocation to people who once rejected them. These people – 'fallen' women, 'bastard' children – challenge Irish people's view of themselves as compassionate. And they challenge Ireland's preferred victim narrative of its past.

Interestingly, Foucault notes how Victorian morality made limited, disapproving concessions. If expressions of sexuality it deemed 'illegitimate' could not be outlawed entirely, they could be confined to 'places of tolerance' – brothels or institutions. Whether selling sex or doing laundry, the Victorian moral code tolerated taboos once they could be monetized. Reminders of hypocrisy are as unwelcome as reminders of scandal.

Reading this reminds me of the question Justin Keating posed in his review of *The God Squad*: how did we lose our wits? The idea of deep trauma and Victorian control brings some clarity to an unanswered question of the 2,000-plus pages of the Ryan Report: from where did Ireland's prevailing culture of harshness come?

A crucial step towards really acknowledging harshness is acknowledging the trauma that produced it, and the wounds it left behind. Dr Judith Hermann, a leading expert on the subject, says that a trauma wound – a victim – cries out in its attempt to tell us of hidden realities or uncomfortable truths. Yet the trauma, to protect us, may close down mind and feeling because the 'ordinary response to atrocities is to banish them from consciousness. Certain violations of the social compact are too terrible to utter aloud: this is the meaning of the word *unspeakable*,' says Dr Hermann.

'Atrocities, however, refuse to be buried.'

Not only do atrocities refuse to be buried, the idea of simply 'moving on' is difficult if not impossible because, as therapist Bessel van der Kolk writes, trauma is not just an event that took place in the past, it is also an imprint left by that experience, on mind, brain and body. This imprint 'has ongoing consequences for how the human organism manages to survive in the present'.

If we accept now that abuse victims, particularly those abused as children, carry the trauma of that abuse their whole life, is it far-fetched to accept that bystanders – us – carry with them still the trauma that affected their inability to act then, or their struggle to acknowledge the trauma in the present? It is always one thing to know the facts of abusive systems, and to conduct related criminal investigations, and another to move on to the wider, societal reflection behind those facts. Repression may persist, until the passage of time wears down the most oppressive and traumatic aspects of denial. Even when a society begins working through its past, trauma experts say the process is not linear progression but forward and back.

Our Catholic Irish past – a trinity of perpetrators, victims and bystanders – is like a pendulum. It swings in and out of view, offering windows of opportunity to engage or disengage, embrace or shun, deal with it fully or partially, honestly or dishonestly.

The Ryan Report is not the end but the start of exploring our past. At 2,600 pages and seven volumes, it joins *Ulysses* as one of Ireland's most over-discussed, under-read texts. Its dry, linear approach is a rich source of data which researchers at University College Dublin have mined to present the facts in new ways that yield new insights. Their accessible study, available online, provides key facts that everyone should understand about Ireland's residential homes: abuse was not an exception, the product of a few 'bad apples', it was systemic. Ireland's residential home system was as much a product of Ireland as the children it was set up to care for, the UCD study argues, while monetizing neglect and making abuse disappear behind institutional walls. The level of knowing about what went on inside residential institutions went far beyond the religious orders, extending to managers, parish priests, parents, local TDs and government – and the wider community.

'It became very clear that people did know and the biggest node on the network was the Department of Education,' says Dr Emilie Pine, associate professor of modern drama at UCD, also involved in this project.

'I feel this was under-represented when the Ryan Report was publicly launched. The focus has been overwhelmingly on the religious orders when the responsibility is actually more widespread than that.'

What's interesting about the UCD research is how, by reordering the information in the Ryan Report, it links knowledge to knowers, clearing the mist of trauma and amnesia around Ireland's bystander landscape. In doing so, it provides new ways of viewing institutions that Dermot Bolger suggested twenty years ago were open secrets.

'Washing came in, slave labour was hired out,' wrote Bolger in 1999. 'Many people knew it was against their interests to question the system. And in truth, most Irish people felt the inmates deserved what they got.'

Bold claims like Bolger's create emotional conflict that may produce denial, or ambivalent reactions. It overlooks that many people who knew may feel they had good reason not to act, while others chose not to know more than whispers. Knowing something was not the same as being able to change it. Weeping over the Ryan Report is an expression of frustration, helplessness and shame, realizing the past cannot be changed in the present. But it can still be addressed – fully and frankly – if people are ready to go beyond the Ryan Report. While Seán Ryan views institutional abuse as a product of Ireland's 'tunnel vision', UK-based survivor Jim Beresford suggests secrecy – what he calls the 'Irish disease' – was rampant in Irish society then – and was rampant, too, in the report of the Ryan inquiry.

Its remit was so narrow, Beresford wrote in the *Irish Times* after the report's publication, that the inquiry was incapable of turning the mirror on Irish society. This was deliberate, he argued, because the process was controlled by Irish civil servants, politicians and others who, as adults, remained consciously or unconsciously beholden to religious orders – in particular the Christian Brothers – who educated them. All education ministers from 1932 to 1957 were CBS alumni, he pointed out, as was Judge Ryan. (Ryan attended O'Connell's on Dublin's northside and says he received a good education that helped his decision to study law.)

'Ireland made the Christian Brothers and then they made Ireland. To a large extent their mindset is Ireland's mindset . . . home truths are often difficult to acknowledge,' Beresford wrote, calling for another commission conducted by outsiders, free of Ireland's religious and political baggage. 'The Ryan Report is an Irish solution to an Irish problem, an old-fashioned Irish cover-up.'

Seán Ryan is aware of the criticisms levelled at his and other investigations: too legalistic in its approach to survivors, too limited in remit to name and blame those responsible. Though he has dedicated his life to the law, and six years of it to investigating institutional abuse, Seán Ryan concedes no legal exploration of such complex material would ever be wholly satisfactory. Nor should anyone expect that a legal approach could, alone, create social peace. If anything he sounds wary of how some, in hindsight, frame his report as the open-and-shut answer to all of our legacy problems with Catholic Ireland.

One day, he says, the legal examination of our past will end. But he sees little debate about the unfinished business: the approach Ireland needs to adopt now to explore its past in the present. Probing our Irish Catholic legacy needs a fresh push and a novel approach, Seán Ryan says: a new forum to pursue restorative justice.

He suggests a people's forum of 100 people, made up of disinterested citizens as well as interest groups, to explore in a non-confrontational way their perspective on the past and on outstanding issues. This approach is difficult, given outstanding legal issues between survivors and religious orders but, he says, it is, one day, inevitable.

'Reconciliation depends on everyone getting around a table and agreeing to reconcile,' he says. 'The shared question for everyone is: how did we take for granted something that now seems obvious to have been brutal and monstrous? And the question for each of us now is: what is present today that I am overlooking in the same way?'

The present can be changed, trauma therapists agree, by acknowledging the past compassionately and channelling this into action. Ask Marie Collins or Paddy Doyle what they want now and, independently of each other, they say the same thing: a society of people who see today's young Maries and Paddys – and reaches out to assist them. To really acknowledge today's vulnerable, abused children in Ireland comes with a prerequisite: reflecting on the past as a broad spectrum of knowing, and placing oneself on this spectrum. Doing this can create a sense of compassion towards oneself and others – and a greater sense of agency in the present than was available in the past. Researchers who work in the field of restorative justice have a term for this behaviour: ethical witness.

'To function as an ethical witness is not just to see or know something, but to act with compassion in response to what is being seen,' argue UCD academics Emilie Pine, Susan Levy and Mark T. Keane in their response to the Ryan Report.

Almost a quarter of a century on, Marie Collins and Paddy Doyle and other abuse survivors talk with some impatience about how practised we Irish are now in listening and blaming rituals. Like all rituals, they serve a purpose and fulfil a need for those who practise them. Eventually, though, they become hollow rituals unless matched with action – and resources. In 1988, Paddy Doyle set us a challenge: to consider the vulnerable children in our midst. Marie Collins wants us to take off our 'national blinkers' and tackle the child abuse still going on today in our holiest of institutions. Without understanding the bystander component of our abusive Irish Catholic past, we struggle to acknowledge the abuse in our present.

According to the 2002 SAVI report (there hasn't been a more recent one), priests were responsible for 4 per cent of child abuse in Ireland. Given child protection rules adopted by the Church and the current parlous state of priestly vocations in Ireland, One in Four describes clerical sexual abuse now – with no disrespect to survivors of the past – as a legacy issue.

In recent years, One in Four's client profile has begun to change 'quite dramatically', Maeve Lewis says. 'Originally most of our clients were institutional survivors, or survivors of clerical sexual abuse, and that cohort has passed through.' State inquiries and events such as the 2018 papal visit can be triggering events that spark new inquiries – but of One in Four's client base, the total in therapy for clerical sexual abuse is 9 per cent. Over 40 per cent of clients in therapy in 2017 were abused by a family member. The uncomfortable reality for modern Ireland is that childhood sexual abuse is not going to disappear with the priests.

This is reflected in One in Four's main problem today. It is not a shortage of clients – 167 were in therapy in 2017 – but of resources. It cannot treat everyone who seeks its help: it operates a waiting list for dozens of callers, and often has to even close the waiting list. Why does our state – why do we – feel this is acceptable? Older generations say today that the very idea of child sexual abuse – and predator priests – was outside their frame of reference. After twenty-five years of exposure to child abuse revelations, what is our excuse with regard to today's everyday child abuse?

Child abuse was uniquely possible in the past, given the nature of residential institutions run by religious orders – ostensibly with state oversight. But abuse has not vanished with those institutions. There are others out there waiting for Molly, Hugo, Patrick or Leo. And there are bystanders looking on, or looking away.

'People baulk at that,' says Maeve Lewis, 'because if we accept that one in four Irish children are sexually abused, and most of them are abused in their own families, then what does it say about us as a people?'

13.   Between the red doors

'The ghosts of a nation sometimes ask very big things; and
they must be appeased whatever the cost.'

Patrick Pearse

Two red doors, nine buildings apart on Dublin's Lower Baggot
Street, are bookends for Catholic Ireland's glory and shame. Behind
both red doors are remarkable operations set up to improve the lives
of others and repair damage done in the past.

My first destination is number 73 Lower Baggot Street, near the
Grand Canal. Climbing the steps, I notice, to the right of the door, an
oval stone plaque. A carved bird turns over a stone with its beak to
see what lies beneath. The plaque was there when the current occu-
pants moved in, but it describes their work well. The women in this
building know better than most what lies beneath our Irish Catholic
history.

Judge Yvonne Murphy's work began in 2006 when she was
appointed chair of the Dublin Archdiocese Commission of Investigation. Three years later, in November 2009, the commission's final
report into clerical sexual abuse in the archdiocese pulled no punches
in exposing what lay beneath. Along with barrister Ita Mangan and
solicitor Hugh O'Neill, Murphy produced a second report, into the
diocese of Cloyne, which was published in July 2011. The third and
perhaps greatest task for the retired circuit court judge and her team
is to investigate mother and baby institutions run by religious orders.
The commission was set up in February 2015 and was due to report
three years later. Such is the volume of work that at the time of writing (summer 2020) it has yet to do so.

An office administrator with a cautious gaze lets me in and puts
me in the front room. With cream walls, grass-green chairs and

magazines, it could be a private medical practice. Then my eyes fall on the white box of tissues and I tense up. How many tales has this room heard? Are there enough tissues in the world to soak up the fresh tears shed here for old pain?

The team here prefers to let its reports speak for themselves, but the achievements of the authors cannot be overstated: letting the silenced speak; making the once sacred profane; exposing the mighty as absurd – like the bishop who arrived to give evidence about the horrors that took place on his watch, yet still asked the commission's staff if they would like his blessing.

Ita Mangan collects me and brings me to Yvonne Murphy's office. There, in a shadowy space of books and dark wood in the back of the building, we start to talk. Because of the sensitivity of their work in the past, and ongoing work with their mother and baby inquiry, neither woman wants to be quoted. But they are happy to talk about the Murphy Report – in as much as they remember it. To be able to get on with their normal lives, the people who work here have to be able to forget what they hear.

The first investigation's objective was to examine how church and state authorities dealt with complaints of sexual abuse against children by clerics in the Dublin Archdiocese between 1975 and 2004. After complaints against 183 priests in total, the commission examined a representative sample of over 320 complaints against 46 priests. The commission's remit precluded it from establishing whether the sexual abuse alleged by complainants actually happened.

Like the Ryan Report before it, Murphy is a landmark document. It belongs in a time capsule of Irish life, alongside a bottle of stout and a copy of *Ulysses*. We discuss the report for a few minutes before I ask Judge Murphy what she is most proud of in it. She thinks for a few moments before her eyes light up and she mentions the term the team devised to summarize the era under investigation: 'undue deference'. It's an elegant and deceptively simple turn of phrase which can open out in many directions, like an origami bird, when you start to unfold it.

Deference is usually defined as respect shown for another person or group because of its experience, knowledge, age or power. Catholic religious, and the institution to which they belonged, ticked all the qualifying boxes. And as I listen to Yvonne Murphy talk, I consider the phenomenon of deference, undue or not. It is a two-way transaction: demanded or expected, as well as given, willingly or not. I recall reading somewhere that psychologists are unable to agree on how much the deference someone shows is due to their innate personality make-up and how much to social conditioning.

What's crucial for Judge Murphy is that showing or refusing to show deference assumes the freedom to decide, something the commission says most ordinary Irish Catholics lacked in the periods it investigated. Back then, deference was due when ordinary people interacted with priests and, in turn, when priests interacted with their bishops. And politicians, police, judges and others in positions to uphold the law of the land demonstrated deference to a parallel system of canon law.

Murphy's investigation tracked the consequences of this deference: the Dublin Archdiocese saw itself as existing beyond state law and, when confronted with child abuse complaints, proved unwilling to even apply church law. Instead it relied on deference, variously as weapon and cloak of invisibility. Yielding to this deference came at a cost, one that was not borne equally.

Justice Murphy was raised in Kiltimagh, Co. Mayo. She remembers how a priest in rural Ireland had far more power and agency than anyone else in the parish. But even in 1960s Dublin, a priest with a car was a star who could invite himself in anywhere and, as commission testimony showed, often did. He could turn up unannounced for lunch at parishioners' homes, knowing they were so honoured by his presence that a place would be set. Unfortunately, a minority of men exploited their position of privilege to molest their hosts' children. The abuse of trust was complete because the perpetrator was a priest.

Undue deference has a colloquial cousin, a phrase familiar to Irish people of a certain age: 'You don't question the priest.' Like 'undue deference', it's another flash of linguistic ingenuity. It explains everything and nothing. In one case examined by the Murphy team, a widow allowed a priest to spend the night in her spare room, only to discover him later in bed with her young son – but said she thought nothing of it. Deference, masked as respect and underpinned by asymmetry of power, proved a powerful set of blinkers.

The Murphy Report, in spare and sober language, removes the

blinkers and records for posterity how, even in the Irish capital in the last decades of the twentieth century, the power wielded by the Catholic Church was considerable.

The commission said it did not accept the truth of diocesan claims of ignorance about the abuse problem – the so-called 'learning curve' – when abuse claims began to emerge in the 1990s. This was not credible, the report suggests, given the mountain of evidence of abuse over decades in diocesan files.

The report concludes that the prominent role of the archdiocese and religious orders in the lives of Dubliners – making a considerable contribution to society – allowed abuses by a minority in their ranks to go unchecked.

'Institutions and individuals, no matter how august, should never be considered to be immune from criticism or from external oversight,' the report found, putting blame finally in its proper place: with clerical perpetrators and diocesan enablers, not victims.

The commission gave countless Dublin parishes, including my own, crucial and minute knowledge about abusers in their midst – and their accessories on the fringes.

Given the asymmetry of power, the failure of responsibility by the Archdiocese of Dublin is not in question. Archbishop Diarmuid Martin, who handed over diocesan archives to the commission after a fight with his predecessor, has said he stands over the conclusions of the report 'with no ifs and buts'. His clear-the-decks approach assisted Murphy in putting everything on the record. There was nowhere to hide, nothing to deny.

Others were more critical, such as the Association of Catholic Priests. No fans of their church superiors, in particular Archbishop Martin, the organization accused the commission of 'naming and shaming those clerics whom [it] found wanting in child protection at that time', though it had no remit to evaluate the truth of allegations. The legal precision of the Murphy Report, due to its nature and remit, is not the final word.

More than a decade after the report into where undue deference can lead, many in Irish society cling to their own learning curve to avoid arriving at any unflattering conclusions about themselves.

There have been a series of state apologies on the horrors of Catholic Ireland, starting with Bertie Ahern's in 1999, following the third part of Mary Raftery's *States of Fear* documentary series. Others have followed, always dragged out of politicians, always reactive and never proactive. Often well written, and perhaps even deeply felt, these apologies acknowledge survivors' pain and shame – but always in the context of how they reflect back on the Irish state and its people. A cynic might parse them in this way: *we are sorry that your suffering and pain makes us look bad.*

Given her task to map out the minefield of the Dublin Archdiocese, and the commission's legal limitations, I'm curious where Judge Murphy places the religious institution she studied. Out come the Venn diagrams I drew for Paddy Doyle and Seán Ryan. Did the diocesan institutions she investigated exist in her eyes as a circle inside a bigger circle of Irish society? Did the two overlap – half in, half out? Or did the Church exist outside, on its own? Without hesitation Judge Murphy points to the third diagram: the Church, she thinks, existed out on its own. It's the unequivocal answer of a sharp legal mind, yet at odds with others' answers. So who is right?

Before I leave, I wonder what Judge Murphy would like her ground-breaking report to be remembered for, after the details are forgotten.

The judge collects her thoughts before answering. Things in Ireland were known, in various silos, but no one was willing or able to put things together: priest-sin-crime. That took a long time.

Back on Baggot Street, beside the door, the bird is still turning over the stone. The first pass – a legal examination of our Catholic past – was and is a Sisyphean task, given how Catholic Ireland's cellars continue to reveal new sub-cellars to be explored, new outrages and new trauma; so much for such a small country. It's time to call on an organization, nine doors down, responsible for its own share of Irish Catholic achievement and trauma.

The red door of 64A is already open when I arrive for my appointment. Unlike the neighbouring brick buildings, Mercy International Centre is plastered and painted cream, a portico supported by four Ionic pillars over the main entrance.

Loitering outside, I watch two passers-by hurry along, eyeing the bronze statue of the woman responsible for the building with suspicion.

'Who's that?' says one woman to the other.

'I dunno. Some *nun* . . .'

The statue of Catherine McAuley, in a gesture of outreach to a poor bedraggled woman, is oblivious to the venomous tone, but the women inside know it all too well. This is the original head-quarters of the Sisters of Mercy order, founded by McAuley in 1831. Drawing inspiration from the Quakers, McAuley and other well-heeled lay women visited Dublin's poor and opened schools and shelters. A Dublin bishop, fearful of these women beyond his control doing charitable works, ordered McAuley to hand over her work to a religious order or found her own. In a show of either deference or shrewdness, she chose the latter and, nearly two centuries on, what began here is a global operation in healthcare and education that has over 6,000 Sisters worldwide. In Ireland the order is best known for its schools around the country and for Dublin's Mater Hospital.

Waiting inside in the reception area, I flick through a book of McAuley's teachings to her fellow Sisters. She urged them to adopt a 'humble and subdued' tone of voice and manner. If a Sister was to 'become remarkable at all, let it be for not being remarkable and for being the most hidden and unknown'.

In their homeland, things haven't quite worked out that way for the Sisters of Mercy. Two realities now compete and conflict in the public consciousness: nearly two centuries of care for the sick and the poor, the education of generations of Irish children – and childhoods blighted by random violence, humiliation, unpaid labour and fearful silence in Mercy institutions. Care and cruelty are the two sides of the order's reputation.

I'm in Baggot Street to meet Sr Mary Reynolds, a former head of both the order in Ireland and, after that, of the Mercy International Association, which brings together heads of all the order's organiza-tions worldwide. But before our conversation, another Sister gives me a tour of the sprawling building with its spiralling staircase and calm chapel. It's remarkable what's hidden behind the Baggot Street facade. As we move between rooms, the unwavering reverence towards McAuley and her personal effects is palpable. You can visit the original schoolroom or the room where she died of TB, in 1841. Her successors view their founder as a saint, and are lobbying for her canonization in Rome.

It's clear from the tour that the Sisters of Mercy order in Ireland, without its international operation, would be a shadow of its former self today. The international organization insisted that the Baggot Street headquarters be retained and helped finance a huge renovation. A well-produced short film, funded by American donors, explains McAuley's life. It highlights her saintliness and the (male) clerical machinations of the time. The film ends with McAuley's death and spares viewers the harsher reality of what followed – the descent into disgrace that began in 1996, four years after Catherine McAuley's final public hurrah: gracing Ireland's last £5 note.

Mary Reynolds grew up on a small farm in Carrick-on-Shannon, Co. Leitrim with two kinds of Catholicism: a mother who believed in rosaries and novenas and a father who, as she puts it, 'found God out in the field'. Sitting in the quiet ground-floor library, she recalls how her parents made sacrifices to send her to boarding school in Longford in the early 1960s. There Mercy Sisters, excited by Whitaker's economic reforms, drummed into their girls the chances for them in 'a new Ireland'.

After university, making her vows and pursuing a 'gentle' career as teacher and guidance counsellor in Longford, she rose to responsibility in the order just in time for two major events. The first was a major restructuring that brought previously autonomous Mercy institutions into one organization. The second, in 1996, was the tsunami that followed Louis Lentin's TV documentary *Dear Daughter*.

The film by Louis Lentin was the story of Christine Buckley, a former resident of the Goldenbridge industrial school run by the Sisters of Mercy in Dublin. Buckley remembered the home as a fear-filled place where physical and emotional abuse dominated. Children were deprived of food and sleep, forced to make rosary beads and subjected to regular beatings, including for bed-wetting.

Three years after she first told her story on radio, the 1996 drama-documentary provoked a media frenzy. The *Star* headlined its article 'Sisters of No Mercy' while the *Irish Independent* headlined its piece, in reference to Ms Buckley's number, 'The scandal of orphan 89'.

The film touched a nerve in the nation and, Mary Reynolds recalls, set off an earthquake in the order. She remembers how each week brought a new wave of lawyers' letters, all alleging abuse and demanding compensation on behalf of clients. She passed on all such letters to the order's own lawyers – activating, as Reynolds concedes in hindsight, a legal vicious circle.

She felt under siege by the media and turned to communications companies for help. Not that she thought anyone was listening to what the order had to say – particularly about how the order organized its business up to the 1990s. Until then, institutions under the Mercy umbrella were run autonomously. This meant there was no communication with other institutions.

'I would have heard stories too. But they were almost like tales from a fictitious world I knew nothing about,' says Mary Reynolds.

This line cuts little ice with many critics. At best, they see it as deliberate disorganization, something in which religious organizations appear to specialize to give them deniability. Other, less harsh, critics simply see Irish disorganization.

Either way, Reynolds says she had a rude awakening as head of the order, prompting what she remembers as a confused state of denial, similar to bereavement.

Reynolds says she was attracted to the order by what she calls McAuley's 'subversive' plan for Ireland: to care for the sick and educate the poor in the hope of eventually changing society's power structures. But over the decades the order had deviated far from the original plan. Instead of changing things, the Sisters of Mercy were drawn into church structures, subject to episcopal authority, and became part of the power structure.

In its 1919 democratic programme, nearly a century after McAuley set up her order, the first Dáil made its first duty '. . . to make provision for the physical, mental and spiritual well-being of the children'. A century on, Ireland is still grappling with the consequences of those two words – *provision for*. It was the basis on which an impoverished country institutionalized the Church's continuing involvement in education and healthcare. The state did not provide, it *provided for*, like an early public–private partnership.

Seen at a century's distance, both sides of the 'provide for' arrangement seem to have been using the other: the state saved money it didn't have by outsourcing social services, while the Church secured access to the minds and bodies of the faithful. Was it collusion?

Mary Reynolds shakes her head uncertainly. She can't speak for bishops and diocesan religious, but orders like hers, she thinks, were unwitting colluders with a system in which many were helped but many were also hurt.

'We looked at the symptoms – neglected children, poverty – and thought treating them was doing the right thing,' she says. 'Instead we should have been down [outside parliament] on Kildare Street campaigning for a better system.'

While Ireland has produced campaigning religious like Sr Stanislaus Kennedy, it's hard to imagine traditional Sisters in full habit picketing the Irish parliament with placards. Instead, a huge number of religious and lay workers compounded the very authoritarian power structures, social snobbery and misogyny that put people inside their institutions where, for many, their lives were – as Samuel Beckett's narrator puts it in his novel *The Unnamable* – a 'punishment for having been born'.

Mary Reynolds says her order lost sight of its original mission of mercy and compassion, became institutionalized and was blighted by the culture of harshness that hung over the Irish Church and society as a whole.

This makes it sound like a passive process. But working for an order with mercy in its name, did her fellow Sisters not see – or did they choose not to see – transgressions, violence and mercilessness?

'When you have an unquestionable reputation – in our case as good healthcare providers and educators – it doesn't allow you to see the rot,' she says. 'We didn't see how care was being exercised.'

The late 1990s and early 2000s saw a series of incremental apologies, coloured, Reynolds admits, by conflicting loyalties and ambivalence about the dramatic framing of the revelations in *Dear Daughter*. The equivocating influence of lawyers on all public utterances was impossible to ignore.

The order was not alone in criticizing the documentary. On the one hand, the film made a huge contribution to public debate, blowing open the discussion and forcing church and state to listen to survivors of institutions. The bravery of Christine Buckley gave many other survivors courage to come forward and take on the religious. On the other, some contemporary critics pointed out that Buckley's subjective experience had been turned into a universal reality. The Mercy Sisters say they felt the documentary left out positive contributions of their order to Buckley's life.

A month after it was aired, *Irish Times* media correspondent Michael Foley suggested there was 'something about this film and its timing that ensured special treatment by the media. It received wide, uncritical preview coverage. Few questions were asked and little journalistic scepticism shown.'

He wrote that, for the media, 'it was a story of goodies and baddies, with no room for subtleties.' Foley's piece provoked a backlash, but he was not alone in his questioning of how the story had been presented.

The years after *Dear Daughter* saw an increasingly complex picture of Goldenbridge emerge. Although they are in the minority – and often qualified – some survivors' memories of their experiences in Goldenbridge were more positive than Christine Buckley's.

Bernadette Fahy was born into her father's second, 'illegitimate' family. He failed to support her mother, and Fahy was placed in Goldenbridge. She also features in *Dear Daughter*. Yet Fahy's memoir, published three years after the film, recalls Goldenbridge as a place of 'little glimmers of kindness' in a world of 'overwhelming general harshness and cruelty'. However, Fahy, now a therapist, also remembers the Sisters' 'own angry frustrations' towards the 'incompetents' unable or unwilling to care for their own offspring, and taking it out on resident children. In the hierarchy of struggle and shame, the children always came last.

Fahy says many institutional survivors still grapple with a whole variety of abuse. All were institutionalized by a society unable or unwilling to provide for them. Many were traumatized by the institutions' prevailing culture of fear, shame, abuse and hunger. Some endured further abuse at the hands of 'good families' who took them out for weekends, holidays or longer periods. Others were shunned on release from the institutions and, with no chance of work, forced to emigrate. Ireland had no place for them, either as children or as adults. And now many are disappointed and even disgusted by a rec-onciliation process they perceive as disjointed, begrudging and defensive. Religious orders carry a great deal of blame, but they were not solely responsible for all of this abuse.

'The maltreatment of the children who lived in Goldenbridge did not begin with the Sisters of Mercy,' writes Fahy. 'A significant num-ber of us had been rejected before we ever arrived there.'

In his 1996 *Irish Times* report, Michael Foley made a similar point about Christine Buckley's assessment of the industrial school in *Dear Daughter*. In the film she says, 'I couldn't understand, and I'll never understand, how our parents dumped us in this place.'

The descriptions of how inmates were treated in religious-run insti-tutions have lost none of their shock value, even decades on. They are the victims – defenceless against adults who were uncaring and often abusive, perhaps themselves the product of abuse. Given what they went through, their opinion of religious is, understandably, bitter. Many of them will stay with this opinion, as is their right.

But what about the rest of us, in particular my fortysomething generation? Nearly a quarter of a century later, what is standing in the way of us taking a wider, less emotive look at this painful past? A way of allowing the achievements and abuses of religious orders to co-exist.

Any hopes of moving forward, survivor groups say, have been sty-mied by religious orders failing to punish individuals in their ranks and foot-dragging on compensation.

In the library on Baggot Street, Mary Reynolds shrinks a little when I mention that, and other familiar accusations. The order decided not to take action about individual Sisters because, she says, they were themselves inserted into an abusive system that provided them with no training or back-up.

Goldenbridge had around 150 children and just four full-time staff. An internal inquiry the order commissioned in 1996 into Gold-enbridge found its care model 'was created by a dominant and dysfunctional personality'. The 'personality' the report was referring to was Sr Xavieria who was featured in the *Dear Daughter* film.

'The religious sisters who subsequently held management responsibility lived in a tightly controlled and authoritarian world. Questioning was defined as arrogance and led to blaming of the individual.'

The problem with the collective responsibility approach adopted by the Mercy order, and others, combined with a lack of prosecutions by the state, is that it leaves many institutional survivors struggling to get closure on their suffering. Many find it impossible to understand that being part of an order would override someone's basic sense of decency as an ordinary human being, and that Sisters were able to inflict cruelty or abuse – or, at least as bad, were able to turn a blind eye to colleagues or subordinates doing so. Of course, that question also applies to the harshness of much of wider society: how was it possible to consign so many vulnerable people to institutions like Goldenbridge, or to turn a blind eye to their existence?

To complete the picture, survivors' experiences need to be examined alongside the stories of the members of religious orders who operated such places. These were often young people from conservative Irish families where the Church's word was unquestioned, who joined orders as teenagers, cast off their individual identity, took a vow of obedience and then were effectively locked up in stand-alone institutions with women, men, children – and other people's problems. Abandoning the idea of making judgements of your own, or having ideas about your future, was part of the initiation into religious life – you submitted your will to the will of your superiors who were, it went without question, acting according to God's will (or, if your superiors were women, acting in accordance with the will of His Grace, the bishop, who was channelling God's will). Absolute obedience meant accepting whatever work you were assigned without protest, and taking it as given that whatever resourcing was provided – or not provided – was not to be questioned. The tactics and purpose were akin to military training – breaking people down, stripping them of individuality, subjugating their wills to the goals of the collective – to create an effective infantry ready to carry out the mission of the organization, a mission that might not even be revealed to you. And all for the greater good, in God's name.

After our meeting, Mary Reynolds sends me the numbers that spell out what the order has done to meet the compensation commitments it made after the publication of the Ryan Report. It paid €20 million in cash, as well as €931,000 in interest that accrued while it waited for the state to set up the fund. It agreed to transfer 16 properties worth €15 million to the voluntary sector; 14 have been transferred, one was refused by the intended recipient and the last is with lawyers. It has sold 15 of 17 properties it agreed to dispose of, raising €5.4 million for the statutory fund, with the remaining two sales near closure. Finally, it earmarked 17 properties (with a 2009 value of almost €81 million) for transfer to the state. By June 2020, 16 transfers had been completed with the last on hold, ready for transfer, because the order says 'the State has yet to complete their acquisition'.

On two other points, the Mercy Sisters and other religious organizations refuse to budge. Their files remain closed, Mary Reynolds says, because they feel the general air of hostility at present would prevent them being assessed fairly.

Such arguments are frustrating for historians, and difficult for survivors and researchers to stomach, as is the position of Irish religious orders that their €128 million contribution to the institutional redress fund is final – although by 2017 the redress costs had passed ten times that amount. The religious justify their position by saying the exploding cost is not a benchmark of their blame but a bill 'incurred by the Dáil on its own legal and moral responsibility'.

Critics accuse the religious orders of playing for time and of ring-fencing assets. They may well be right. Looking at the world through Sister of Mercy eyes, though, such accusations are unlikely to encourage the Sisters to open their archives. Any hope of moving to a stage of restorative justice is stuck in a vicious circle of claim and counter-claim.

Shuttling between the various camps in this conflict – religious orders, state officials, survivors, researchers and campaigners – is like visiting opposing fronts in a warzone. After years of clashes, followed by periods of resentful fallback, there is little in the way of goodwill left between the rival camps. Each side perceives the others as dishonest, disingenuous and bullying. Many survivors say the trauma of their abusive experiences as children has been compounded in later life by the arrogance of religious organizations. On the other hand, elderly women in religious orders say that, even though they no longer wear habits, they are afraid to be identified in public. One tells me how, after a reconciliation Mass, she was confronted by a well-known orphanage survivor: 'Are you a nun? I know you're a bleedin' nun!'

Often when I return to Ireland and this debate I sense an expectation – demand – to choose a side: back survivors or defend religious. Faced with such a choice, it's hardly surprising many people have chosen apathy, interspersed with flare-ups of concern or anger about the latest revelation.

It is hard to work out what has to happen so that everyone's truth can be heard as part of a larger differentiated narrative. Behind the ongoing hurt and the wounding, I wonder, what is really going on?

The more I delve into this past the more I keep thinking about guilt and shame and how often the two are confused. The commissions, inquiries, court cases and reports were all urgent and necessary and, whatever their shortcomings, they have opened archives and left a paper trail with clear attributions of responsibility and blame. Identifying guilt in this way has served a valuable social function. But almost everything to date has been about addressing narrow guilt – in the legal, Murphy Report, sense – not wider shame.

However, the more I consider it, the greater my sinking feeling: could it be that the last twenty-five years of exhausting legal action and shocking revelations was the easy part? Still ahead of us is how to deal with collective shame, far more complicated because it involves all of us.

Researchers say that a major impediment to acknowledging and feeling collective shame is the perception that it exposes unflattering flaws. There is little motivation, as a result, for an 'active drive to make reparations', writes social psychologist Brian Lickel, 'but rather a more passive desire to hide, disappear, or escape from the emotion-eliciting event'.

When you have the option, you choose not to acknowledge the

emotive event; when you have no option, you do. Embarrassing revelations – particularly the kind that attract international attention – prompt a rush to react. But the reaction passes. This is what we do in Ireland and the consequence, say survivors and researchers, is that Ireland has yet to adopt a cohesive approach to its Catholic past. Instead we take a piecemeal approach that is less than the sum of its parts.

'Irish society, especially the Irish State, Church and legal system, remain fundamentally unaltered by the process of addressing the past,' argues James Gallen, a lecturer on international law and transitional justice at Dublin City University.

Perhaps Ireland is stuck in the guilt gear, struggling with the shift to shame. Or perhaps the state is responding in the way voters want – with public displays of outrage over religious orders sealing their archives being matched by public indifference to the government's decision to seal its own records, and commission files.

After months talking to survivors, delving back into religious institution reports, and reading heart-breaking memoirs of blighted lives, I find it unsurprising that most people struggle to embrace this story. The scale is staggering for people who work in this area full-time, let alone people with full-time jobs, trying to raise their families and make ends meet.

And even if we chose to reflect on our Catholic past, how and where would we begin? What would we hope to achieve? With little guidance or encouragement to do so, it's easier to escape shameful events by disassociating from the parties involved. In Ireland this can mean no longer identifying as Catholic, or even belittling Catholicism. Researchers in the area would flag such actions as standard responses to shame. Another action is for people who, unconsciously, share a sense of collective shame to act quickly to identify a subgroup to blame for past events. This is natural human behaviour. However, disavowing a sub-group, Brian Lickel warns, stops us understanding how the action of the sub-group reflects the 'real nature' of the collective.

Once Catholic Ireland was 'us': our sons and daughters were God's holy anointed, spreading the faith and creating a glorious Irish spiritual empire around the world, and keeping the show on the road at home. Our pride knew no bounds. Then came scandal and the fall. A new narrative was written, framing the same religious as a disgraced 'them', with each of the group's members responsible for the acts of their institutions and their colleagues. We reserve for them a collective blame that it doesn't seem to occur to us to apply to ourselves as a people. We assume they knew exactly what was going on and we seem to think lay people knew nothing at all. In other words – now, as then – we see 'them' as having nothing to do with 'us'. The pedestal many of us reserve for our religious now is one of blame. I wonder what would happen if we questioned the deference pedestal of then, and the blame pedestal of today. Doing so might help us acknowledge the legacy of Irish religious as two conflicting sides of the same coin: achievement and abuse.

Back on Baggot Street, I'm sitting in the half-light of the Mercy International Centre library with my eyes on the Catherine McAuley statue outside the window, and my ear with Mary Reynolds. After everything I had heard about how closed religious orders are to journalists, I'm surprised at how open she is. Perhaps I expected a tight-lipped Sister who would give me some pre-cooked legalities and a few bland platitudes. Instead I got someone who is open to questions and happy to talk, who wonders deeply about the nature of God and mercy, and how the legacy of her order – the good and the bad – will all measure up in hindsight.

Hers is a life lived in a state of permanent consideration: once to her order and superiors and now, in addition, to those hurt by the order and its members. She knows any mention of the Sisters of Mercy and other religious orders will remain a trigger for those who were traumatized. Anxious not to minimize survivors' suffering with a careless word, every time she opens her mouth she tries to weigh what she is saying. It must be exhausting to be her.

'We didn't invent abusive people, families or clergy, or a mentality that found sex outside of marriage so terrible that they would disown a child,' she says. 'What you really want to shout is, "We're only part of the story." But you can't.'

As we wrap up, I tell her I'm not clear on whether the abuse and the public response have encouraged deep reflection among the Sisters of Mercy – or a defensive withdrawal.

Reynolds concedes that some Sisters took longer than others to realize that their story of achievement in education and healthcare is now, for ever, also one of cruelty and abuse. When this realization struck her, she says, it pushed her into a personal and spiritual crisis.

'From there on out it wasn't a question of me as a merciful woman, but me as a woman in need of compassion and mercy,' she says. 'It was a very dark moment, I was dependent on God to give meaning to stay with this.'

Her low voice and urgent eyes suggest she is still grappling.

After walking back from Baggot Street I go into St Stephen's Green and sit down on a park bench. I watch a swan dunking into the pond to wash itself.

My mind is racing. An ongoing struggle continues over whether competing narratives of our past can exist as part of a bigger story. And somewhere between those red doors – 64A and 73 – lies a version of the past I am trying to understand for myself. Exploring our past is about deciding how close we feel to one door and how far from the other door – while acknowledging that both buildings, and what lies behind both doors, are part of our past.

The work to apportion guilt will end eventually but the story won't. Perhaps the only thing survivors, the state, religious and ordinary people share is disgust – an unexpressed fear of being contaminated through ongoing contact with sickening elements of our past. The need to disassociate from such elements is human, but it brings the risk of retaining or repeating old habits and narratives.

As I watch the young swan dunk itself again and again, its grey feathers refusing to wash white, I think of grey-faced women facing mountains of other people's laundry. And I consider the tragic irony of words of Catherine McAuley's: 'How can we teach the love of God if our own hearts are cold?'

14.   We don't want to know what's buried here

'We make out of the quarrel with others, rhetoric,
but of the quarrel with ourselves, poetry.'

W. B. Yeats, 'Anima Hominis'

Hurrying alongside the Liffey quays in an evening shower, I pass Adam and Eve's Church on Merchant's Quay. Straight away I think of a calendar on my desk back in Berlin. A gift from a friend, with pictures from the archives of Irish religious orders, I view it as an ironic celebration of Ireland's former spiritual empire. The image for July shows an Irish nun sitting on an elephant in India in 1903. August has six Irish Sisters of Charity squinting out from a sea of billowing black as they board a California-bound TWA plane to set up a new mission in the early 1950s. And so forth.

But my favourite image in the calendar is a view of this very spot, outside Adam and Eve's Church, showing a priest and two assistants blessing a fire engine, aboard which stand four men in dark uniforms, stoic and alert. Dozens of bystanders look on. It's a scene that was totally normal then and would be utterly exotic now.

I think of the young boys in the picture and wonder how many are still alive. Did they really believe that a blessing of holy water by a priest would somehow help the work of the fire brigade? Help them get to fires faster? Protect the firefighters from harm? Or ensure a passage to heaven if they perished? What did they actually think it was for? Did they think about it at all, or just go along with it?

As I pass the church and think of that emblematic image from my calendar, it highlights a theme I have been grappling with on and off: whether we confused religious belief with church presenteeism.

How much did the people's mere presence at that quayside blessing – along with their presence at Masses, novenas and missions, at baptisms and funerals and other significant life moments – contribute to the Catholic nature of a past Ireland? Even if they were just part of a national rent-a-crowd, a large group of people can change the picture – and the dynamic – of the past. Presence implies attachment and fidelity. Presence creates institutional legitimacy. Presence suggests approval. Presence aids impunity.

How many people really think that their absence from church now has somehow resolved the past? Voting with their feet may be an eloquent vote of no confidence, of disapproval, but it still leaves a lot of unfinished business and exasperates survivors like Paddy Doyle. And, if we're honest, as a small, conservative country, we've always been good at the 'done thing' – going to Sunday Mass then, staying away from it now. Mass passive absence today does not address the effects of mindless Mass presence yesterday.

There's a remarkable similarity between how older generations talk about going to Mass then, and how younger people talk about staying away today: it's just what you do. Writing this book, asking Irish people randomly how they feel about Catholic Ireland, the most common reaction is a blank stare. While some express anger about the abuse scandals and the institution, most don't seem to have any deeper knowledge or feelings towards the Catholic faith. Few recall being a part of Catholic Ireland.

On one level, I understand the apathy. On another, though, I find it surprising. Regardless of one's own views, Catholicism and Christianity remain among the most influential cultural, spiritual and ideological influences on our country and its history. They have helped define almost everything about who we were as a people then, and now – as well as, for many, everything we no longer want to be. Considering most of us were there, it could be expected that we would have thoughts and feelings about this. But instead we have 'moved on'. Or have we?

I wonder if the silence is an absence of feeling towards our Catholic past, a cautious silence, or a conflicted struggle to associate with the era. As time moves on, and there are no abuse survivors or perpetrators left – what story will we tell ourselves then?

After nearly thirty years grappling with the appalling facts, perhaps the very idea of understanding needs to be addressed and redefined. A new phase of emotional comprehension is required. And looking at Ireland from the outside, I see green shoots – new story-telling and fresh narratives that acknowledge the emotional challenges of understanding a complex past. And following such a narrative trail has brought me down the quays in the rain tonight to Dublin City Council's exhibition space on Wood Quay. I'm here to observe a post-abuse narrative unfold, to see who witnesses it and who claims ownership.

Officially 'I am One in Four' is a photographic exhibition. In reality it is an emotionally charged archaeological excavation, brushing away the clichés that populate the discussion of child abuse and bring-ing non-survivors to a place that words cannot reach. It is based around Photovoice, a method of bringing out hidden stories. In this instance, to access and understand their experiences of abuse, shame, silence and recovery, abuse survivors have taken photographs and written accompanying texts.

By going public with their experiences the eight participants here this evening are taking a calculated risk: that the potential gains of helping others understand even a fraction of the devastation of abuse outweigh the risks of being retraumatized themselves.

As I walk around the exhibition hall studying the images – crashed cars, barbed wire and locked doors – I notice that clerical child sexual abuse is represented here as one part on a wider canvas. The panel discussion with survivors is preceded with a video where they tell their stories and repeat the evening's message: 'I am One in Four. I am you.'

Assisted by One in Four, the exhibition has been organized by Dr Maria Quinlan, a UCD sociologist, and Patrick Bolger, one of Ire-land's best-known photographers. Both are also survivors of child sexual abuse: Maria familial, Patrick clerical.

Patrick Bolger's pictures tonight – cracked asphalt, concrete churches – are very different from his usual work in newspapers and glossy magazines. Alongside the images are angry poems detailing a priest grooming and seducing a child, and the child's parents smiling, bowing and thanking the abusing priest: Tom Naughton.

Naughton's story fills fifteen pages of the Murphy Report into sexual abuse in the Dublin Archdiocese. He abused children for nearly a quarter of a century and was shifted from one parish to the next amid complaints. When auxiliary bishop Donal Murray confronted Naughton with complaints he had received, the priest was dismissive and told his superior not to listen to 'cranks'. His superior listened to him, rather than the complaints. Eventually, Naughton was charged for his crimes. He pleaded guilty to sexual abuse of a child and served six months in jail.

In one poem, Patrick Bolger lists the 'secrets of Valleymount', the parish in Co. Wicklow, where he grew up. The second secret, he writes, was that Tom Naughton's abuse was 'never a secret' in Valleymount.

> Fathers knew.
> Mothers knew.
> The waters rippled to the whispered truth . . .

It's clear that Patrick takes issue with Ireland's us-and-them framing of clerical sexual abuse. As an adult looking back, he views Tom Naughton not as an 'other', but as an ill man whose clerical stature made him feel 'bulletproof'. He understood intrinsically 'the power of the collar and the power of silence and the bended knee of the community'. Even if people knew, he says, the priest was confident they would 'doff their hat, that no one would challenge him'.

Going public with his clerical sexual abuse story has prompted every kind of response, he says, from those who mutter 'it was a different time' to others who flag the power disparity between priest and parishioners. No reaction, he says, can justify passivity and its consequences.

Bolger's neighbours simultaneously knew nothing of what was going on, or say they had no power to do anything about it, yet had enough knowledge and power to instruct a garda living locally to pay a quiet visit to the local parish priest and have Fr Naughton moved. In such a way, even parents' protective instincts were part of a culture of collusion. Naughton was shifted to Donnycarney, on Dublin's northside, where he continued to abuse. Two of the priest's victims in other parishes have since taken their own lives. Naughton was a small enough problem to shift elsewhere, but too big to solve. The result: silence.

Patrick Bolger writes about this silence in one poem:

> Silence is not not knowing
> Silence is a deliberate action
> Silence is a decision to say nothing
> Silence is a decision to do nothing
> There is power in silence
> And human agency.

The Photovoice project has energized Patrick but also stirred up old anger. Anger towards the Catholic Church official who, in recent years, explained Naughton's crime to him as being based on 'the occasion of sin': that if there hadn't been altar boys like Patrick around, maybe the priest wouldn't have done anything. Anger, too, he says, towards the Murphy commission for hearing his testimony but not using it in its final report.

That was a wounding and sobering experience, he said, and made him realize that not even the Murphy Report could explain fully this part of his reality. Its legalistic approach – good for fact-finding – was, he says, not characterized by empathy and was 'not enough' for the future. The Photovoice project, on the other hand, has allowed him to take stock of his ongoing struggle with his feelings about what happened, as well as his parallel struggle with denial about abuse, which he still senses in his family and in Irish society.

If Patrick is angrily eloquent, Maria Quinlan is empathetic and analytical. The youngest of nine from a working-class background, she says she experienced sexual abuse within her family that has taken her decades to overcome. Her empty, vacant photographs – a muddy pool or the word 'cunt' spelled out in flower petals – represent the isolation and loneliness she felt as an abused child. That word – 'cunt' – was one she remembers hearing frequently in her childhood and remains for her an expression of her home's toxic masculinity and downgrading of female identity and sexuality.

Experiencing abuse as a child, she writes in her contribution, 'leaves you wide open for manipulation . . . the wounds are invisible'.

She adds, 'I was born into a toxic cesspit of addictions, secrets, lies, abuse and violence of all kinds.' Normalizing the toxic elements of her life only burdened her more as an adult, she explains.

She sees decades of work ahead for Irish society to acknowledge and heal the abuse it has suffered and the traumas it has sustained. A starting point, she says, is honest and non-judgemental analysis of how, even if its visible parts have been pruned back, Catholicism remains part of Irish life: from the unconscious 'God bless' to the ringing of the Angelus bell by the national broadcaster twice a day. 'It's like that Japanese root – once it gets into your garden, we're infested.'

Maria hopes an approach like Photovoice can offer new ways for people to think about this Catholic presence and explore how they feel about this. And she suggests that allowing time for this to happen, allowing people to feel understood rather than judged, may, paradoxically, even open a door back to spirituality.

Maria's own life has been enriched by practices such as yoga and meditation. 'I'm a spiritual person and I love the Bible. It is full of nothing but empathy,' she says. 'But if we can't forgive ourselves we can't forgive anybody else.'

She believes that Ireland's unaddressed Catholic heritage – our unresolved discussion over church and societal responsibility – has created a blockage. If we can't look back, forgive the Church and forgive ourselves, Maria thinks, then it's hard to see a way forward. Things will remain frozen, with new generations continuing to go through 'vacuous' First Communion and Confirmation rituals for the sake of it. She believes these formulaic rituals may be doing more harm than good, blocking off the possibility of young people opening their minds to spirituality.

'We are just creating more people who don't love themselves,' she says. 'We need to step up.'

Patrick nods his head when he hears Maria talk of spirituality. Tom Naughton robbed him of his ability to believe, he says, but he is working slowly to rebuild some spirituality. Now his religion is hiking, and the Wicklow Mountains are his church.

These two survivors of sexual abuse – clerical and familial – say they discovered that working through their pasts has opened a deeper perspective on the society that was home to their abuse. This is not unusual for people who've been through something like this. Just as Marie Collins thinks endless health system scandals are a symptom of unquestioned Irish attitudes towards authority, Patrick and Maria flag how we allow government to outsource our homeless crisis to charities. For Patrick and Maria this is twenty-first-century Ireland repeating a pattern.

'Everything is ad hoc,' says Maria. 'We have a reluctance to put in place services and strategies because that would mean admitting problems they are meant to address.'

Beneath the shadows of clerical sexual abuse, Maria Quinlan and Patrick Bolger argue, are solutions not only to historical traumas but also to modern riddles of Irish life. Witness, empathy, honesty – with others and with oneself – are, they say, the first step to really owning problems, and prerequisites for progress in resolving them.

Days later, in Berlin, I'm still thinking about the remarkable 'I am One in Four' exhibition: a portal into private abuse hell but also a glimpse into the possibilities of healing. All participants walked the perimeter of their suffering, describing the structure but also survey-ing the foundations on which it was built. It was quite appropriate, then, that the launch took place in Dublin City Council's Wood Quay offices, before the numbered stone bricks of old Dublin's city wall. The wall, incorporated into the exhibition space, is living testi-mony of the almighty battle here, four decades previously, to erect new civic offices on a site of Dublin's Viking origins.

Back then, archaeologists discovered how early Dubliners burned their old wattle houses to the ground to build on the same foundations.

'Excavators know this because black scorch marks are still present at the bottom of the wooden foundations [and] as many as three layers of houses have been found,' notes the *Dublin Historical Record*.

Sometimes I wonder if we are doing the same today as we grapple with our Catholic past: torching our (religious) buildings, meta-phorically, only to rebuild new structures on the same, scorched foundations.

This approach works fine – as long as you are aware of how the hidden foundations will come to define the shape, scale and ambition of what is built on top. But what happens if you are not aware of the foundations, or insist the foundations of the previous structure have nothing to do with what you want to erect now?

A little while later, on a freezing Sunday morning in Berlin, I'm out walking with a friend. I tell him about my dig through Ireland's Catholic history, as well as about the churches now earmarked for demolition. My friend, a psychotherapist who has no time for organized religion, points at two church steeples on the horizon and says, 'You can topple as many steeples as you like, but what counts is what lies underneath.'

Soon he's explaining the conscious versus subconscious mind. You can view it as an iceberg, with the conscious mind – those thoughts of which you are aware – as the visible tip. Just below the surface is the preconscious mind – a kind of mental waiting room where thoughts remain until, as Sigmund Freud put it, they 'succeed in attracting the eye of the conscious'.

At the third level, well below the surface, lurks the unconscious mind. This is where Freud saw mental processes inaccessible to consciousness but which can still alter our judgement, feelings or behaviour. Trauma is stored in this unconscious mind, the mind you cannot see.

Demolishing churches due to shrinking congregations is a significant marker in our history as a country, but that doesn't eliminate our Catholic past and its legacy any more than shaving the tip off the iceberg would have saved the *Titanic* back in 1912. The real action happened beneath the surface.

My friend uses the example of someone who decides to get away from their parents, viewing them as a toxic influence. They move to another country, change their name, hairstyle, job. Yet without excavating their home foundations – the only rules they have for living their life – it is likely they will draw unconsciously on these same rules. They will keep living life and experiencing reality based on the very rules they supposedly now reject, learned at a young age from their parents – or their priest.

Acknowledging this reality – the unconscious part of the Irish Catholic iceberg beneath today's sea – is one step towards understanding our then and our now. And sometimes the best way is via the side door to our brains – through art.

It's a cold Saturday afternoon in January but the front door of the Georgian building is open, an invitation to a crowd that isn't here.

We're at the city end of Gardiner Street, between the railway bridge and the Customs House. For decades, a sign advertising the headquarters of the *Irish Catholic* hung from the facade of number 56. That's in the past – the newspaper now has new premises – and I'm next door in number 55, exploring the Irish Catholic legacy.

It's an exhibition of interventions by artists, shocked into action by the revelations of Tuam woman Catherine Corless about the former mother and baby home in the Galway town, in particular uncertainty over the remains of around 800 children who died there. With a story so difficult for the mind to grasp, art offers another way in.

One of the works on display is a white shop-window mannequin wearing a pretty hat and a puffy dress made up of missing children's birth certificates. Nearby are glittery gold baby shoes with elongated laces, on to which are printed self-explanatory texts: 'Patrick Munnelly 3 months. John Lavelle 6 weeks. Anne Ruane 11 days.'

Keeping a lonely vigil inside the gallery, drinking coffee against the cold, is survivor Sheila O'Byrne. Originally from Dublin's Sandymount, Sheila's life changed after a party in 1976 when she went back to a friend's house. A short encounter with a man at the party – 'nobody told us about the birds and the bees' – left her pregnant.

When the man vanished she ended up on the steps of St Patrick's on the Navan Road, working all day for no pay for nuns she remembers as 'heartless, ignorant, bitter to the core'. But she hasn't forgotten the Ireland she encountered during her crisis pregnancy: a well-oiled machine of interlocking cogs to control and conceal 'shame'. The Navan Road was her second stop, after being placed with a Greystones couple from whom she eventually fled.

'This was arranged by the monsignor in Sandymount: the medical, the religious, the state, all in it together, like one big co-op,' she says. When her baby was given up for adoption she returned home but never discussed the episode with her parents or how she decided to disappear on her own from Sandymount.

'I was a big embarrassment and shame on my family,' she said, 'and I knew I had to get out.'

The most haunting exhibit watched over by Sheila is in the cellar: grey, ghostly christening robes made out of glass, suspended and dangling, waiting for babies that will never return.

A few months later I encounter the robes again, this time at the opening of *(A)Dressing Our Hidden Truths*, in the National Museum of Ireland's Collins Barracks outpost. The exhibition of work by artist Alison Lowry is a full-frontal attack on Ireland's heartless defence of morality. Here the nine christening robes dangle in the dark, moving with the air currents. Like the local Irish brand of Catholicism, the dresses appear soft and yielding but are actually brittle and impenetrable. Literal and figurative skeletons in our Catholic closet, the garments started out white but here have ended up grey and scorched. Lowry uses a technique called *pâte de verre*, covering a garment in glue and glass powder, burying it in sand and firing it to a high temperature in a kiln. With fabric and glue burned away, the glass remains.

Standing beside the dresses, rendered almost speechless by the exhibits' awful beauty, two older men grapple with the eternal question of Irish life: *how much was known?*

One says simply: 'Enough people knew.'

In the museum foyer, the speeches make similar points. Minister for Family Katherine Zappone, whose department is in charge of working through the toxic legacy, says the incarceration, forced adoptions and unexplained burials were made possible by the collaboration of government, Church, religious orders and society.

'It is simply not feasible, credible or believable that people did not know what was happening in our cities, towns and villages – and for many families happening in their own home,' she said. 'This was an injustice carried out on a national scale – and the response must be just as wide-ranging.'

Following the minister on the podium, Alison Lowry says she hopes her art can help foster understanding, dialogue and forgiveness to ensure such shocks from the past won't be replicated in the future. She quotes a line from César Cruz, a gang violence prevention advocate: art should comfort the disturbed and disturb the comfortable.

Six weeks later, when I catch up with Alison, she's just back from visiting the exhibition with her two sons. They're ten and thirteen and, at that age, she says, less impressed by content than scale.

'I heard the older one say, "It's four rooms, not one," ' she says.

The boys don't yet know that Ireland's Catholic past – its glory and shame – could fill an entire museum. They don't know that such a museum doesn't exist. Nor do they know that the National Museum of Ireland initially didn't want their mother's exhibition. But some museum staff fought for it – and the public response speaks for itself.

Staff say it has been very busy, with people asking specifically for her exhibition. In the guest book, filling up fast on the first evening, someone wrote: 'At last, at last . . .'

Clearly, there is a public appetite for this. But will it, picking up on her César Cruz quote, disturb the comfortable?

Not enough, says Lowry, ever the self-critical artist. She's been mulling over one reviewer who suggested the exhibition didn't do enough to hold a mirror up to Irish society of the recent past.

'And she's completely right, I think Irish society was complicit in it,' she says. Even Northern Ireland, where she lives, had mother and baby homes. Her mother told her of one for Protestant women on the Malone Road in Belfast. Researchers estimate around 7,500 women went – or were sent – to such homes in the North.

'We all knew this was going on. Perhaps we didn't know what was going on behind the closed doors of the institution, but it was hiding in plain sight,' she says. 'Nobody wanted to blow the whistle. What is it – a part of our nature – we don't want to stand up and call this out?'

Perhaps acknowledging complicity in hindsight is post-Catholic Ireland's new version of that old familiar phenomenon of Catholic Ireland: knowing and not knowing.

Like the 'I am One in Four' exhibition, Lowry's work encourages reflection and, in its Collins Barracks home, raises uncomfortable questions about what it means to be Irish. Getting to her haunted glass dresses in the museum means passing an 'Erin go Bragh' ('Ireland for Ever') tea set in a display case and the 1919 declaration of the first Dáil 'to the nations of the world' about an emerging Irish nation believing in 'equal rights against the vested privileges of ancient tyrannies'. The young Irish state and its people demanded rights and recognition from others but did not extend the same rights and recognition to the women and children remembered by Lowry's work.

In a darkened room at the opening of Alison Lowry's show, Anna Corrigan is keeping vigil at an exhibit in the show to her mother

Bridget who died in 2001, aged eighty-one. Anna grew up believing she was an only child but in 2012 learned that, before she was married, Bridget had two sons at the Tuam mother and baby institution. Unsure if her half-brothers are dead or alive and adopted illegally, Anna is another tireless campaigner for a story she isn't sure Ireland is really interested in hearing. She understands the lack of appetite for it, attributing it to people's struggles today. 'Someone will say, "Yeah, that was terrible, but I don't have a house."'

Standing in the darkened room in Collins Barracks she admits having mixed feelings about the exhibition. The artistic approach may be educational for some but, she fears, there is a risk with it of skipping important stages in the process of coming to terms with the past.

'We need truth, justice, accountability and restitution and only when that is done, and the papers have been released with everything in the open, can we look at ourselves and how we ended up in the position we found ourselves,' she believes.

Like other survivors and campaigners at the opening of *(A)Dressing Our Hidden Truths*, Corrigan says tensions persist between them, religious orders and the government. Survivors say they are exhausted by obstacles to accessing files and information. Used to this behaviour from religious orders, Anna Corrigan says it is tiresome to experience this from successive governments too. She is yet another activist who notes that the political rhetoric of openness is at odds with bureaucratic inertia, with officials refusing to acknowledge survivors' human rights – and the Irish state's role in the violations of these rights.

It's not totally surprising that ordinary people hang back in this process. Instead of treading the road to reconciliation, the main interest groups grappling with Ireland's Catholic past remain trapped on a roundabout. Alongside are ordinary people who have conscious disgust towards past abuses and subconscious disgust towards survivors and those who remind them of the failings of the state. Survivors see Ireland trapped in a long-running game of official announcements, pushback and retreat on one front only to pop up with something equally infuriating elsewhere. Most survivors and campaigners cannot work out whether the strategy is callousness or carelessness. Anna

Corrigan is not prepared to give up, although she says keeping tabs on religious orders, the wider Church and the state is a full-time job.

'It's like whack-a-mole,' says Anna, 'but I have quite a big hammer.'

Though decades of burdensome revelations about Catholic Ireland has left them exhausted, survivors, artists and activists are finding new ways of telling what many see as a familiar story.

Like an archaeological dig, this is painstaking, multi-stratal work and there is disagreement over the correct order: should campaigners keep after the institutional Church for full acknowledgment and disclosure? Or supplement that work with a second line of scrutiny? For instance: how much of Catholic Ireland's structure was clerical imposition and how much was simply a manifestation of the underlying class and power structures in Irish society at the time?

To see a younger Irish writer's take on these issues, I'm in Ballymun, on Dublin's northside, prowling the first floor of The Apex arts centre. On the walls, between the top of the stairs and the men's toilets, are images of Ireland as we like it to be: a dozen paintings of rugged rock coastlines, calm blue lakes, fizzing white waterfalls. Inside the walls of the theatre, however, we're about to be confronted with another reality entirely.

We Don't Know What's Buried Here, a new play by Grace Dyas, promises to hold up a mirror to a less flattering image of Ireland. Onstage two women, Tina and Bernadette – ghosts – dig for their pasts and their babies in the shadow of their former laundry building.

'It looks like something from Nazi Germany from the back,' says Tina of the building, 'but from the front it looks respectable.'

'Work will set us free,' Bernadette says. 'I would have installed a neon *Arbeit macht frei* sign on the building if I had the budget.'

Despite some nods towards the vacant, absurdist style of *Waiting for Godot*, the play is, in fact, bursting with issues. Instead of a promised memorial, the ghosts say their laundry will be razed for a hotel. Catholicism and its legacy are being sidelined by a new Ireland's dominant neo-liberal doctrine.

'We are worthless . . . poor people on rich land,' says Tina.

The play identifies the laundries as manifestations of power abuse, fuelled by gender and class discrimination. And, though rough around the edges, it is an energetic attempt by a young writer to call out our past by dragging it into the present, where one ideology is buried under the next with little debate.

Dyas is treading in the footsteps of Patricia Burke Brogan's ground-breaking play *Eclipsed* which, three decades earlier, took an approach to the laundries that was calmer yet no less menacing. Burke Brogan based her play on her time as a novice with the Mercy Sisters. She left the order after spending time in a laundry where 'the women looked at me as if I was a gaoler, and I suppose I was'.

Just like Dyas, Burke Brogan pulled no punches about identifying the laundries as manglers of humanity. Nor did she airbrush out the uncomfortable, unspoken contract with Irish society, Irish people.

'We give them food, shelter and clothing . . . no one else wants them,' declares Burke Brogan's Mother Superior. Silencing a conscience-plagued novice about their treatment of the women, she adds, 'We are eclipsed. But blind obedience will carry you through.'

In Ballymun, after the final curtain and polite applause, the audience files out and reaction is mixed. 'It ended up touching everything and nothing,' says Áine, wife of a German journalist friend, taking issue with the Holocaust comparisons and its broad-brushstrokes capitalist critique.

'The whole point of the laundries was the complicity. We were all complicit, right down to how you could only leave if you were collected by your family. And many of the women were just not collected.'

Outside the venue, a group of students say they really enjoyed the show. Then two of their friends turn up with curry chips and the play is forgotten.

Standing at the bus stop I get talking to a young woman from Berlin who says, 'The repeated references to *Arbeit macht frei* were really shocking. And I'm not sure in a good way.'

Waiting for the bus, it's clear Dyas is anxious to stir up debate about the lack of agency of the working class – and women in particular – in Catholic Ireland, and how they are memorialized today. They have yet to be accepted into the invitation-only heroes' narrative of our recent past. Across from the bus stop, on the walls of Ballymun's derelict shopping centre, is a mural with the faces of

leaders of the 1916 Rising. 'Is cuimhinn linn' – *we will remember you.*
We didn't always. For decades, particularly after the outbreak of violence in the North in the late 1960s, mainstream Ireland struggled
with how to remember its revolutionary origins, and reacted allergic-
ally to those who did. In recent years the state's foundational event
has been reclaimed, explored and commemorated. Not so the damage done to vulnerable citizens of the new state. While the words of
the 1916 Proclamation were addressed to 'Irishmen and Irishwomen'
and vowed that, in pursuing the happiness and prosperity of the
nation, Ireland would cherish 'all the children of the nation equally' –
the new, independent Irish state fell far short of this.

The bus comes, and I get on board thinking a better name for
Grace Dyas's thought-provoking play would be: *We Don't Want To
Know What's Buried Here.*

PART THREE

Among the ruins

15. A stone phoenix

'Because of his fear of a priest's power he made
sure to give the appearance of a welcome.'

John McGahern

Ireland is still grappling with the legacy of three aggressive nineteenth-
century imports.

The first, the rhododendron, became popular in the UK during
the 1700s but, in Ireland, is best known through its introduction
around Muckross House in Killarney a century later. Once praised
for its beautiful blossoms, today many view the rhododendron as an
invader that shades out indigenous plants, is poisonous to livestock
and hosts organisms that attack oak and beech trees. Something
embraced for its beauty has, in hindsight, revealed an ugly side.

The second import was Victorian morality. After emancipation in
1829, Catholics constructed facades of moral respectability behind
which they obsessed over sex, the sin of sex, how best to control sex
and how best to deal discreetly with sexual accidents – make them
disappear or emigrate. Sex was everywhere and yet nowhere. While
Ireland's rural poor starved en masse in the Famine, or emigrated,
Ireland's aspiring middle classes craved something more than
potatoes: respectability. In their understanding this meant learning
self-restraint, resisting emotional or physical drives in order to separate themselves from the lower classes who, in turn, aimed for their
own idea of respectability. For historian Joe Lee this mid-nineteenth-
century Ireland was a sluggish society where 'envy, jealousy and spite
would become rampant'.

Dropped in on top of this was the third import: a reformulated
religion that transformed ragged Famine-era faith into shiny, earnest
Sacred Heart Catholicism. What many assume is age-old Irish

Catholicism is nothing of the sort. It is just nine years older than the *Irish Times* and thirty-four years older than the GAA. Like the Gaelic Athletic Association, it recodified and formalized a much older tradition. And both emerged out of the heartland of Ireland, Thurles.

It's a grey and cold day, no weather for a staring match with a stone phoenix. Yet that's what I'm doing at the gates to St Patrick's College in Thurles. The mythical bird of renewal atop the pillar has caught my eye because I recognize it from the scan of an *Illustrated London News* article I'm holding. The article is about the day that Ireland's Catholic Church stirred from the ashes of despair – 22 August 1850. Looking at the drawing beside the report, I realize I must be standing in the same spot as the illustrator did back then.

The Synod of Thurles that August was a big enough story to warrant significant coverage in British newspapers like the *Illustrated London News*. It told its readers that the first gathering of Catholic Church leaders in Ireland since 1642 was 'to deliberate and pronounce upon questions of the deepest moment to the interests of that religion, the purity of faith and morals, the strength and dignity of the Church and the general well-being of the community'.

The report describes a procession of 300 religious men – in full garb, altar boys carrying their trains – passing through the gates of St Patrick's at 10 a.m. The paper's correspondent is rhapsodic about a 'gorgeous . . . array of coped and mitred bishops, their vestments of the richest and costliest materials – velvet, brocade, or cloth of gold; and their mitres glistening with jewels.' The procession's entry through the gates is illustrated, but instead of focusing on the bishops, my gaze is drawn to the onlookers kneeling in the dirt. Amid tolling bells and Gregorian chant, they were part of the 40,000 people crammed into Thurles for the occasion.

Like the rest of the country, Tipperary in 1850 was still feeling the aftershocks of the Famine and many still bore the 'shrunken looks and sharpened features' described on a fact-finding tour for relief purposes by a Quaker gentleman, Robert Davis, three years earlier. Perhaps some people in Thurles that day were from nearby parishes hardest hit by hunger and unspeakable trauma – like Clonoulty, 15km outside town, where the population had halved to 3,500 after the Famine. The Thurles locals and visitors no doubt picked up on what the *Illustrated London News* correspondent called the 'stir and bustle which give unmistakable indication of the approach of some remarkable event'.

This is the symbolic starting point of modern Irish Catholicism: a people in rags, soiled capes and tattered bonnets, survivors of hunger, fever, eviction and violence, literally on their knees, as well-fed clerics glide by like demi-gods with a rustle of silk, the glisten of gold. Alongside the bite of incense, I imagine the air was heavy with awe, perhaps even hope.

The people's hope had expired three years earlier when an ailing Daniel O'Connell, the leader of Catholic emancipation, departed on a pilgrimage to Rome and returned in a coffin. Following him home in 1849 was the new Primate of All Ireland: Archbishop Paul Cullen. Appointed to Armagh at just forty-five years of age, the man considered the 'lowliest and meekest' in a report of the synod procession was at the start of his mission from God. And it was here in Thurles that a deeply traumatized people met a spiritual leader historians say was moulded – but also traumatized – by three decades in Rome.

Paul Cullen was born outside Athy, Co. Kildare in 1803. One of sixteen children from a prosperous farming family, he was just seventeen when he left for Rome to study for the priesthood. His sharp mind attracted the Curia's eye and, after his 1829 ordination, Cullen became a fixture at Propaganda Fide, the College of the Society for the Propagation of the Faith. His proximity to the pontiff made the Irishman adept at court politics and, as an obedient ultramontanist,[*] he was deeply convinced of papal prerogative and power. Internalizing Pope Pius IX's antipathy towards the modern world, he saw the Enlightenment and the French Revolution not as liberations but threats to the truths of Catholic absolutes.

Cullen saw figurative enemies at every gate and, in 1848, those

---

[*] In Roman Catholicism, ultramontanism emphasizes centralized papal authority. Derived from the medieval Latin *ultramontanus*, 'beyond the mountains', it reflected how northern European church leaders looked southward beyond the Alps, to Rome, for guidance. After centuries of struggle with liberals, ultramontanists expanded their power and influence after the First Vatican Council of 1870, which defined the dogma of papal infallibility.

enemies became real: gathering Italian republican forces that forced the Pope to flee Rome. Cullen remained and helped hold the fort, literally and metaphorically, as outsiders forced their way in and the world he had known vanished. The Papal States, under the sovereign rule of the Pope since the eighth century, were no more.

His traumatic brush with revolution left Cullen shaken and wary of anyone professing revolt on his return to Ireland. Irish nationalists, hoping for a leader to fill O'Connell's shoes, sensed his reticence to back their cause and would have to wait for Charles Stewart Parnell. Paul Cullen had other priorities: as primate and papal legate, he had a mandate for reform and planned to use it. In doing so, he spear-headed another kind of revolution in Ireland.

Walking up the drive to the limestone facade of St Patrick's College, I realize it was a relatively modern building at the time of Paul Cullen's synod – it had opened as a secondary school and seminary in 1837. It ceased being a seminary in 2002 and is now a third level college. I am here to meet local priest Fr Christy O'Dwyer. He leads me through the empty corridors of the college where he once taught and upstairs to the old library where, in 1850, the bishops met.

Images of the synod show an attic-like room with timber beams supporting the roof. Now the room is a library, dominated by wooden shelves and dusty books. On a shelf is a forgotten mitre, on the wall a portrait of the one-time Cashel Archbishop Thomas Croke – of Croke Park fame – with a piercing gaze. A stained-glass window reading 'Synod Thurles A.D. 1850' is the only visible reminder of a gathering that consolidated reforms that had been creeping in unevenly for decades and merged them with new standardized rites, practices and structures. Thurles was less the birth of a new Catholicism in Ireland than its baptism.

'They put a structure in place to stop people doing solo runs,' says Fr O'Dwyer, suggesting the legacy of Thurles was a new defensive culture in Irish Catholicism. 'There was a fear at that time that sparked a need for control, which in turn encouraged a perfectionist view of the world.'

Several major decisions were made here, but their significance is more apparent to historians now than at the time. By a tight majority – 15 to 13 – bishops came out against interdenominational Queen's Colleges set up by Sir Robert Peel's government in Belfast, Cork and Galway. They decided they were dangerous to faith and morals. This was a key moment in the bishops' battle for denominational education – a battle that continues up to the present day.

The Thurles synod agreed, too, to adopt a more stringent approach to the Catholic faith. Sacraments like Baptism, Confession and funerals were brought back inside the walls of the church. New traditions and rites were introduced after Thurles and others popularized: veneration of Our Lady and the Sacred Heart, devotions such as the Forty Hours* and First Fridays.†

Also crucial after Thurles, Irish lay Catholics were collectivized and activated in societies and sodalities for prayer, social events and fundraising for church building and decoration.

After Thurles, the Catholic Church in Ireland was going places. Catholics, used to kneeling in the dirt, could now point with pride to their new parish church and an adjacent presbytery that signalled a new prosperity and 'respectability', that all-important currency in Victorian society.

A new generation emerged of serious young curates with cassocks, Roman collars and careful manners. Drawn from Ireland's well-off farming families and business owners, these young clerics represented a consolidation of power both in the middle classes and in the Church. The new generation could draw on the moral credit earned by an older generation of priests in the Famine. At the same time they had spare capacity to raise the quality of religious worship – having just 1,500 people to minister to per priest, compared with nearly twice that before 1845.

One of my favourite paintings in the National Gallery of Ireland, from 1883, shows this collision of Catholic Ireland, old and new. In

---

* Forty Hours' Devotion – from the Italian *quarant'ore* – is an exercise of 40 hours' continuous prayer, day and night, before the exposed Blessed Sacrament i.e. the consecrated Communion bread removed from the tabernacle and put on display in a special receptacle on the altar.

† First Friday Devotions are a set of practices – Mass attendance, Communion and Confession – dedicated to the Sacred Heart of Jesus on the first Friday of nine consecutive months.

Mass in a Connemara Cabin the faithful kneel on a rough floor for a station Mass said by a blushing young curate in white vestments. By including an image of the Sacred Heart on the cabin wall and, on a chair, the young curate's black coat and pristine top hat, painter Aloysius O'Kelly signals the decline of old traditions, as the station Mass tradition was slowly wound down by priests in favour of church Mass – on their turf. The power dynamic is clear: the priest towers over the locals. The clerical pedestal is already in place.

Overseeing this transition – as Archbishop of Armagh and, from 1852, Dublin – Paul Cullen used his power and strategic skill to bring Ireland's previously strong-willed bishops in line with Rome. He supercharged the momentum for reform by inviting religious orders into Ireland. In 1800 there were just 120 nuns in Ireland, by 1850 there were 1,500. Twenty years later, that figure was 3,700 and it reached 8,000 in 1900. In Cullen's 25 years in Dublin, from 1852 to 1878, religious orders opened some 37 institutions: hospitals, schools, convents and laundries. What some historians now call Cullen's 'devotional revolution' triggered, in turn, revolutions in Irish health, education and welfare.

I wonder how many of the young boys and girls watching the procession in Thurles in August 1850 were pulled – or pushed – into this energized Church?

Young men with no hope of an inheritance, or harbouring sexual desires outside the norm.

Young women attracted by religious orders' leadership opportunities – in many cases far beyond what they could expect from wider society.

By nudging offspring towards the Church, their parents solved a problem with a solution that gave them bragging rights: a priest or a nun in the family.

Once inside the Church, meanwhile, their children found a channel for their faith, their ambition – positive and negative – or maybe they just found a place to hide from life.

After centuries of humiliation, this rewired Catholic Church offered promise and pride. Many of the surviving old traditions began to fall away because there were so many new ones. Who had time for holy wells in the rain when the new church had a bustling calendar of events with space for all – and a new slate roof against the elements?

Just as important was the moral structure offered by Cullen. Leading Irish historians and sociologists agree that this rigid Catholicism was less imposed from without than demanded from within – to protect the patriarchal order and the economic interests of an emerging Irish middle class. Key to the new post-Famine economic order was the need for stronger farming families to hold together land and assets – which required a strict control of sex, through moral rigidity and ignorance – in a bid to avoid errant offspring.

At this time a rapidly industrializing Britain with a rising middle class had its own impetus for tight social control. Victorian novels and popular pamphlets reordered the control of physical and sexual needs via 'a message of self-abnegation as the way to happiness on earth and afterwards'. With Catholic-hued prudery now the social norm in Ireland, Victorian views – seeing the denial of sex, pleasure and self as morally superior – survived longer in Ireland than in the country of their origin. In this period, historian Joe Lee suggests, sex was denounced 'as a satanic snare' because it 'posed a far more severe threat than the landlord to the security and status of the family'. Sex was banished to the confessional; self-control and restraint were idealized and, eventually, internalized.

Within a decade of the Synod of Thurles, as sex was reigned in, social control via the Church grew as Sunday Mass attendance, well below 50 per cent before the Famine, became near universal. Slowly, surely, two things were happening. First, the Church in Ireland caught up with changes agreed in the Council of Trent – Catholicism's reforming response to the Protestant Reformation – three centuries previously. Second, Cullen's Church grabbed the Catholic political identity as shaped by Daniel O'Connell – and ran with it.

Wrapped up in expensive, elaborate rituals, overseen by tight, top-down structures and communicated in authoritarian messages, the rebranded Irish Catholicism presented absolute loyalty to Rome as an attractive counter-model to British rule. By 1879 in Thurles, when the town's new Cathedral of the Assumption opened, a Romanesque nod to Pisa Cathedral, local archbishop Patrick Leahy made clear what was on the spiritual menu: 'Roman usages . . . Roman chant, Roman ceremonies, Roman everything'.

Rereading the 1850 newspaper reports of the synod, as I wait for the train back to Dublin, I find it easier now to understand the significance of what happened here. Under Cullen, Ireland's Catholic Church identified – and moved quickly to fill – deep-seated needs in the people: for order, safety, pride, education and economic security. This institution, unlike any other, offered the promise of status, salvation and consolation in the desolation of post-Famine Ireland. Looking at the illustration of the locals kneeling in the dirt, I imagine many found in this brand of Catholicism a balm, or anaesthetic, for what later generations would dub 'survivor guilt'. The 1850s was too early for that. Instead it seems likely that, for Famine survivors, what was offered to them after Thurles would have seemed like a sign of hope, a phoenix rising from the ashes – something to embrace rather than a demanding imposition. As the train leaves Thurles, I consider some of the defining characteristics of Cullen's Church – devotion, defensiveness and obedience – and decide it's time to see what traces remain.

First stop: devotion. In the hope of getting a flavour of traditional devotion – even in its twenty-first-century form – I travel to Galway for the annual novena that attracts huge crowds from across Connemara and Munster. Novenas never featured in my Dublin childhood. My hazy sense of them is that, if a regular Catholic Mass is a sprint, the novena – derived from the Latin for nine (*novem*) – is the marathon of Catholic religious practice: nine days of Mass, rosary, petitions and blessings. I have no idea what to expect.

I arrive in Galway on a miserable February day. As I round a corner, I see my destination on the other bank of the surging River Corrib: the limestone facade of – deep breath – The Cathedral of Our Lady Assumed into Heaven and St Nicholas. It's not yet lunchtime but the third Mass is over already and a crowd is spilling out into the chilly sunshine. I push past them into the muggy gloom and find a priest handing out gold-coloured miraculous medals. They have an image of the Virgin Mary surrounded by an inscription: 'Mary conceived without sin pray for us who have recourse to thee.'

An older woman beside me pockets ten medals: 'They're all for my grandchildren in the US.' I'm sure they can't wait.

A queue has formed at a metal urn of holy water. Above it is a golden Byzantine icon of the Virgin Mary, with an angular elongated nose and narrow pursed lips, and infant Jesus, known as 'Our Lady of Perpetual Help'. The original was first venerated in public in 1499, and the image has remained central to novenas around the world – and in Ireland under the Redemptorist order since 1943.

Over the coming hours and days, in whispered conversations in the cathedral shadows, people tell me stories of hope and despair. Amid the ritual and repetition, a word I will hear often is 'comfort'.

'I battle depression sometimes but I find the atmosphere here special and a real help,' says Winnie, a woman in her early fifties. 'There's energy and calm at the same time, and when I hear of other people's trials here, it puts my own in perspective and makes me more calm and thankful.'

The cathedral opened in 1965 and combines Galway limestone, Connemara marble and ecclesiastical extravagance. The overall design is an eclectic nod to the Renaissance, though it's hard to know – architecturally – what exactly the building is trying to be. Locals dubbed it 'Taj Micheál' after its powerful patron, Bishop Michael Browne.* Footage of the cathedral opening shows a clerical show of force – much like an animated version of the Thurles synod illustration just over a century earlier. Amid the economic struggles of 1960s Ireland, the Catholic Church was strong – and arrogant.

My sculptor friend Imogen Stuart designed the doors of the cathedral and, at the opening, remembers the bishop asking why the

---

* The year after the cathedral was opened, Trinity student Brian Trevaskis caused uproar on *The Late Late Show* when he dubbed it a 'ghastly monstrosity' and called Bishop Browne a 'moron' for spending money on building a church when unmarried mothers were being treated like outcasts. Trevaskis compounded the injury by returning to *The Late Late Show* to apologize for calling the bishop a moron – which he did. He apologized for his crude use of language but said, 'I would ask whether the Bishop of Galway knows the meaning of the word "moron". I doubt very much that he knows the meaning of the word "Christianity".'

doors were not more like an English cathedral he'd seen. Though he had approved a detailed model she'd given him, Berlin-born Imogen was oblivious to his telling-off and began explaining her concept. Browne cut her off with a stinging put-down: 'You Germans, you all have a touch of Hitler about you.'

Imogen remembers turning bright red as the bishop moved on. He extended his hand to her daughter Aisling, who refused to kiss his ring. At just ten, she demonstrated to the assembled adults how deference can be given – or withheld.

Bishop Browne is long gone and today's crowd is more eclectic than deferent. Elderly nuns in full habits glide past a young woman in gold lamé platform shoes and a black T-shirt emblazoned with the slogan 'Cutie with a Bootie'.

Doing his rounds in the cathedral is chief steward Tom McGrath. With snowy hair, striking blue eyes, and purple sash over his grey suit, I ask him why, in spite of two scandal-filled decades, he thinks the crowds still come here.

'People are very good at knowing the difference between their own faith and the institution,' he says. 'Terrible things happened in the institution but it doesn't deter people from practising their religion.'

The novena couldn't happen without the local branch of the Legion of Mary, the Catholic lay organization founded by civil servant Frank Duff, in Dublin, in 1921. In the sacristy, local legion head Bernard Finan is checking the Communion distribution plan with a blueprint of the cathedral. At a push they can accommodate around 2,200, he says, and distribute Holy Communion from 40 stations. In some years up to 45,000 hosts have been distributed.

'The novena is a chance for the Church to reach out to people,' says Bernard. 'People face huge pressures today, with family and work, and yet so many still make a huge effort to come.'

Down the corridor in the cathedral kitchen, on a break of tea and buns, Bernard's wife Dymphna and her friend Anne are discussing the deferential attitude to the clergy in their youth. The deference was 'just there', they say, the combined effect of a priest's education and clerical status as 'God's holy anointed'. The visiting priest was venerated in the never-used sitting room, they remember, and given tea in a special cup and saucer. The women think everyone contributed to this group mindset.

'It was us who put the clergy up there on their pedestal and it was us who kept them there,' says Anne. 'That the pedestal cracked and they crashed down is a good thing. They're more human and at ease and everyone is happier now.'

And what of today?

From their vantage point inside the church, Dymphna suggests Ireland's group-think about the clergy is alive and well – it has simply flipped from deferential to disrespectful.

'On Shop Street I saw a woman pull her son away from a passing priest,' she says. 'Imagine. My heart goes out to the ninety-nine per cent of good priests.'

Next morning, after early Mass, the celebrant, Fr Pat, jokes that his order, the Redemptorists, have a lot to answer for in Ireland. Before they got into novenas, Redemptorist priests were in demand across the country for their sulphurous sermons at parish missions – raucous religious revival meetings set up in the nineteenth century to counter Protestant proselytizing. The Redemptorist hell-fire missions were a long way from the moderate theology of the order's founder, St Alphonsus Liguori, but were hugely popular across the island – both as faith rallies and as social outings.

Sitting alone in the cathedral refectory, Fr Pat, originally from Boherbue, Co. Cork and now living in Belfast, has an unsentimental take on what he sees today. A thinker and a reader, his story echoes that of many Irish priests. He entered the seminary in 1964 and struggled under rigid superiors who were suspicious of Vatican II. After ordination in 1970, he found his personal enthusiasm for reform and renewal strangled by congregations as conservative as his superiors. As the years passed, he watched from the pulpit as liberal, thinking Irish Catholics departed. Left behind: the devotional remainers.

'The Catholicism planted into the Irish did not have deep roots, didn't have the elemental side, yet it completely took over,' he says. 'There was no intellectual tradition that touched the average person, no thought about how they felt about their faith.'

Working inside what he jokingly calls the 'devotional monolith', he sees an irony in an institution that presented religious faith as a

rulebook now being strangled by its own historic, controlling
instincts: the very top-down rigidity that once gave it immeasurable
power has become its fatal flaw.

As he talks, I watch elderly women bobbing in and out of the
room. With their helmet hairstyles and down jackets, these fragile
birds of faith can be found in churches around Ireland – for now, at
least. Often when I see them I'm reminded of Judith Hearne, novelist Brian Moore's tragic fictional spinster. She lives out her days in
furnished rooms, drinking discreetly and avoiding the gaze of her
abusive spiritual spouse, the Sacred Heart of Jesus with His 'kind yet
accusing' eyes.

Like Judith Hearne, many of these women remember an Ireland
where religion was 'just there . . . not something you thought
about'. Faith was a mixture of fear – 'begging God's pardon' – and
comfort. Judith Hearne, Moore writes compassionately, 'put loneliness aside on a Sunday morning'. Ireland had little time or space for
people like her, who had not married and met the social norm.
Already isolated, she knows that breaking with her faith risks complete isolation. With Catholic identity the flip side of Irish identity,
Moore writes, 'if you don't believe, you are alone . . . no faith, then
no people'.

Leading the Galway novena is Fr Brendan O'Rourke. During a
break he shows me the cathedral crypt, recently renovated in cream
marble. Fr O'Rourke is also a therapist and, sitting between the
tombs of two infamous bishops – the severe Michael Browne and
charismatic (and disgraced) Eamonn Casey – he suggests that Ireland's intertwined social and church community of yesterday is today
akin to a traumatized and estranged family.

'Many members are gone – absent, or unwilling to participate –
but the therapy can continue without them, regardless,' he says. And
for some, he says, the novena is a quiet part of that therapy.

An hour later, upstairs, in his final homily of the novena, Fr
Brendan addresses the old, painful secrets in many Irish hearts – and
the Catholic Church's role in defining, and policing, social taboos.
He recalls being the celebrant at the funeral of a friend's mother. Just
before the woman's death, she spoke for the first time of a baby she
lost shortly after birth, a baby who was unbaptized and banished to

'limbo'* by a callous priest. Fr Brendan felt his graveside task was to honour this woman and give an identity back to her dead, disappeared baby.

'Then others at the graveside began to speak of their baby sister, a brother, a stillborn son,' he says. 'People were grieving over secrets not spoken of, prayers for decade after decade. It's a testament to their endurance and the power of love – family at its best.'

It's not an explicit apology for another Ireland's clerical bullies, but the crowd listens to his acknowledgement of the deep wounds they caused.

Fr Brendan says this is the real purpose of a novena today: 'less a miracle request show than a forum to reflect on one's sufferings and bear witness to others'. He reads out a sample of the prayer intentions: for parents struggling with Alzheimer's, for sons battling with addiction, daughters with eating disorders, a separated father fighting for access to his child. For many here, attending the novena is an outlet and a crutch, a means of witnessing pain, coping with impossible situations and gaining a handle on the resulting emotions.

Still, an element of the otherworldly hasn't been abandoned and as the Mass nears its end, Fr Brendan announces the blessing of holy objects. A rustling begins around me as people produce statues, rosaries and other less identifiable items.

Seeing a few stricken faces, he adds, 'Don't worry if you've left it in the car. God's blessing is powerful so it travels.'

Feeling I've seen enough, I slip out ahead of the crowd. Looking back up at the limestone facade of the Taj Micheál, I'm reminded of what writer John McGahern called Ireland's 'fortress church'. Though bishops condemned his early writing, McGahern was careful to separate his affection for the Catholic faith in which he was reared, with its simplicity and connection to nature, from the 'peculiar' Church the

---

* Limbo, which comes from the Latin word meaning 'border' or 'edge', was considered by medieval theologians to be a state or place reserved for the unbaptized dead, in particular babies. Though never officially part of church doctrine, it was taught to Catholics well into the twentieth century. It was effectively abolished by the Catholic Church in a 2007 document, saying limbo reflected an 'unduly restrictive view of salvation'.

Irish fashioned for themselves: 'Very much like an army, it demanded unquestioned allegiance.'

In Galway this devotional version of the Church seems to be thriving but the Redemptorist priests here tell me not to be deceived by the optics. A unique kind of Catholic faith and practice – a collectivized source of comfort and spiritual structure for some; a manipulative prison for others – is slipping away before our eyes.

Waiting in the car park is Oliver Hanratty from Carrickmacross, Co. Monaghan. From his trailer he sells souvenirs from another Ireland: laminated prayer cards for hanging in cars; holy air fresheners; keyrings promising 'whoever wears this will not suffer the everlasting fire'. Considerable shelf space is devoted to the Irish holy trinity – the Virgin Mary, Padre Pio and Mother Teresa.

After years travelling to religious gatherings all over Ireland, Oliver says his souvenir business will end when he retires. His children are 'red-faced' when he asks them to fill in for him. 'They aren't into this, and maybe they're right,' he says.

Oliver follows my gaze to look up at the cut-stone cathedral facade. His sentiments echo those of the priests inside – big changes are afoot with this version of Catholicism. The next decade will bring so much change for the Church that no one stone will be left on top of the next, he predicts.

'When we're gone,' he says, sweeping his hand out over his holy trinkets towards the cathedral, 'not even the memory of us will remain.'

16.   Lost in the thicket

'The Irish priesthood . . . hold possession of the people's hearts to
a degree unknown to any other priesthood in the world.'

Archbishop Thomas Walsh of Cashel

My journey to the heart of Catholic Ireland has taken me into the
past and all over the country: to the leafy glens of ancient Glendalough and to a nearby Penal era Mass rock; to Thurles, the baptismal
font of a reformulated Irish Catholicism; to Galway's novena, a lingering vestige of its devotional character. Now, continuing my
exploration of Paul Cullen's version of Catholicism, I'm on a far tip of
the western seaboard to meet a man with painful personal experience
of its waspish defensiveness.

For Fr Kevin Hegarty, Belmullet Co. Mayo has become his refuge after a wounding experience of being brought into line by
Irish Church authorities after trying to ask questions about the
direction of the institution. Looking out over the churning Atlantic Ocean, Fr Hegarty pulls himself straight, breathes easy and
loses himself for a moment on this wild outpost of the country.
Before us is Inishglora island and, to our left, three jagged walls of
the fifteenth-century Cross Abbey. As the sun sets for another day,
winking through the crooked Celtic cross gravestones as it has for
centuries, this is a good place to reflect on the longevity of Ireland's –
and Europe's – Christian heritage.

'When I stand here I have a feeling of a vague but definite continuum, despite everything,' says Kevin, as he asks to be called. With
tousled grey hair and searching eyes, it's hard to picture him as a
morale-sapping mischief-maker. Yet that was the verdict of Irish
bishops on his three years as editor of *Intercom* magazine in the 1990s.
He transformed the clergy's sleepy in-house journal into a lively

publication that flagged the institution's blind spot towards child sexual abuse. Instead of listening, the defensive Irish Church banished Kevin Hegarty as far west as it could.

It's All Saints' Day in Belmullet, with a round of graveyards to bless, and I'm joining him on a tour of his beautiful kingdom. The yellow bogs and violet mountains look like a real-life Jack Yeats painting, I tell him. He tells me how Yeats and the writer John Millington Synge came this way in 1904. In a travel piece for the *Manchester Guardian* Synge told readers that Belmullet was 'noisy and squalid, lonely and crowded at the same time, and without appeal to the imagination'.

The town has scrubbed up since but, separated from Ballina by a vast, boggy expanse, it still has a lonely feeling. Ballina native Hegarty knows Belmullet well: after his ordination in 1981, he worked here as chaplain and teacher of history, English and religion. Then in 1991 he was appointed editor of *Intercom* and began commissioning daring articles challenging the male monopoly on the priesthood and flagging the neglect of priests' emotional and mental health.

Though this was already robust fare for the previously cautious magazine, everything changed for Hegarty with the publication of an article headlined 'Twenty Questions for the Bishops'. The piece had been submitted on spec by a social worker, Philip Mortell, and appeared in the December 1993 issue. Mortell wondered if – in light of clerical child sexual abuse allegations in the US, Canada and Britain, and ever-louder whispers at home – Irish bishops would 'acknowledge and apologize for the hurt and damage inflicted on victims and their families'.

In a series of pointed questions, Mortell asked if they would 'take responsibility for their previous ignorance, denial and minimization of child abuse in general and clerical child abuse in particular?'

The one-page article touched on every issue that would convulse Ireland for the next two decades and continue to preoccupy us today: clerical training; compensation and rehabilitation of survivors; treatment of perpetrators; adequate prevention work.

Immediately after publication, the defensive Irish Church leapt into action. One bishop told Hegarty his 'card was marked', another that it was 'none of *Intercom*'s business to be asking these questions'. Not satisfied with that, bishops – many of whom would later feature in the reports of state abuse inquiries – began to gaslight the editor priest. Fr Hegarty was the problem, they implied, not the Church. His editorship of *Intercom* was, they said, a 'source of disillusionment' that was 'undermining the morale of the priests'.

Hegarty made a final appeal for support to his bishop, Thomas Finnegan, who said he would meditate on the issue during an upcoming trip to Lourdes. 'He came back and said Our Lady had told him at the grotto that I should leave *Intercom* – as infantile as that.'

Hegarty was relieved of his duties in 1994, just as Fr Brendan Smyth was sentenced to four years in prison for abuse of children in Northern Ireland.

At our first graveyard blessing, a gaggle of barnacle geese swoop overhead as Fr Kevin says a few prayers and leads a decade of the rosary with thirty people. It's a quiet ceremony, like hundreds of others taking place around the country today. After the prayers, watching the easy affection of the locals towards Kevin, I wonder what will happen here – and elsewhere in Ireland – when the priests vanish.

As their chat drags on, I explore a hill above the modern graveyard and discover a much older plot for people who couldn't afford a proper burial for their loved ones. The rough stones they erected here still lean on each other, as if still in mourning. In the long shadows of the winter sun, it reminds me of the old Jewish cemetery in Prague. Then from death springs life: a hare pops up from nowhere and bolts off down the hill. As I look around again, I realize there is something far older here than Cullen-brand Catholicism.

As the day draws in, Kevin brings me to Teampall Deirbhile (Deirbhile's chapel). The two surviving gable walls are believed to date from the twelfth century, constructed to strengthen or replace the sixth-century originals built by St Deirbhile and her community here. Said to be a noble beauty and contemporary of St Colmcille, legend has it she plucked out her eyes to head off a persistent suitor, before having her sight restored at a local well. Centuries later, it remains a place of pilgrimage for people with sight issues – and for those looking beyond the ruins of today's Catholic Church.

Kevin describes how every Easter morning over 200 people gather in the roofless chapel to watch the sun rise and pierce the dark through the eastern wall's intact window.

The sun is setting now and a chill has set in. What was intended as a banishment has proven a liberation for Fr Kevin. Far from the scandals and mind games of the institutional Church, he has reconnected with what is more important for him as a priest: witnessing births and deaths and life in between.

'There is such majesty in the nature here, these thin places – *caol áit* – are particularly close to heaven,' he says. 'If the Church rids itself of wanting to control people's lives, of all traces of triumphalism, if it can return to this here –' casting out his hand on the wild landscape – 'then people will respond.'

Hours later, trudging the lonely streets of Belmullet, I see a dull glow in the distance. As I approach, an outline emerges of a woman – the Virgin Mary – staring desolately from a wooden box, behind a glass pane that is cloudy with condensation. It's a disturbing sight: Mary drowning under a sheet of ice – or is it a glass coffin for a dying, devotional Church? I study her doleful eyes and her hands joined in prayer. She doesn't look happy.

Obedience was a third, controlling characteristic of Cullen-brand Catholicism. To see what part obedience plays in the Church today I'm in Maynooth, Co. Kildare. Walking through the gates of St Patrick's College, once the largest seminary in a Catholic country where size mattered. This is an institution founded in response to the gradual lifting of the Penal Laws. Once, generations of young men were forced to leave Ireland for training, but the upheavals of the French Revolution closed many of the seminaries they attended. St Patrick's was the answer, and this cradle of Irish Catholicism opened its doors on 5 June 1795.

Decades of growth and expansion followed. By 1845 Irish bishops, who condemned their starving flock for 'taking the soup' of Protestant missionaries during the Famine, accepted a capital grant of £30,000 and an annual grant of £26,000 towards the college's running costs from the Westminster government.

Once Cullen's reforms kicked in, Maynooth came into its own. By 1855, half of Ireland's priests had been educated here and two-thirds of its seminarians walked its corridors.

These home-grown clerics had many attributes but, for former St Patrick's professor Patrick Corish, the typical 'Maynooth priests' were 'good labourers, not good thinkers'.

Some suggest the clerics produced here were shaped by Cullen's defensive world view, others argue that generations of priests – and, later, their congregations – were moulded by professors imported from France with a love of Jansenism. This school of theology emphasized a perceived tendency of humans towards sinfulness and depravity, and the need to stamp it out. Others contest this.

One thing is not contested: most of the seminarian intake was drawn from Ireland's middle classes. Maynooth did not equip them with supernatural powers to control the Irish and raise them from spiritual lethargy. Instead Canon Patrick Sheehan joked in his 1900 novel *My New Curate* that any youthful ambition of new priests was soon broken by 'the inertia of Ireland'.

That presumes, of course, that young priests' enthusiasm was still intact after leaving Maynooth. German historian Knut Jongbom Clement, in an acidic travel journal of Ireland after a visit in 1839, suggested the new seminary 'has certainly not promoted the progress of intellectual education in Ireland' and said the training on offer was 'restrictive, one-sided, paltry and monastic, supervision stringent and distrustful'.

He observed, 'That is how it was among people of the Middle Ages and how it is in the cabal of clerics in Maynooth. Such creatures become blind zealots from prejudice and lack of experience and think of themselves in their dwarf-like existence as giants.'

At its centenary celebrations in 1895, Bishop John Healy of Clonfert announced proudly that St Patrick's was 'not a university', nor did it encourage 'transcendentalism in any form whatever, nor does it set itself up as the exponent of any fantastic school of thought either in science or philosophy . . . It is, so to say, a machine for turning out fully equipped a certain number of missionary men annually, destined to preach to and teach the Irish people the faith of their fathers.'

The Maynooth machine has fallen silent now. Walking empty corridors, with parquet floors that smell of floor polish, it's impossible to ignore the dwindling numbers of seminarians photographed in annual wall charts.

Rector Tom Surlis says he's well used to tropes about the rambling building – built for 600, now housing 23 seminarians – as a symbol for the decay of Catholic Ireland. 'But there are still twenty-three here,' says Fr Surlis. 'We're in a liminal space: a foot in the past and one in the future, being dragged in two directions. It's a difficult time but also full of opportunity.'

The future of the college is uncertain. In 2016, the Archbishop of Dublin, Diarmuid Martin, complained of 'strange goings-on' in Maynooth and moved all of his seminarians to the Irish Pontifical College in Rome.* In 2020, discussions were under way to move the remaining seminarians here into parishes.

St Patrick's staff say they have responded to complaints and scandals† with a tighter selection process and a broader formation programme. But many admit a growing tension between the seminary and diocesan bishops on new admissions.

'The bishops' attitude is that anyone is better than nobody and, given they are trying to maintain their dioceses, I don't blame them,' says one staffer in Maynooth. 'But, like any dying system, Maynooth is now getting the remnants, and I'm not sure we can build a future on the men coming out now.'

Another staff member says an institution that once had its pick of any generation now attracts young men hopeful that church structure and doctrine will provide them with certainty. A counter-cultural conservative shift happening elsewhere in the world, this staff member suggests, is already under way in this shrinking seminary.

'Many of the men who come to Maynooth now are reactionary to

---

* Dr Martin spoke of a 'poisonous' atmosphere in which there were allegations of widespread gay sex, arranged by smartphone dating apps, and this in turn was the subject of anonymous letters and blog posts. Other allegations included student harassment by staff members.

† Among the scandals, former seminary president Micheál Ledwith was defrocked in 2005 after a series of sexual abuse allegations from teenagers and seminarians – which he has denied. One former seminarian remembers Prof Ledwith as a 'vain man with three wigs – just cut, normal and in need of a cut – who liked taking guys up to his room'.

the dominant culture, and not always in a good way,' the staff member says. 'They . . . attempt to construct a form of religiosity that gives them no way to grow and develop.'

During my visit I meet two seminarians, with Fr Surlis sitting in.

Ricky O'Connor had a circular route to the seminary. He moved to Our Lady's Island, a small Wexford village, from the UK with his family aged twelve and was raised outside Irish Catholicism. After school years picking fights with his religion teacher, aged nineteen he picked up a Bible and read it from cover to cover. He contemplated joining the British Army then became Mormon before, aged twenty-one, he found himself being drawn to the Catholic Church. His Baptism, Communion and Confirmation were on the same day – Easter 2011. A year later, he decided he wanted to be a priest. Even before taking his vows, in June 2019, he said he had fewer problems with a smaller Church than with the Church's 'clinginess' to old ways and structures.

'The Church is clinging to a system that isn't working, saying that's the way it's always been,' he says. 'But the whole point of the Gospels is to shake us out of what we do.'

Shane Costello from Claremorris, Co. Mayo worked as a teacher for three years before entering the seminary. His family and friends were surprised, he says, but supportive. Before his ordination, in June 2019, he says he understands why many people in Ireland struggle to see anything beyond the recent horrors – the laundries, residential homes and abuse.

'We probably have to stay in this cloud for a generation – and that is probably a good thing,' he says. At the same time, Shane notices how many people, when they find out what he does, feel instinctively they have to explain to him that they believe in God but don't go to Mass.

'They don't have to justify themselves, I don't care about that,' he says, 'but that suggests to me a bedrock still there somewhere.'

To understand the bedrock culture – and legacy – of Maynooth, it's worthwhile, too, talking to men who left here not as priests but as laymen. 'Robert' was nineteen when he began training for the priesthood here in the early 1990s. Growing up in small-town Ireland, he was fascinated by religion, liked Mass and was intrigued by what he saw as the radical kindness of the Christian message.

It took just twelve months in the seminary to kill all that. As he sits opposite me, around thirty years later, his pain is still palpable.

'The place had an insidious nature, people creeping around, secrets, laughing at people outside,' he says. 'I had to get out and, when I did, I felt an important part of me had been ripped out, a flame quenched.'

In hindsight, Robert says he was naïve and innocent, going in. But he says his honest curiosity about what he could learn left him ready to accept the regimented days, starting at 6 a.m., the ban on radios and other contact with the outside world.

There were over fifty in his class, and he remembers young men of every type: the gentle ones, the bitchy ones, the ones avoiding their sexuality and the others obsessed with it. Some talked incessantly about women, he says, others were open misogynists, while a final group hunted for lovers among the new arrivals.

Robert says he was propositioned several times in Maynooth – on walks, over coffee – by older seminarians and says their aggressive come-ons left him feeling threatened, angry and, for a time, homophobic.

Many seminarians already had a fully formed sense of entitlement. Some were 'second-rate intellectuals looking forward to their career pontificating at the pulpit', Robert recalls, while others had simpler needs. He recalls a stilted conversation with an older seminarian who approached him one day at lunch just to ask him what kind of car he wanted when he was ordained. To Robert's amazement the other seminarian announced, 'I'm getting my parishioners to buy me a BMW.'

With a sinking feeling, Robert sensed he was in a minority in Maynooth with his wish to earn the privilege of conferring the sacraments. While he had felt no pressure from his family to enter the seminary, he faced considerable disappointment from his parents when he decided to leave.

After two weeks back home, Robert remembers a phone call from a nun he had never met before who'd heard he had left Maynooth. 'She said I shouldn't lose heart with God or Jesus,' he says. 'The Maynooth seminary, she said, was corrupted, the Devil was there and there was too much evil in it.'

Nearly three decades on, Robert still feels Christianity is special and is envious of those who still have a faith. But, echoing survivors of clerical sexual abuse once close to the Church, he doubts he will ever recover his.

For people like Robert, Maynooth represents a monolithic, institutional Irish Catholicism that lost its way in structure and rules and, in the end, was entrapped by its own unforgiving rigidity. Though he knows his experience is limited and not universal, he suggests that the very rigidity drilled into generations of seminarians makes it unlikely that, as priests, they are emotionally able to fully understand the damage done by their institution.

As he talks, a smile appears on his lips as he remembers one of his first lessons in Maynooth. Decades later, the idea still intrigues him: *you cannot be truly sorry until you are forgiven*. Confused by the seemingly counterfactual message, I ask him later to explain what the lecturer might have meant.

'It had to do with the grace of forgiveness,' he says, 'and how wretched someone might feel with sorrow, and thus be truly sorry, after they have felt the grace of one who has pardoned or forgiven them.'

That unsettled feeling, the struggle with incomplete sorrow, hangs over many conversations I've had with Irish priests about their time in Maynooth. Most made friends for life here, but many harbour lingering unease about the seminary's narrow education, its efforts at total control from above, and the ongoing effects of both today.

In Belmullet, Fr Hegarty remembered his years in Maynooth as a time when a liberal push for reform among some seminarians and even some staff was eventually strangled by the institution's defensive conservativism. After the 1979 papal visit, he suggested, those in power in Maynooth failed to spot – or chose to ignore – the far-reaching social change taking place in the society beyond its thick stone walls. They knew best.

'In the age of the satnav,' he said of his former seminary, 'they hung on to antiquarian maps.'

Prowling the high-ceilinged corridors of the seminary, as I watch the dwindling numbers of seminarians on one wall, I am watched from the opposite walls by bishops in ecclesiastical purples, once pungent, now faded. Those here in St Patrick's, and outside, have strong opinions on whether the seminary fulfilled its purpose and lived up to its potential. Uncontested is that this place, a very Irish hothouse of Catholicism, is on its last legs after a two-century run. Yet, while the patient may be brain-dead, the relatives are conflicted and locked in denial and disagreement about how to proceed. No one wants to be the one to make the call to switch off the life-support machine. Apart from a deep sentimental attachment, they are inhibited by the thought of the inevitable row over the legacy – and this in a family already battle-fatigued. Whether you can imagine a Catholic Church in Ireland after Maynooth depends very much, it seems, on whether you believe in life after death.

Back in Berlin after my latest journey around Ireland, I'm walking through the Tiergarten Park near the Brandenburg Gate with a friend who is an enthusiastic gardener. We come upon a large rhododendron section in full bloom. Stroking a leathery leaf, she tells me how the rhododendron's roots remain extremely shallow yet, given half a chance, the shrub can take over everything. Those powerful roots are out of sight but my eyes are fixed on the beautiful blossoms of dusty, ecclesiastical purple.

There were already many shoots of growth in the Irish Church before the 1850 Thurles summit. Paul Cullen pruned and fertilized and created the conditions for abundant growth. He pressed Irish bishops to regularize celebration of the sacraments, reformed how clergy were to behave, and contained British influence over educating Irish Catholics. He left a remarkable structural legacy – churches, schools, hospitals – but also created a deeply dysfunctional clergy on a pedestal.

Cullen was a man of fragile physical and mental health, and the great historian of nineteenth-century Catholicism in Ireland, Prof Emmet Larkin, has suggested the Church he left behind reflected his own controlling defensive nature as an 'ecclesiastical imperialist' living in 'a perpetual state of siege'.

Even if he imposed an alien Roman model of the church on Ireland, the speed at which this Roman rhododendron took off says as much about the acidic Irish soil as the transplant. 'Cullen was successful because he cut with the grain of Irish history rather than against it,' argued Prof Larkin, 'and also because the Irish people eventually found his ultramontanism as congenial and agreeable in meeting their needs as he did.'

Like a blossoming rhododendron, Paul Cullen's Roman rigour offered an aesthetically pleasing windbreak against the arbitrary gusts of fate – or at least a refuge and framework for processing life's cruelty and rebuilding the post-Famine economy. But, paired with the 'respectable' Victorian morality of Ireland's middle classes, Cullen Catholicism blocked out light, strangled sexuality and choked thought.

Where the British failed with the stick, Paul Cullen succeeded with a carrot that was as much Confucian as Catholic. 'Lead them with excellence and put them in their place through roles and ritual practices,' wrote the Chinese philosopher, centuries before Christ, 'and in addition to developing a sense of shame, they will order themselves harmoniously.'

It's a testament to Cullen's absolutist ambition that, 140 years after his death, many who have never heard of Ireland's first cardinal assume that his defensive and arch-conservative brand of Catholicism – the one they have abandoned – is the only one there is.

Today's slump – jaded priests, dwindling devotions, empty seminaries – may be the end of 1,600 years of Christianity in Ireland. Or it may be simply the end of a very Irish hybrid of Catholicism.

Wandering in the Tiergarten, the rhododendron bushes have grown tall and dense. If you don't watch out, it's easy to lose your way.

17. 'The most devoted of all the children of the Holy See'

'His Holiness is sick and tired of Ireland and does
not want to hear the word mentioned.'

Mgr John Hagan, Rector of Pontifical Irish College, Rome (1919–30)

The young man's long, blond hair curls over his ears. He's wearing a white, collarless shirt with puffed arms, a silver waistcoat and blue breeches with one knee exposed. Crouched down, arms spread wide, he gazes in fascination at his reflection in the still pool of water below.

I'm standing in Rome's Palazzo Barberini, taking a break from interviews about the slippery relationship between Ireland and the Holy See. Now, standing before Caravaggio's *Narcissus*, I feel as drawn to the luminous young man as he is to his own flattering mirror image in the pool. I know a lot of the magic is down to Caravaggio's mastery of light and dark, with figures of cinematic luminescence seeming to vibrate out of a shadowy background. This afternoon, though, his work is speaking to me as metaphor: I can't help but think that people in Catholic Ireland's clerical republic were as transfixed by their own self-image as Narcissus.

'Narcissistic' is a problematic term these days, a medical term that has become a colloquial term of abuse. But narcissism is simply a phenomenon within the natural range of human behaviour. The father of psychoanalysis, Sigmund Freud, maintained it was crucial for self-preservation and saw daily life as a constant battle to balance self-love with a need to give love to others. Psychologists say healthy individuals are ones whose dependence on others' affirmation develops, in time, into a more adult self-esteem. This maturity brings a realization that other people have worth and deserve respect, too. Problems begin when, somewhere along the way, a person fails to move beyond infantile narcissism.

The more I learn about Catholic Ireland of the past century and beyond, the more I understand the struggles of a young state and the effect of these struggles on its people. The Irish stepped on to the world stage properly in the early 1920s, after centuries of hardship, hungry for recognition and appreciation, expected to be the centre of attention and given special treatment to reflect a unique status. Gripped by post-colonial trauma and small-nation insecurity, Ireland now looked to Rome instead of London as its mirror. What were we hoping to see?

What happened next provides answers to that question.

Diving into the story of the Irish people's relationship with Rome, and official relations between the Irish state and the Holy See, is less a journey into the past than into another dimension. For a millennium – more – the Irish made Rome a place of pilgrimage or refuge. The remains of Donnchad mac Briain – king of Munster and son of the legendary High King of Ireland, Brian Boru – who died in 1064, lie in the ancient church of Santo Stefano. But across the city, Gianicolo Hill, with its spectacular views, is perhaps the most Irish spot in Rome. Here you'll find San Pietro in Montorio, a simple, shabby Renaissance church and end point of the Flight of the Earls; when members of Ulster's noble O'Neill and O'Donnell families fled Ireland, they ended up here in 1608. Welcomed by the Pope and supported by local noble families, they didn't last long in Rome. The summer heat and the mosquito-plagued Tiber River proved too much and Rory O'Donnell was the first to die, in July 1608. Other family and servants followed, and Hugh O'Neill was the last to die, aged seventy-six, in 1616. The exiled Ulster Gaelic aristocracy now lie buried in San Pietro's crypt, beneath ornate grave slabs urging the faithful to support Catholic Europe. O'Neill's death, taking with him the old Irish order, is the final entry in the Annals of the Four Masters: 'God was pleased with his life when the Lord permitted him to have no worse burial place than Rome, the head city of the Christians.'

From the arrival of the earls onwards, successive Popes offered words of comfort, soothing balm for the souls of weary Irish Catholic visitors, battered by British rule. And centuries of Irish bishops were happy to present their Church as a channel of continuity. Archbishop

John Healy of Tuam wrote in 1908: 'Those silent graves on Montorio have been, and will be for ages to come, a bond of union stronger than steel to bind the heart of Ireland to the great heart of Rome.'

To be honest, the great heart of Rome has seen better days. Trudging uphill from the Colosseum through narrow, dirty streets, I pass a wheelie bin and rotting boxes of cabbage leaves in my search for Sant'Agata dei Goti. The church, dating from 1729, one-time chapel of the Irish College, is dedicated to a martyr who lost her breasts for refusing to deny her faith. I find it at the back of a shabby courtyard where a group of teenagers smoke a joint and a homeless man sorts his possessions in plastic bags. The church inside is dark, grubby and depressing: from the ceiling, images of bad-tempered Irish saints glare down at me.

No doubt things were smarter here in 1847 when Daniel O'Connell, The Liberator, the 71-year-old father of Catholic emancipation, made his dying wish in Genoa: 'My body to Ireland, my heart to Rome, and my soul to heaven.'

Leaving the soul to take care of itself, and the body for collection in Genoa, his doctor extracted O'Connell's heart for the journey to Rome. A funeral Mass – with O'Connell's 'inurned heart lying on a catafalque in the centre of the nave' – was held in Sant'Agata's. Days later, a two-day memorial service took place across town, this time in the golden gleam of Sant'Andrea della Valle. This spectacular basilica is the resting place of the bodies of Popes Pius II and III, where Puccini's opera *Tosca* opens and where, in a discreet corner, a plaque to O'Connell implores: 'Whether you be a guest or citizen, supplicate heaven with a pure mind for peace and repose for his matchless spirit.'

Four years later, visiting transport entrepreneur Charles Bianconi commissioned a marble memorial for his late friend O'Connell from sculptor Giovanni Benzoni. Today the two-panel memorial is at home in an outdoor arcade of the current Irish College. In the upper panel Mother Ireland, with a wolfhound and a harp, is greeted by an angel. Below it, O'Connell in the Westminster parliament refuses to take the anti-Catholic oath which 'one part I know to be false; and another I believe to be untrue'.

Calamity struck in 1925 when, shifting the memorial here from Sant'Agata, the movers realized that the urn – and O'Connell's heart – had vanished. Rector of the Irish College, Mgr Ciarán O'Carroll, believes the theory that someone saw the gold and silver urn going into the wall of Sant'Agata in 1847 and figured out that by loosening some bricks on the outside wall of the church they could get it out again.

'No one knew anything had happened until the monument was moved,' he says. 'I'd say O'Connell's heart landed at the bottom of the Tiber.'

The Irish College was founded in 1628 and is the last of a network of such institutions set up around the Continent to train Irish priests during Penal times at home. Around the same time, Waterford man Luke Wadding created a monastery of Irish Franciscans in Rome, Sant'Isidoro. It was Wadding, effectively Ireland's first ambassador to the Holy See, who pushed for St Patrick to be recognized by the Church. Born into a middle-class family in 1588, Wadding left Penal Ireland to join the Franciscans in Lisbon. On a mission to Rome for the Spanish King, his superiors asked him to take over a small unfinished church near the Spanish Steps. He remodelled the complex and founded the monastery, named after Spain's St Isidore, in 1625.

These powerful institutions, and the city's connections with great Irishmen, created in many Irish a visceral pull towards Rome. On a beautiful spring morning, I retrace their steps. Turning into a narrow street near St Peter's Square, the soft morning sun cuts through the morning haze and catches the dome of St Peter's Basilica. I stand in awe, as its architects intended, and imagine the scores of pilgrims for whom this sight ended a long and arduous journey of faith – even from as far away as Ireland.

A nineteenth-century local newspaper account of a visit to Rome captures visitors' sense of awe. In February 1893, a Fr J. Nolan from Ballymena, leading a group of 250, recording the ladies and gentlemen's response to attending Mass in St Peter's Square, wrote that 'every heart was moved, and every eye was wet with tears'. A few days later, the group gathered in the papal apartments where Pope Leo XIII, braving a chest infection, was carried in on a sedan chair to dispense blessings and silver medals to the visitors. The pilgrims departed the Eternal City 'weary, but believing they had been highly favoured by God', Fr Nolan wrote. Almost a century later, in 1990, another man of Ulster – Donegal's Packie Bonner – had a similar response after the Irish football team's private audience with Pope John Paul II. The Pope rested his hand on Bonner's shoulder, goalkeeper to goalkeeper. 'The moment lasted only seconds but what a moment it was,' he recalled later. 'I was transfixed by his presence.'

This atmosphere of reverential enchantment was the backdrop for Ireland's twentieth-century relationship with the Holy See. Yet, beyond regular Irish proclamations of filial loyalty, from the outset communications with the Vatican often had a peeved tone. On a visit to Rome in 1920, Seán T. Ó Ceallaigh, a member of the first Dáil, professed in writing his 'devoted loyalty' to the Holy See. But the rest of his scorching 3,000-word memorandum to Pope Benedict XV demanded more Holy See attention and support for the independence struggle of 'the most devoted of all the children of the Holy See'.

The memo is a psychogram and blueprint for the Irish approach to the Holy See in the coming century: devout, submissive, wounded, paranoid and reprimanding – all at once.

In 1923, Desmond FitzGerald, the Free State government's Minister for External Affairs, visited Rome to complain about unwarranted Holy See interference in Ireland's internal affairs. The cause of tension: a warm Roman welcome for two anti-Treaty visitors and an ongoing and highly divisive papal fact-finding mission to Ireland headed by Mgr Salvatore Luzio.

Prickling with polite indignation, Mr FitzGerald told the Vatican's Secretary of State, Cardinal Pietro Gasparri, that Dublin expected the Holy See to put things right and ensure that 'no hitch could in future occur' between the two states.

Beyond this no-nonsense tone, the official report of the visit is filled with other telling clues: it explains at length the level of slavish detail provided to Cardinal Gasparri, and the author notes with satisfaction how several other visitors to the cardinal – including the Minister for Hungary – were sent away while the Irish visitors preoccupied the Secretary of State. The Irish demonstration of firmness yielded instant results – a promise to withdraw Luzio. And then – mission accomplished – filial firmness flipped back to filial loyalty: Mr FitzGerald asked immediately for a chance to kiss the Pope's ring.

Anxious to re-establish authority, the Pope made the Irishman wait five days but granted him a thirty-minute audience, ending with a papal benediction for the four-man Irish delegation. Soon after the Irish departed, ending a period of furious lobbying, Mgr John Hagan, then rector of the Irish College in Rome, reported that 'his Holiness is sick and tired of Ireland and does not want to hear the word mentioned'.

Leading a pilgrim group to Rome in 1925, William T. Cosgrave, the Free State Executive Council president, told Pius XI – presumably recovered – that his Irish children, 'humbly prostrate at the feet of your Holiness . . . offer our loyal devotion and deep affection'. Returning the compliment, the Pope praised the 'truly pious and Catholic people' of Ireland.

Four years later, the Lateran Treaty of 1929 opened the door to a bilateral relationship and the exchange of envoys. Ireland's first representative in Rome was Charles Bewley, a shrewd diplomat and world-class anti-Semite who delighted in the flattering reflection of Ireland he saw in the Roman pool. His early reports are a unique melange of self-belief, wishful thinking, insecurity, projection and entitlement. He wrote to Dublin that, as well as the Holy See's 'very real knowledge and admiration of Ireland's fidelity to the Church', he sensed 'a strong feeling that today the Irish people are as genuinely Catholic as any race in the world'.

But the foremost cheerleader for Irish prestige in Rome was Joseph Walshe, for two decades head of the Department of External Affairs. The Tipperary native was shaped by thirteen years with the Jesuits, initially as a novice, and then teaching in Clongowes College, while studies in the Netherlands gave him a continental outlook and grasp of French, Dutch and some German. When appointed Ambassador to the Holy See in 1945, he spoke of Ireland's 'profound homage . . . and unbreakable faith and strong love . . . for the Holy See' as he presented his credentials to Pope Pius XII.

It was not their first meeting. A decade earlier, Mr Walshe had met Cardinal Eugenio Pacelli, hoping to secure a papal blessing for the 1937 Constitution. Walshe returned to Dublin with the next best thing, when Pius XI declared: 'I do not approve, neither do I disapprove; we shall maintain silence.'

One of Walshe's priorities when posted to Rome was to find more auspicious premises for the embassy. And so, after his arrival in 1946, Mr Walshe was granted permission from Dublin to buy the seventeenth-century Villa Spada from a Jewish émigré in the US for $150,000 – adjusted for inflation, roughly $2 million today. This a year before the Irish government could afford to set up health and social welfare systems.

During the bidding Mr Walshe, in an aside worthy of Charles Bewley, noted: 'We shall not really have our Jew until the instruments are signed, sealed and delivered, but I have little or no fear that he will now withdraw.'

As secretary of the Department of External Affairs for twenty-three years in Dublin, Walshe insisted that the young state's diplomacy should be characterized by 'modest dignity'. Dublin's dealings with the Holy See, he added, should be defined by 'care and self-sacrifice'. The villa he acquired meets none of these criteria. Visiting the Villa Spada today, four kilometres south of the Vatican on the Gianicolo Hill, is to step back in time to the Roman spring of Irish relations with the Holy See. The grounds are spacious, airy and carefully maintained. The villa is impressive as a showpiece but, as an embassy, it is utterly impractical: gleaming representation rooms sit empty most days, while diplomats are squeezed into a modern, cramped annex out the back. (The villa is now the home of Ireland's embassy to Italy.)

Practicality was not a priority for Joseph Walshe, once in Rome. Instead, on behalf of the impoverished Irish state, his priority was to secure a lavish status symbol. Walking through its reception rooms of gold leaf, stucco and marble, it all reminds me of an old Irish tradition – the good room kept for the priest – multiplied many times for Holy See officials.

The years that followed continued the conveyor belt of unprompted declarations of 'filial loyalty' from Irish leaders to the Holy See: Taoiseach John A. Costello in February 1948; Éamon de Valera in 1951. Though there was a mutual interest in keeping things cordial, historian Dermot Keogh suggests that Irish officials learned early on that, whatever notions it had of itself, Ireland's was not as exceptional a relationship as many Irish expected: 'Irish diplomats were to discover repeatedly that their country's solid commitment to Catholicism did not necessarily give it a position of privilege.'

Far from a relationship of scrupulous Roman control, the Holy See and Dublin favoured what you might call discrepancy diplomacy. The private, professional relationship was at odds with public expressions of gratitude and devotion, but the arrangement suited everyone. By the mid-1990s, the gap between the public politeness and private realpolitik had become too wide and, when the clerical sexual abuse scandal exploded, the diplomatic relationship collapsed under the weight of its own contradictions.

There's never a dull moment in the Rome apartment where I've rented a room for my stay. My host Gonzalo, I discover, is a leading male burlesque – boylesque – performer and the apartment he shares with his husband is redolent of gay Italian Catholic pragmatism: a mix of puffy ball gowns, crucifixes and, in the bathroom, an icon of a saint topped with a real crown of thorns that I inspect while shaving. Gonzalo performs in clubs, he tells me in the kitchen, and takes private bookings in all manner of places.

'I used to work quite a bit in the Vatican, they paid quite well, but it's slowed of late,' he says between sips of prosecco.

That evening he takes me along to a performance in a backstreet gallery, far from tourist Rome. On the walls are a new collection of artworks. A striking photograph shows a white-clad Pope taking a lie-detector test administered by a red devil as Death looks on with interest, hoping for some trade. The lights dim, the show begins. A woman performer, citing a recent book about gay priests in the Catholic Church, rolls around the floor as she performs 'The Ballad of the Lonely Masturbator' by American poet Anne Sexton.

Half an hour later, Gonzalo appears in his signature outfit: top hat, suspenders, and a voluminous dress made entirely of white balloons. With a wink, a sharp needle and cheers from the crowd, he pops one balloon after another until there's nothing left but a twinkling cover on his private parts. The crowd is delighted, as is he. I wonder how this routine went down in the Vatican.

I get talking to a local woman, Miriam, who remembers the thrill of being on St Peter's Square when Pope Francis emerged to give his first *buona sera*. As a practising Catholic, she allowed herself a brief moment of hope that the Church would reform, in particular regarding women. But she's since slid back to realistic Roman Catholicism.

She says centuries of living with the Medicis and Borgias – powerful clans who snatched the papacy for their own, often criminal, ends – has lowered Italian expectations of their religious and decoupled the institution from private faith. Living here, you learn early on, she says, to defend yourself from 'holy men' – her eyebrows arch.

'At this stage,' she laughs, 'people who still claim to be shocked by the Church and the Vatican have, I think, the wrong perspective.'

Six hours later, bleary-eyed from too little sleep and too much wine, I'm at a show far more spectacular than Gonzalo's. Everyone I've met in Rome agrees that on a Sunday morning the only place to be is Santa Maria Maggiore, the hulking papal basilica built originally in the fifth century and with mosaics to match.

Precisely at 10 a.m. a bell signals a procession of thirty-six people: wardens, servers, deacons, priests, bishops, archbishops and an elderly cardinal. The hierarchy is strict, the service modern but delivered largely in Latin, as translated by St Jerome, who lies buried beneath our feet. There's a Gregorian schola, billowing incense and two collection baskets as big as family picnic hampers. Large, hungry families. The crowd is mixed: conservative Italian Catholics, visiting religious, tourists with roller suitcases and selfie sticks, older women on their own and clusters of thirtysomething gay men.

The service glides by like a long, articulated lorry of ritual, tradition and aesthetics. Beside me, a woman in a leopard-print cat suit snorts at the Gospel's message: 'Can a blind person guide a blind person? Will not both fall into a pit?'

Mass over, the procession glides back out of the church, the cardinal bringing up the rear with regal, benevolent waves. He looks familiar. Minutes later, in an adjacent cafe over coffee and cornetto, I realize I've just seen Cardinal Angelo Sodano, the most powerful churchman of modern times.

For twenty-five years, until 2006, Angelo Sodano was the Holy See's Secretary of State – effectively its Prime Minister – and, until 2019, dean of the College of Cardinals. 'Sodano had a formidable

reputation – but not as a pastor,' says former Irish President and qualified canon lawyer Mary McAleese. 'Sodano ran John Paul II, not the
other way around.'

Sodano was, critics say, a Godfather figure straight out of the
Medici/Borgia playbook. He had close contact with disgraced US
Cardinal Theodore McCarrick.* Many believe he was the protector
of notorious paedophile Fr Marcial Maciel, founder of the Legion of
Christ, an institution for the formation of priests, and a crucial donor
to the Holy See during the John Paul II era.

When the clerical abuse scandal broke in Ireland, Sodano turned
the considerable force of his position and personality on Irish politicians. Mary McAleese says that during a 2003 meeting in Rome
Sodano sounded her out on a concordat between their two states. She
was surprised by his suggestion of a concordat – a framework document to define the relationship between the Holy See and the respective
state in matters that concern both. In addition to regulating privileges
enjoyed by the Catholic Church in the state, such an agreement may
regulate secular matters that have an impact on church interests. Dr
McAleese says her mind was whirling at the potential consequences.
She warned Sodano such an interstate treaty, at that particular time,
could be a 'knock-out blow' for the Catholic Church in Ireland,
already on the back foot due to mounting abuse claims.

Cardinal Sodano appeared to be under the impression, says Dr
McAleese, that the issue had already been raised with her ahead of their
meeting.† It hadn't, she says today, but he pressed on, mentioning
'extensive services the Catholic Church had provided in healthcare, in

* Theodore Edgar McCarrick is a laicized American former cardinal and bishop
of the Catholic Church, accused of abusing or sexually harassing seminarians as a
bishop and abusing children since early in his career of more than sixty years as a
cleric.

† At the outset of their meeting she remembers Sodano mentioning that he understood the issue of a concordat had been raised with McAleese. She looked at her
Irish government representative, sitting in on the meeting, and both shrugged.
McAleese says she told Sodano she had not been briefed by any archbishop or cardinal and had no idea what he was talking about. Cardinal Seán Brady had visited
her the evening before the Vatican meeting – she was staying in a cottage on the
grounds of the Irish College – with an envelope. It contained a calendar for the
Armagh Archdiocese and she says that was their only topic of conversation. 'He

education and other areas, and obviously it had extensive files and archives and materials which they would wish to protect'.

She says, 'There was no doubt in my mind where this was going. The message he wanted to get across was that the Holy See had huge power and he wanted to use that muscle to persuade us to take a particular course of action.' She cut the conversation short.

A year later, Sodano tried again: asking then Minister for Foreign Affairs Dermot Ahern for an indemnity deal with Ireland, similar to the one he had just agreed for the US Catholic Church. Two years before the release of the Ferns Report,* and six years out from the even more explosive Ryan and Murphy Reports, Sodano saw what was coming down the tracks and perhaps hoped to sound out what, if anything, remained of Ireland's filial loyalty. Mr Ahern says he rejected what he remembers as a 'quite blunt' request.

Mary McAleese believes these Sodano encounters were the beginning of the end of a kind of bilateral relationship that began nearly a century earlier in a very different world. Given the confidential nature of bilateral talks, the Holy See declines to comment on what happened. But a fuse had been lit.

A century before it became an Irish embassy, the Villa Spada was the field headquarters for Giuseppe Garibaldi's forces in their 1849 battle to defend the revolutionary Roman Republic against French forces, determined to restore the temporal power of the Pope over Rome. A second temporal battle broke out here in 2011.

On 20 July, a week after Justice Yvonne Murphy released her

---

didn't raise with me any hint or suggestion of a concordat. Maybe he decided it was a foolish idea. I would credit him with a lot of common sense.'

* The report of the first Irish state inquiry into clerical sexual abuse. The inquiry into abuse allegations in the Diocese of Ferns was established in 2002 following the transmission of the BBC documentary *Suing the Pope*, which followed the efforts of Colm O'Gorman, founder of the support group One in Four (see Chapter 12), to investigate how Ferns priest Fr Seán Fortune was allowed to abuse him and other teenage boys in Wexford, and the progress of O'Gorman's lawsuit against the Church. The report documented over a hundred allegations of child sexual abuse involving twenty-one priests and a consistent failure of church and state authorities to deal appropriately with allegations that came to their attention.

second report into clerical sexual abuse and its cover-up, this time in the Irish diocese of Cloyne, Taoiseach Enda Kenny called time on Ireland's filial loyalty to the Holy See. The two states had reached this 'unprecedented juncture', he told the Dáil, because the Cloyne Report had 'exposed an attempt by the Holy See, to frustrate an Inquiry in a sovereign, democratic republic'.

In her report Judge Murphy said that requests for assistance were unanswered by the Papal Nuncio, while the Holy See's Congregation for the Clergy claimed that child protection measures drafted by Irish bishops in 1996 were 'merely a study document' containing 'procedures and dispositions which appear contrary to canonical discipline'. For Justice Murphy, the effect of this intervention was clear: 'This effectively gave individual Irish bishops the freedom to ignore the procedures which they had agreed and gave comfort and support to those who . . . dissented from the stated official Irish Church policy.'

For Taoiseach Enda Kenny the behaviour of the Holy See in the present, compared to historic wrongs in other investigations, was evidence of the 'dysfunction, disconnection, elitism . . . the narcissism . . . that dominate the culture of the Vatican to this day'.

The Taoiseach's remarks prompted surprise and widespread praise in Ireland. It felt as if the lid had finally blown on decades of pent-up frustration with Rome.

The Holy See's response was cool, pushing back responsibility on to Irish bishops for child protection policies, saying the Irish hierarchy 'could adopt them without having to refer to the Holy See'. It asked Dublin for clarification on what exactly the Holy See had 'frustrated' in the Cloyne investigation, as Mr Kenny claimed, and said that 'a Government spokesperson clarified that Mr Kenny was not referring to any specific incident'.

Even today, Archbishop Paul Gallagher, the Holy See's Secretary for Relations with States, effectively its foreign minister, says there was 'no little misunderstanding of this episode'. At twenty-five years' distance, he says the Holy See viewed the child protection regulations it was sent from Ireland as a 'study document' – because this is how they were framed by Irish bishops. He points out that Cardinal Cahal Daly, in a letter to the Holy See on 4 January 1996, described the guidelines enclosed as a 'report' and a 'framework for addressing the issue of child sexual abuse'.

The Irish bishops' document, Archbishop Gallagher says, 'did not constitute binding canonical legislation, as it was never intended to be'. As far as Rome was concerned, Irish bishops were keeping the Holy See in the loop, not requesting its final word on the matter. Archbishop Gallagher insists the Holy See's response did not encourage Irish bishops to sit on their hands because, then as now, it already insisted on canonical trials and penalties for priests accused of the kind of crimes emerging in Ireland.

'The difficulty was that many bishops preferred to follow instead what we might call a therapeutic model,' he adds. 'Such a model was very common in all sectors of society at that time, a fact sometimes conveniently forgotten.'

The verdict of the Holy See's foreign minister is clear. One camp of Irish bishops sought Rome's view on its child protection strategy. Rome declined to issue an authoritative word because none was sought and it felt none was needed because canon law was clear. The absence of a definitive Holy See command then offered cover for another camp of Irish bishops resistant to binding child protection provisions. Read between the lines and Gallagher's message is clear: *Don't blame us for your chaos.*

Opinions differ on this matter among senior Irish diplomats who have served in Rome. Some agree with Yvonne Murphy and Enda Kenny's anger at Roman rebuffs. Others see blame on both sides. Rome has a great deal to answer for and Irish politicians were justified in calling them out, says one former Irish diplomat, but Justice Murphy's approach was not tactically astute. She headed an inquiry independent of the Irish state, but with an independent status without basis in international law. The Holy See insisted on answering questions only through correct diplomatic channels, her critics say, persisting with an approach that a legal mind like hers should have known would, in all likelihood, yield no results.

'The Holy See was using diplomatic practice to get off the hook and we were foolish to give them the get-out,' says the former diplomat. 'Had the government made a request for information, the Holy See would have been obliged to respond. The pity is that no such request came from Dublin, then or now, and Rome has been able to avoid being asked.'

Instead of pressing for information through proper diplomatic channels, even after the publication of the Cloyne Report, Labour leader and Minister for Foreign Affairs Eamon Gilmore dismissed the Holy See's response to the criticisms as 'technical and legalistic'. Two months later, he announced the closure of the Villa Spada as Ireland's embassy to the Holy See. As leader of Labour, the junior partner in government, Gilmore could not afford to be outflanked by his condition partner on outrage towards the Holy See. Sources in Dublin and in Rome say the cost question should not be underestimated in the decision, given Ireland's tight EU-IMF bailout corset following the financial collapse in 2008. It suited the government to maintain ambiguity around its motives: anger, cost or both.

'The Holy See embassy was always known for getting the best of everything, sometimes to a ridiculous extent, with parties and considerable waste,' says one Irish government official. A former local staff member of the embassy says successive ambassadors struggled to manage the Villa Spada, historic premises that had become a money pit. Daily operations were hobbled by encrusted legal structures and labour laws that contributed to institutional dysfunction. The former staffer laughs at the popular idea in Ireland that the closure was prompted by outrage towards the Holy See. 'Closing the embassy,' the former employee adds, 'was the only way to break the service of the local receptionist and the driver.'

In hindsight, the broad consensus in Irish diplomatic and political circles is that the fallout of the Cloyne Report was a timely moment for an overdue decision. The Villa Spada was an appropriate place to receive princes of the Church, but that era had passed. When the diplomats departed the villa for the last time, they switched off the lights and the internet, banishing the ghost that haunted both the relationship and the Wi-Fi. The internet password: 'JosephPWalshe'.

18.   Wizards of Rome

'They are bossed and controlled till they
have no sense of responsibility.'

John Kelleher

In the soft morning light of the Roman spring, I'm standing at the point where the Italian capital ends and Vatican City begins. Looking around at the expanse of St Peter's Square – the curving colonnade, the Egyptian obelisk from Caligula's circus – I think of the generations of Irish entranced by this sight. Would any recognize the glorious Italian capital now? Would Caligula? A toxic mix of bureaucracy, austerity and crookedness has seen Rome sink beneath its own rubbish, collapsing in on its own infrastructure.

In contrast, St Peter's Square is spotless on this early weekday morning, cobbles polished by centuries of pilgrim soft-shoe shuffle. Yet, where the visible dirt of Rome ends, the invisible dirt of Vatican City begins. In a meditation on the Stations of the Cross during Good Friday ceremonies in 2005, Cardinal Joseph Ratzinger – standing in for the dying Pope John Paul II – took issue with the 'filth' in the Church, 'even among those who, in the priesthood, should belong entirely to Him'. Less than a month later he became Pope Benedict and would eventually face his own claims of abuse cover-ups. In 2018, survivors of clerical sexual abuse in Ireland were told by Pope Francis in Dublin that the cover-up of their torment by church officials was '*caca*' – which, the translator explained, was 'the filth you would see in the toilet'.

Yet, under these two Popes, efforts in the Vatican to address clerical sexual abuse and cover-ups have been of a piece with the too-little, too-late approach of Irish bishops: deny, report, apologize, repeat.

In 2019, all senior Catholic clerics from around the world were summoned to Rome to discuss the growing crisis and left with a warning from Pope Francis: 'No abuse should ever be covered up, as was often the case in the past, or not taken sufficiently seriously, since the covering up of abuses favours the spread of evil and adds a further level of scandal.'

But one bishop attendee I spoke to says he met many bishops from other parts of the world – particularly Africa and Asia – who still see clerical sexual abuse as a problem of Western decadence and moral decay, not a structural problem shared by their growing churches.

'This,' sighs the bishop, 'is only getting started.'

Over lunch at the foreign press club, just off Via del Corso, journalist Paddy Agnew has no illusions about the Holy See – and wonders why so many Irish did. After three decades reporting from Rome, until 2017 for the *Irish Times*, he views the Catholic Church as a global institution captured by parochial Italian thinking and bad habits. That echoes the disgust expressed by Pope Francis in 2013 over the Roman Curia's defensive nature, which he called the 'leprosy of the Vatican'.

'They set the ground rules and then claimed it left everything to local churches, which is an easy way of claiming they didn't know about it,' says Agnew. 'Abuse put Ireland on the map, Ireland became the Ground Zero, but [Dublin] Archbishop Diarmuid Martin also set the bar on how you deal with it.'

It seems a sad irony that, after decades of valiant – and expensive – Villa Spada diplomacy, it was rapist priests that made Rome notice Ireland. And then only temporarily: like many I meet in Rome, Paddy says Ireland's clerical abuse scandal was soon eclipsed by similar US revelations, on a much greater scale. Leaving the press club after lunch, I see a street cleaner – the only one I will see during my time in Rome – trying to shift rubbish on the street with a power hose. It's a pointless approach worthy of the Catholic Church that just moves the mess around. As my mother would say: 'lifting and laying'.

In Luke Wadding's time, four centuries ago, around eighty Irish monks lived and worked in the monastery of the Irish Franciscans in Sant'Isidoro, near the Spanish Steps. That number is down to just six today, including three students and another in his ninth decade.

Germans and Americans complete the community of fifteen. My tour guide through Sant'Isidoro is Br Hugh McKenna, a native of Foxrock in Dublin. After a fascinating trip through four centuries of Roman history, we sit for coffee in the loggia and our conversation turns to more recent Irish history. Br McKenna tells me of his four years, until 1979, as a boarder at Gormanston Franciscan College in Co. Meath.

His time there as a pupil coincided with the era of abusive school bursar and sports master Fr Ronald Bennett. Everyone knew to avoid him, says Br McKenna, but nobody owned up to knowing what he did to the boys he collected from the dormitory – or had summonsed via the school intercom.

'When that happened the entire class would go "oooooh" as a boy left,' says Br McKenna. Teenage boys can have a unique obsession with sexual innuendo, usually of a naïve nature. In hindsight, it was desperately inappropriate in this case.

'When they came back, the boys just seemed quieter than usual,' says Br McKenna. 'We all knew something was going on in front of us but we never spoke about it, we had a mental incapacity to imagine this, no one was able to find the language.'

The past caught up with Br McKenna years later, in an unexpected way. As Franciscan provincial in Ireland for six years, he found himself on the front line of almost weekly revelations about his order, including revelations that complaints at the time against Bennett yielded no response from college authorities. Br McKenna's task, as provincial, was to apologize to those abused by the Franciscans. Among the victims were three former schoolmates.

Sitting in the courtyard of Sant'Isidoro, staring into his now empty cup, Hugh McKenna says that the shame of sexual abuse is now as integral a part of the Irish Franciscan story as Luke Wadding's proud legacy here. McKenna's professional life has forced him to grapple with his conflicting private feelings of knowing/not knowing – or knowing how much not to know.

Looking in on Ireland from Rome, he sees much work yet to be done among the ordinary population to take on board the clerical sexual abuse story as an integral part of Ireland's collective past, rather than something external to it.

'So many people buy into the negative group-think about the Catholic Church, though many know how much they owe to religious orders – be it their education or whatever,' he says. 'It's very complicated for people to balance this. Some are trying, but I think others have yet to get beyond their teenage anger towards the Church. They need to reflect, to grow up.'

This is an argument many religious make in private, as Irish men and women, but are wary of making in public in case they are accused of relativizing church blame – or distracting from ongoing conflict between liberals and conservatives inside their Church.

One of those enmeshed in the latter conflict is Mgr Ciarán O'Carroll of the Irish College. The college was subjected to a Holy See investigation after complaints from more doctrinaire Irish seminarians about teaching staff, subsequently seen as too liberal and sent back to Ireland. And, as mentioned in Chapter 16, a 2016 church row featured the Irish College after all Dublin seminarians were transferred here when Archbishop Diarmuid Martin complained of 'strange goings-on' in Maynooth. With a regular stream of Irish visitors – from visiting officials to wedding parties – being located 2,000km away from Ireland is no distance when dealing with public anger at how the Irish Church handled clerical sexual abuse.

'Anger management is part of the job now, but I don't have to own everyone's anger,' says Mgr O'Carroll over a gin and tonic in his college living quarters. 'I'd say, "Someone did something terrible to you, I'm not disputing that, and if I were you I'd be angry, too." But they know it wasn't Ciarán O'Carroll.'

Living in Rome offers a historical perspective to events, Mgr O'Carroll says, insisting the Catholic Church in Ireland is far from at an end. What is at its end is Cardinal Cullen's version of the Church. The challenge, he thinks, is to train young priests to look beyond the era of top-down rules and social pressure Catholicism.

'The Cullen Church ended up in a position it should never have taken: of power, trying to control sex, and of huge wealth,' he said. 'It's important the men emerging from here have flexibility in the face of whatever changes are to come. We are at the brink of a new model of Church, and I think this is an exciting time.'

★

Bishop Paul Tighe is one of the highest-ranking Irishmen in the Roman Curia. In October 2017 the Navan native was appointed the Holy See's Secretary of the Pontifical Council for Culture. His official job description is to analyse what's happening in world culture and see if there is a way of bringing Catholic values and Christian tradition to the debate. The unofficial job description came during an audience with Pope Francis, who told him on his appointment, 'I want you to get out there.'

And he has gotten out – even to unlikely places like the iconic South by Southwest (SXSW) festival of music, media and politics in Austin, Texas. To the ambitious film-makers, tech entrepreneurs and hipster hangers-on, Tighe has an unusual message: their fundamental, inherent worth is not dependent on achievement or success.

Meeting in his office, we pause our conversation regularly for the squall of sirens as police cars outside whisk VIPs up and down the Via della Conciliazione to the Vatican.

Born in 1958, Tighe studied at UCD and Holy Cross College in Dublin and grew up in a modernizing Ireland with a Church he remembers as uninterested in assisting an increasingly educated population to reconcile their faith with intellectual reason.

'The Church discouraged people who asked questions. It became a lazy Church, and we're reaping that legacy now,' he says. What many in Ireland forget, he says, is how the evolution of Catholicism in Ireland is not universal. 'I know a lot of people from elsewhere in the world who have great difficulty recognizing Irish Catholicism as Catholic.'

Working in Rome, he encounters the legacy of Irish Catholicism's positive characteristics, too: many visitors from Nigeria, the Philippines or beyond express gratitude for Irish missionaries who gave them an education and a start in life.

Given Tighe's day job, I'm not surprised when he brushes off as 'naïve' the concern in Ireland that Rome was closely involved in the Irish Church's response to clerical sexual abuse. Any mistakes made in Rome, he argues, were down to geographical and cultural distance and its hands-off approach. Ireland, he suggests, has never been good at heeding advice, orders or criticism from outside.

'When the child abuse issue came along, I think it shattered many

Irish people's faith,' he says, 'but it was faith in an institution more than in the ideas the institution was there to represent.'

I've passed through the Sant'Anna gate and am standing deep inside Vatican City. The working side of Catholic HQ is closed to tourists, close to them yet very far away: a mash-up of medieval city and university campus. My destination looms above me to the left: the Apostolic Palace, its high stone foundations visible. The far side of this building has a light ochre hue and the familiar window where Popes appear to cheering crowds. But this unseen side, the dark side of the Holy See moon, has an unpainted grey stone facade and a forbidding air that reminds me of Colditz Castle.

Once inside the palace, the first thing I do is get lost. A passing priest appears from nowhere, takes pity on me, looks at the note with my destination and beckons me silently to follow him. We enter a wood-panelled lift and exit on the third floor, *III Loggia*. I follow as he glides down a corridor of golden coffered ceilings, marble floors and, on the wall, the largest map I've ever seen: two globe frescoes of the known world, six metres high, painted in the late sixteenth century. The Holy Land and Italy are rendered in gold, I notice, while Ireland is squeezed into the extreme left top corner, trapped in the ceiling line. The misshapen island of saints and scholars looks like an afterthought. I recall Paddy Agnew's words: *only clerical sexual abuse put us on the map.*

Dragging my eyes from the map, I realize I've arrived at my destination and turn to thank the priest, but he has vanished as silently as he appeared. Another priest shows me into a room and closes the door behind me. Nobody makes a sound here.

I look around at golden wallpaper, Louis XIV chairs upholstered in red satin, and a marble-topped table. The orchids on the table seem like the only real thing in a room that makes me feel like I'm in a David Lynch movie set in a Renaissance palace.

From here, behind solid sixteenth-century walls, the world sounds distant and dull. A clock ticks frantically, its bell chimes urgently, then a door swings open and Archbishop Paul Gallagher enters. The Holy See maintains relations with 180 nations and international organizations, and all conversations – whether on human rights, religious freedom, conflict resolution or climate justice – and all lines lead back to Archbishop Gallagher, head of the oldest diplomatic service in the world.

He speaks with precision, his words as carefully groomed as his grey beard. A Liverpool native, he says his family, despite its name, has yet to discover any Irish roots. He took up this position, effectively the Holy See's foreign minister, in 2014 after an active career in the field that has taken him from Uruguay to Burundi, Guatemala to Australia.

Archbishop Gallagher brushes over recent tensions with the Irish government. Asked whether the crisis of the Church in Ireland is over, he answers carefully.

'The present crises in Ireland – and elsewhere – bring out the humanity and fragility of the Church and its people, clerical and lay,' he says softly. 'People can be driven away, by events in their own life or in church institutions. But they've still got to respond: "Where am I going to find that spiritual nourishment that I need?" '

Before Gallagher's ordination in 1977, the year I was born, he visited Cork and Dublin as part of the Christian Life youth movement. A lingering memory of his visit: surprise at the influence and reach of the two cities' respective archbishops, Cornelius Lucey and John Charles McQuaid, whom he mentions by name.

'These were figures that inspired fear,' he said. 'The government would tremble if the archbishop was going to say a bad word or come out against them. There was bound to be a payback time. They have fallen from a great height, they have been publicly humiliated, it is a great shock.'

Archbishop Gallagher is a busy man, with many files open on his desk – ranging from pressures on the multilateral world order, to the future of the Catholic Church in China. Ireland is not a priority and, given the state of the world, it's hard to see how it could be otherwise.

A senior Curia official tells me later that, with a staff of under a thousand, the Holy See's central administration is more of a haphazard organization than an efficient all-seeing bureaucracy. Gallagher's secretariat has around forty people to cover the world, with desk officials covering up to eight countries each. One official says that, because of its small size, Ireland's growing clerical sexual abuse crisis failed to register in Rome.

'As a result the Irish are doubly angry, because they have the under-standing of us as a very efficient organization that must be doing this deliberately,' the Curia official tells me. 'The reality is an institution where, thanks to history, culture and geography, people are not used to being held accountable. There is no word in the Italian language for accountability.'

The problem with this explanation is that it sounds like an excuse. The Holy See's administrative apparatus has perfected the art of moving both fast and slow. It can strike quickly – silencing anyone it believes has veered from church teaching – and yet it can take years, or even decades, to respond to grave crises or its own failings, like the global clerical sexual abuse scandal.

Irish sexual abuse victim Marie Collins experienced this first-hand. She resigned from the Vatican's Commission for the Protection of Minors after three years. The final straw for her was a refusal by the Congregation for the Doctrine of the Faith (CDF) to change its work practices and respond to letters from abuse survivors. The CDF consistently sees blame and guilt elsewhere, but rarely in its own ranks. In a 2010 letter to Irish bishops, Pope Benedict – CDF prefect for over two decades, prior to becoming Pope – said clerical sexual abuse in Ireland, and the Irish bishops' response, had 'obscured the Gospel to a degree that not even centuries of persecution had suc-ceeded in doing'.

Sitting in the Apostolic Palace, as part of my mind listens to Arch-bishop Gallagher, I remember how infuriated I was by that papal letter. So infuriated that I wrote to the Pope – in my best, blunt German – noting how neither he nor the Holy See was taking any responsibility whatsoever. I didn't expect him to see the letter, or to get a reply, I just wanted it said. A month later, a creamy white enve-lope arrived from the Holy See. Inside: papal rosary beads. The Holy See's equivalent of a corporate form letter: 'Your opinion is import-ant to us.'

My attention swings back to the film-set room in the Apostolic Palace, and to Archbishop Gallagher. He thinks it is up to Irish people to reassess their relationship with the Catholic Church. I think back to the past century of diplomatic exchanges between Dublin and Rome: Irish demands for Roman recognition, papal control and

Holy See mediation, followed by indignant protestations against external interference if any intervention came from Rome. And I think of today's relationship with Ireland, which – Curia officials say – is more relaxed, professional and mature.

'Through all of this comes a certain amount of emancipation of Irish Catholicism. I think that is a process that almost has just begun,' says Archbishop Gallagher. 'In the future, people are not going to have their faith based so much on a tribal identity – characteristic of the Catholic Church in the first half of the twentieth century.'

Inside the impenetrable walls of the Apostolic Palace the clock ticks its own time. Before I go, my Liverpudlian host opens a door in the thick wall and shows me an extraordinary sight: the only private bathroom in the world to have walls decorated with Raphael grotesques.

Hearing of my trip to Rome, an experienced Irish diplomat who once served here tells me that, eventually, all envoys to the Eternal City realize the head of the Holy See is like the great and powerful Wizard of Oz: much huff, little puff – essentially an old man behind a curtain. Catholic HQ has much influence, but little power, leaving the countries it deals with considerable discretion in defining the relationship. How much of Ireland's problems were caused, I wonder, by failing, or refusing, to discern that crucial distinction between influence and power? The effect in Ireland of our official stance was not seeing, or not wanting to see, the reality behind the Roman curtain? How many of our problems were caused by Wizards of Rome, and how many by Irish Dorothys boarding the Holy See hot-air balloon?

In 1912, Cornish novelist and Methodist minister Joseph Hocking claimed that Ireland faced 'complete domination of the country by the priests, who receive their orders from Rome'. His claim was effective propaganda that simplified the chain of command. Over a century later, many Irish cling to this Rome rule idea because it offers an escape clause, a way of disowning our past. In exploring our difficult and troubling Catholic past, though many roads lead to Rome, most lead back to ourselves.

Commenting on Irish government foreign policy documents from the mid-century, historian Ronan Fanning described Ireland's then relationship with the Holy See as 'the most cringingly servile and sickeningly obsequious Catholic foreign policy in the history of the State'.

One former diplomat who served in Rome begs to differ, suggesting Ireland mostly got the Catholic Church it wanted. 'We were always a country that wanted to be part of something bigger but in hindsight that is not always a good idea. There's lots of finger-pointing towards Rome, but for decades the Irish state and the Irish bishops were always well able to keep Rome at a distance – when they wanted to.'

Exploring the renovated Villa Spada, I notice that the old plaque declaring the villa's Holy See accreditation has found a new home – tucked away on the wall of the stairwell to the attic bedrooms and roof terrace. I wonder how Joseph Walshe would view his legacy ending here in the shadows, like an embarrassing gift from an ex-girlfriend.

Villa Spada sits on its hill, a stone-and-stucco memorial to our young republic, a reflection of the hunger for appreciation and status, and of our gauche approach to so many of our official dealings with the Catholic Church. By establishing Ireland's Holy See embassy just 300 metres away from the Church of San Pietro and the graves of the Earls of Ulster, Joseph Walshe hoped Ireland could overcome lost centuries and restore Catholic Ireland's seat in a global spiritual empire. He believed that Ireland's needs were best served with its interests aligned with those of the Holy See. Taoiseach Éamon de Valera did too, telling the Irish diplomatic corps in 1945 that 'close contact with the Catholic clergy is absolutely essential for all our representatives'.

He added, 'If you succeed in impressing the clergy with the role filled by Ireland as a Catholic nation, you will secure through them the sympathy and interest of the people amongst whom they work.'

Joseph Walshe was dead over a year by the time de Valera visited Rome, in 1957. Leaving the Villa Spada, passing the pool in the garden, I can see him standing here – the former revolutionary, now an elder statesman – chatting proudly with a cluster of cardinals on a mild autumn evening. Even with his failing eyesight, the imagined Ireland de Valera saw in the gleaming surface of the Villa Spada pool was more flattering than the reality back home. He had left behind a country where, in Fethard-on-Sea that summer, locals had boycotted Protestant shops because a local woman from a Church of Ireland background, married to a Catholic, refused to raise her children as Catholics. In Dublin, gardaí raided a production of Tennessee Williams's *The Rose Tattoo* and arrested its director because an actor mimed the dropping of a condom onstage (mimed because it wasn't possible to find a real condom to use as a prop). Meanwhile, emigration was at its height – by the end of 1957 nearly 60,000 people would have left the country – and Ireland's economy was in a 'prehistoric state', according to economist and politician Ken Whitaker. While de Valera toured Rome, Whitaker was working on a plan to remake the country, retool its economy and, eventually, loosen its ties to Rome. Poolside at the Villa Spada, like Audrey Hepburn's fictional princess, perhaps de Valera wished his brief Roman holiday would never end.

Diplomats say today that Walshe, de Valera and many of their successors laboured under delusional ideas of Ireland's relationship with the Holy See. Misreading this crucial relationship to exaggerate our importance – or maintaining the illusion Ireland enjoyed a special relationship in Rome – had far-reaching consequences. It may have been in the Holy See's interest to keep the dream alive, but these were Irish dreams and Irish illusions.

In 2014, Ireland reset its diplomatic relationship with the Holy See. That year a new resident ambassador, Emma Madigan, reopened the embassy in a modest office suite opposite Passetto di Borgo. This is the escape passage that links the Apostolic Palace, visible to the left, with the fort of Castel Sant'Angelo, to the right. By moving its Holy See representation here, Irish relations with the Catholic Church had finally escaped the past for a more mature present.

One admiring bishop in the Curia remembers how Madigan hit the ground running with an 'aggressive, feel-good campaign . . . She was very effective: she used to come up and hug old cardinals, throwing them completely off guard.'

Hugging cardinals rather than kissing rings marks a radical shift in the Irish state's approach to the Holy See, one that is less fearful and deferential. It represents a maturing of the relationship. Ireland has greater self-confidence and no longer needs to see itself reflected flatteringly, like Narcissus, in the Roman pool of Holy See opinion.

Given that, it would be easy and convenient to dismiss the Villa Spada diplomatic approach as naïve or cringeworthy, as having nothing to do with us. But that, too, dismisses the cost of that approach – to the country and, in particular, to our weakest and most vulnerable citizens.

In its early years, allying the new state to the Holy See was seen as a wise strategy and a means of building pride and confidence. Even de Valera's successor as Taoiseach, Seán Lemass, insisted that a modernizing Ireland should retain its Christian spirit and missionary tradition. They were more potent weapons than armies and economic might, he said, because of their 'unselfish dedication to worthy aims, a clear understanding of the fundamental purpose of human existence'. He added, 'We hope and pray, divine guidance in whatever we may undertake.'

Six decades on, it is clear that this went terribly wrong. Our task today is less to judge than to try and understand the unquestioning alliance Ireland sought with Rome. To accept – and own – the cost of our own insecurity that saw Ireland willing to spend money it didn't have on a villa to impress Roman cardinals before it could afford healthcare for its own citizens.

Taking abuse survivors seriously means owning the Dublin–Rome relationship – all of it. Ireland was once a state that wooed the Holy See, not the other way around. No one forced us to collectively kiss the papal ring. There was only ever as much Rome rule in Ireland as Ireland wanted.

19.   Stopping the Sacred Heart

'Between them they succeeded in degrading the Mysteries. But it was
the only way that was open to them of showing off their souls.'

Brinsley MacNamara

Once upon a time, Ireland went to great effort – particularly in
Rome – to present itself as 'the most Catholic country in the world'.
But at some point within my lifetime, that claim was exposed as a
threadbare cliché. Whenever I hear someone make that claim about
our past, as the best Catholics in the world, I wonder to myself: *by
what measure?* Bums on pews? Crowded seminaries and novitiates?
Overflowing collection plates? The warmth of our smug glow of self-
satisfaction with our socially perpetuated self-policing conformity?

Some still talk of the strength of 'the faith' in a vanished Ireland,
but I hear little reflection today on what that faith meant, either then
or now. If Ireland of the past had been a truly religious country – in
a genuine spiritual sense – why the reflexive need to reach for super-
latives? Genuine spirituality is modest, quiet and, by definition,
beyond measure.

Religion was never discussed in my home when I was growing up,
let alone personal faith. Like many families of a particular era, Sunday Mass was a given – at least until we were teenagers – but there
was no practice within our four walls. Things were different in rural
Ireland but my parents, who moved to Dublin in the 1960s, seemed
happy to have left the Angelus and the family rosary behind them.

At some point in the last forty years, a quiet shift began. Collectively, quietly, Ireland took down its Sacred Heart pictures, papal
marriage blessings and holy water fonts – and kept them down. Fre-
quent attendance at 'devotions' shifted to the duty Mass on a Saturday
night or Sunday morning, which in turn became a monthly or annual

excursion to the chapel. Such private gestures were part of a more significant secularizing transition: realizing that many of your neighbours were, as you were, simply going through the motions was freeing. Eventually people realized that, in their unbelief, they were now in the majority, were able to walk away without much thought – or social cost.

The lack of sentimental attachment of these people to 'the faith' tells its own story. And the alacrity with which we shrugged off a faith that was once so pervasive and defining is, in turn, reflected in the widespread lack of interest in faith as a historical, cultural or sociological artefact.

After spending an afternoon rediscovering my school religion books in the Central Catholic Library, I have dinner with a Jewish friend originally from New York. Now married and raising two children in Ireland, she is non-practising but anxious her children understand the rituals and traditions of their Jewish heritage. Given that, she is puzzled by the absence of religion or religious traditions within Irish Catholic family homes. Jewish friends point to many religious services at home, such as the Seder meal on Passover where the story of Exodus is recounted and the youngest at the table asks the Four Questions. The ceremony is there to remind Jews of their roots and why this night is different from other nights. It is self-evidently important and precious, a touchstone, not a source of embarrassment.

'This is where Catholics lose out. Jews bring religion into the home,' says Carina, who has lived in Dublin for over twenty years. 'Obviously synagogue is important, but plenty of people celebrate the holy days without going anywhere near.'

Other non-Irish friends, living in Ireland and of different faiths, are surprised by how the permanent presence of religion in our Catholic schools belies its absence in further education. Of my friends from continental Europe, none are priests but several found it normal to read theology – the study of religious faith, practice and experience – at university. In Ireland, we abandon all focus on religion – such as there was – when we leave school.

'People never get the nuances in a classroom,' says Brendan O'Reilly, a retired teacher and catechist, noting the low uptake among Irish adults of theology or scripture studies. 'We engage in religious education from the cradle in Ireland, but the grammar of religion is lacking.' And this lack of grammar can become an important issue, he says, with teachers obliged to offer thirty minutes of religion a day in schools, regardless of motivation, knowledge and personal conviction.

Schoolteacher friends say the current religious education syllabus has broadened its gaze, is more inclusive of other faiths and more intellectually rigorous as an exam subject. But that is little help to me and my generation, lacking the grammar to frame their thoughts and attitudes to religious faith and practice. Many of us are the former teenagers the Irish Jesuit Michael Paul Gallagher once identified as 'threshold' Catholics. We have 'less an attitude of rejection as of non-acceptance, of inability to cross the threshold into some level of commitment'. 1980s Irish teens, he suggested, had moved from their parents' 'passive but shallow belief' and into their own 'passive but shallow unbelief'.

In his book *Help My Unbelief* Gallagher sketched out what he called a continuum of alienation, anger and apathy. At one end, a small number of teens had made a conscious, informed decision against God. At the other end he saw those for whom religious belief had not yet been totally eclipsed by modern distractions, trapped between old doctrinal Catholicism and new ideas of personal faith.

The slump Gallagher predicted in his 1983 book came to pass, with Mass attendance in various surveys down from over 80 per cent in 1990 to around 40 per cent in 2010. So, when it comes to Catholic faith in Ireland, is my fortysomething generation at the end of something old, the start of something new, or frozen somewhere in between? An Irishman I met in Rome put it another way: 'In our lifetime we have gone from believing we were the last Catholic country of Europe to thinking we are now in the vanguard of philosophical secularism. Maybe we need to get over ourselves.'

I seek out Ann Hession, who teaches religious education and spirituality at Dublin City University. My generation, she says, was caught in the middle of a drastic swing away from rigorous religious display and practice, both in society and in education. Speaking in broad terms, our parents' generation parroted their religious knowledge without any idea of the content. We got the start of child-centred learning, with the fear factor removed. But the attempt to open a door to a personal understanding of faith, pushed after the Second Vatican Council, was superficial and anodyne. It was built on an old, flawed assumed accept-ance of God and knowledge of transcendence. There was no definition of terms, no taste of theology, no historical foundation. Looking back, it reminds me of how I learned the piano in 1980s Ireland: taught to follow the notes and never to enjoy the underlying harmony.

The shallowness of many people's religious belief allowed prosper-ity and secularism to erode Catholic Ireland's foundations, with great speed. Our country caught up fast with the rest of the Western world, a process catalysed by exposure of clerical abuse and the Church's incompetent response. In our teenage years, initial shock turned to cynicism and, for many, apathy. Given what was going on outside the school walls, the well-meaning fare served up as religious education – described in Chapter 6 – had not a hope of making an impact. Seventies and eighties teenagers – vaguely encouraged to take on religious belief, but perplexed by the need to do so – called a halt to the charade. And yet, here I am, reflecting on our Catholic legacy, wondering if I have missed something.

'Pupils left school without a sense of the systemic sweep of the story of salvation,' says Hession. 'I was twenty-five and at Boston College when the penny dropped that there is a salvation history story from the Old Testament to our time.'

I'm intrigued by her mention of salvation history and recall, with some nostalgia, my schoolboy fascination with the sweep and revolu-tion of the Reformation. I was given few opportunities to deepen that knowledge – we dealt with Martin Luther in history class and not religion – or even feel it might be worthwhile. Given the increas-ingly hostile atmosphere to religion and religious education among my schoolmates, instinctively I kept my fascination to myself and did not pursue it further.

The clerical abuse scandal has boosted the number of people who say religion is of no interest to them and should have no place in mainstream Irish education. And yet – trapped between religious epochs, educational experimentation and their experience of flimsy attempts at faith formation – many of my fortysomething friends in Ireland now struggle to make informed choices on education and religion for their children.

With or without the Church?

Catholic ethos, yes or no?

Religion lessons and/or religious instruction?

Inside or outside the classroom?

And that great modern Irish dilemma: First Communion for the children – yes or no?

Ann Hession suggests it is understandable, yet mistaken, to assume that Ireland is riding a one-way water slide away from religious belief. Our spiritual needs remain intact, she says, the question is how they are met. She senses Ireland is moving away from a mythic-type religion through a rational era and into a post-rational period.

'We are in an in-between phase where we begin to think for ourselves, question myth and move into post-rational forms of spirituality,' she said. 'It doesn't mean we are going to throw the tradition out; we are going to relate to it in a more adult way.'

Just how much or little my generation can relate to Catholic spiritual teaching, she thinks, will depend on finding like-minded people, beyond traditional church circles, who know that being Catholic does not always mean the Irish Catholic experience. It can be more than mindless box-ticking or defensive nationalism.

And instead of being sold a package of doctrines and rules that is spoon-fed, Catholicism can be a self-starting approach that, by its nature, encourages a critical engagement with what you are exposing yourself and your children to. 'When I bring my eleven-year-old to church – and she has to listen to a lot of nonsense in homilies – I sometimes wonder: am I actually damaging my child's spirituality by bringing her into a bad liturgy?' says Ann Hession. 'Sometimes we just don't go at all.'

The more I think about my frustration with the religion textbooks of my schooldays, the more I accept that much of this feeling is about me and not those books. Previous generations were limited in other ways, forced to read the dry-as-dust Irish Catholic instructional 'Sheehan's Apologetics'.* I feel I fell between stools and have been left

* *Apologetics and Catholic Doctrine*, by Archbishop Michael Sheehan, was first published in two volumes in 1918 by M. H. Gill & Son, Dublin. For decades it was a standard school text in several countries and sold an estimated 500,000 copies.

with a truncated vocabulary on spirituality and religious belief that I feel has limited, not liberated, my thought processes. I think back to the comments of my Swedish friend Lotta about the limitations of secularization, and her fellow Swedes' inability to engage with anything beyond the literal world. I wonder: have I been robbed of the ability to read a religious metaphor or grapple with spiritual questions, by not being exposed to the ideas, the language, the sweep of history, and the place of belief in it? Or have I been spared?

I can see vague shapes moving, fuzzy ideas struggling to form, about our age of anxiety. I realize I am on this journey because I have a niggle to satisfy. How can you make an informed choice for or against something – in this case a religious faith with a global reach – if you've only ever had a subjective, superficial and hyper-local experience of it?

As today's Ireland settles into its new prosperous, secular present, it's interesting to watch how continental European countries – already far ahead in their own secularization process – have begun moving on to reflect a post-secular society. Everyone has an opinion on this, even German philosopher Jürgen Habermas, for many the pope of Germany's post-war secular left. Though no friend of organized religion, he argues that an ideal society is one that 'accepts an interpretation of the relationship between faith and knowledge that enables them to live together in a self-reflective manner'.

This follows a 2004 public debate he had in Bavaria with then Cardinal Joseph Ratzinger on the subject of faith and reason. At their meeting, the man who would be Pope a year later suggested that a liberal society based on reason 'must be willing to listen to the great religious traditions of mankind'.

Audience members hoping for a grudge match, between two high-end German intellectuals from a similar generation but very different worlds, were surprised when the philosopher agreed with the future Pope. Without conceding his conviction and belief in the moral autonomy of the liberal state, Prof Habermas acknowledged the limits of human reason and the achievement of faith in having 'kept intact something which has elsewhere been lost'.

As an important source of 'citizens' consciousness and solidarity', Prof Habermas argued that faith and its institutions – when working as they should – deserve the liberal state's care as an ally in its own struggle against the alienating forces of the modern world. It was a memorable meeting of minds. Reading through the German texts of their debate from fifteen years ago, I try to imagine a similar debate – no anger, no interruptions – taking place in Ireland. I'll be trying for some time.

Modern Ireland views itself as largely secular yet still broadcasts the Angelus twice daily on national radio. German national radio, meanwhile, is intrinsically secular yet still broadcasts a daily half-hour programme each weekday morning at 9.30 a.m. Called *Day by Day*, it is an engaging attempt to address religious and spiritual questions in a broad, inclusive manner. The reports touch on everything from the history of faith in times of pandemics to the historical significance of the number 666. A similar, probing approach is taken by Germany's liberal weekly newspaper *Die Zeit* on a dedicated page, called 'Belief and Doubt'.

One searching article in 2018 by Verena Friederike Hasel asked why so many people – those of faith and none – find it embarrassing to talk about religious belief. If we feel we have no need for religion as enlightened people, she asked, surely being able to tolerate the difficult questions posed by religions, and by religious leaders, is also part of what makes us enlightened people?

Hasel noted how Germans are obsessed with Islam and love to demand its Muslim community engage in debate about their religion and its effects on German society. 'But what right have we to demand a fundamental debate about Islam when we can barely tolerate speaking of a faith that has formed all of us?'

After her daughter demanded to be baptized, Hasel attended a six-week religious course and remained as firm as ever in her unbelief, 'but I've become aware of the beauty of the Christian faith'.

The German media's relative ease with religious topics comes to mind when I stumble upon a speech by Fr Arturo Sosa. In it the Superior General of the Jesuit order wonders if mainstream Western secularism may be moving towards a point where 'fighting against religion is over'.

'Indifference moves into an investigation of the phenomenon of religion,' he says. 'In this way, out of curiosity, many young people

come close to a faith community in order to see what they can discover and learn.'

When I read that sentence, made in a Vatican address, I laughed
with recognition. I wouldn't consider myself young any more, but he
could have been talking about me. Rather than fighting or cheering
secularization, the Jesuit head suggested changing one's perspective
to see it as a liberation from old burdens and battles. It frees non-
believers from the pressures of inherited faith, while encouraging
believers to find out for themselves why they believe. And it can lead
to a new societal understanding – if there is goodwill on all sides.

This appears to be what Taoiseach Leo Varadkar suggested in his
Dublin Castle address to Pope Francis in 2018, calling for a 'new cov-
enant for the twenty-first century . . . It is my hope that your visit
marks the opening of a new chapter in the relationship between Ireland and the Catholic Church.'

But is this call likely to be followed, or is it coming too soon?
Given everything Ireland has been through with its once dominant
Church, who under the age of fifty is really interested in a deeper
relationship with the lingering brand of Catholicism on offer? And
for those who are interested, or at least not vehemently opposed to
the idea, where to begin? Sometimes answers lie in the most unlikely
places.

I'm nosing around Dublin's Holy Cross College in Clonliffe, the
archdiocese's former seminary. Like in St Patrick's Maynooth, the
corridors here are populated with ghosts. Looking into an empty
classroom, behind the heavy wooden door I encounter the sacred and
the profane: a metre-high crucifix on a stand, facing a meeting-room
flip board. On it, a handwritten question from a long-ago session:
'What is missing?'

I look at the board, then the crucifix, thinking: *if Jesus knows what's
missing, he's not telling.*

Instead I go looking for answers outside, in the corridor of red-
brick arches and dark-stained parquet, where around fifty people
who won't see fifty again are drinking tea and chatting like giddy
teenagers at a buttoned-down school social.

All are participants in Pathways, a two-year course run by the

Dublin Archdiocese. The Pathways brochure says its purpose is to give adults the opportunity to 'explore faith and ministry'. Pathways began life under another guise, nearly forty years ago, but now the Dublin Archdiocese is taking a final gamble: that it can activate new, lay evangelizers who do not have the time or interest in a full academic course in theology, such as that offered at Trinity College's Loyola Institute.

The participants are from all walks of life – teachers, doctors, solicitors, homemakers – with one thing in common: they haven't let go of their Catholic faith, though some are clinging on by their fingernails. They – and others like them in similar courses around the country – have come to realize just how many blanks were left by school religion classes. They are here to fill in those blanks, particularly before the priests vanish. These people are effectively preparing for the end of Catholic Ireland as we know it.

'We have a mix of traditional Catholics and people struggling to get something out of their faith,' says Sr Eileen Houlahan, who oversees the course. For her, the decline of faith in Ireland is complex but an under-reported factor is our passive response to religion and low levels of religious education. The course here is making an offer, she says, to correct that. 'These are people who want to make an adult choice.'

Pathways offers a self-contained, relaxed lecture each week on topics such as approaching the Bible or understanding the changes of the Second Vatican Council. I can identify with the people here tonight who were last spoon-fed religion in school and now want to enrich their spiritual diet by knowing how to feed themselves.

During a break, I chat over tea with Keith, a doctor in his second year of the course. He has no problems talking about what he learns here at work in a busy Dublin hospital.

'When I talk about it with my peers I'm struck by how they are surprisingly open and would like to learn more,' he says. Nursing his cup, he is optimistic that Ireland's shrinking Catholic Church will see 'the whole hierarchy thing die out' and spark a greater sense of community.

Keith's hopes fit with this week's first-year lecture topic: early Christian communities. Course leader Fr John Joe Spring, a friendly

Kerryman, suggests the future of the Irish Catholic Church lies in getting back to its early church roots, when the priest was only one of many roles on offer.

'Any plan for the Church's future based around priests is doomed to fail,' he says during the break. 'But I've a feeling there are a lot of cul-de-sacs to be explored before the pathway ahead is found.'

After the break, groups deliver their feedback on what they heard from the priest. Essentially, all have the same question: at what point did clerics become the be-all and end-all in the Catholic Church?

It's complicated, Fr John Joe says, struggling to summarize centuries of theological debate in a few sentences. Course participants don't let up, though, demanding to know when a small group grabbed the power in the Church and created the current clerical model. Others want to know when the clerics are planning to hand back power.

One man is particularly persistent: 'People want to get involved but often you have priests stopping the laity doing things and then that's that. This comes up at every class.'

Fr John Joe, picking his words carefully in his Kerry sing-song, suggests that some priests are products of a certain model of priestly formation and have never quite made the shift to the new reality.

'They need to complain to the bishop,' whispers Sr Eileen beside me.

'Good luck with that,' I whisper back.

Drifting out of the class, I start talking to Sandra from Tallaght. She tells me about her struggles with her faith and family life, her divorce and how much the course means to her. As well as attending Pathways, she's now in her third year of a theology degree and loving every minute of it. Pope Francis is changing things, she says with a confident smile, and her talents are now welcome in the Catholic Church.

Does she believe talk of lay involvement is serious or lip service?

'We're reaching breaking point but we all here have the voice now, not them,' she says, gesturing around her. 'Look at me: a divorced woman in the Church, and I have a voice.'

The crowd is thinning out now, leaving behind course staff and facilitators like Carmel. Since completing Pathways, Carmel says friends approach her with questions about everything from weddings – she's also a marriage counsellor – to bereavements. Her old Pathways course notes are a 'toolbox', she says. Often she photographs passages with her smartphone and sends people things she learned here. The feedback, she says, is always positive and grateful. 'We're all multipliers, sending things out, not sure where it ends up, but we don't need to be.'

With her warm Dublin accent, down-to-earth approach and calm enthusiasm, she is more convincing than any religion teacher I remember. If she was selling, I can imagine buying.

Carmel and the others don't have to be here. Unlike the people who once walked these corridors – priests and seminarians – they are not being trained in obedience and hierarchy but in thinking and empathy. Unlike our religion teachers, their spiritual thought is motivated by curiosity – not because it is a job requirement. Many Pathways participants say they are getting something here that modern, secular Ireland – with all its consumer choice – is not offering them.

'Thanks to Sr Eileen here I've learned to pray. That keeps blossoming out like a flower and it's not going to stop,' says Carmel. Beaming like a lantern as she heads off into the night, she shouts after me, 'It's infectious!'

Realizing I've forgotten my bag, I walk alone back down the empty college corridor. The ghosts of Catholic Ireland are out in force now. All evening I've imagined them listening – some in horror, others with delight – to the creeping coup being planned by the people here tonight in Holy Cross College, once a belly of the beast. For the people here tonight, walking away from the Church was not an option, but neither is sticking with Ireland's pay-and-pray, car-wash Catholicism: put a coin in the slot and expect the full service. They feel empowered and are trying another approach because they still need a spiritual strand to their lives. With language, knowledge and the confidence to speak their mind, they are on their way to being enabled Catholics, not cowed and silenced – either by religious figures or by a secularizing society. For them, both sides – believers and non-believers – remain part of Irish society, even as numbers shift between sides.

These spiritual seekers are interested in keeping two things in view: the rear-view mirror of Catholicism, but also the road ahead. If revelations of clerical sexual abuse and their cover-up were the explosive charge, it was the shoddy structure and weak foundations of Irish Catholicism that aided its sudden collapse. Fr Vincent Twomey, a former professor in Maynooth, suggests it is impossible to discuss the collapse without including all who contributed to its existence – and longevity. 'What was the ultimate cause of the implosion of the public face of the Church over the past thirty years? Could it be that unquestioning faith which marked Irish Catholicism?'

At the Pathways course, rather than lose themselves in the language of religion, the participants are retooling that language and their teenage faith, fleshing out more mature ideas of personal belief for real-world use. If they grow in number, as priest numbers dwindle, it could mark the greatest power shift away from the clergy in the Irish Catholic Church since the Penal days.

As I hurry along the corridor, still looking for my bag, I wonder if another me, one that stayed in Ireland, would have walked away in disgust from the Catholic Church. Or would I have embraced the Pathways course as remedial work on the ruin left by my despised textbook, *The Christian Way*?

In the gloom I pass a bust of a gaunt John Charles McQuaid. Fancifully, I conclude that he is unimpressed by this evening's interlopers. I find my bag in the empty room where the class took place. As I close the door behind me I notice a sign on the outside, a holdover from the seminary days, reading: 'Theology'. It should read: 'Last Chance Saloon'.

20.   Us and them

'The past does not stop, it examines us in the present.'

Siegfried Lenz

Berlin's former Stasi Headquarters exudes malevolence. The seven-storey secret police building, with a facade of blank windows and weathered grey screed, stands at the heart of a drab complex of apartment blocks just east of the city centre. Even before you learn what happened here, it feels oppressive.

On my first visit, in July 1999, I spent hours drifting in a daze down airless corridors of a building that is now a museum. In one office, above a cheap veneer desk and rotary telephone, a wall calendar showed the date January 1990. That was the month when, weeks after they toppled the Berlin Wall, East Germans stormed the complex to preserve evidence of the state's mass surveillance, before it was destroyed. The museum is one of Berlin's most visited sites and, since 1990, the agency charged with managing the facility here has processed 7.3 million applications to access files kept here by the German Democratic Republic's Ministerium für Staatssicherheit* – the Stasi. Though numbers are dropping, there were still nearly 57,000 applications in 2019 alone.

For four decades until 1990, the Socialist Unity Party (SED) ruled East Germany in a 'dictatorship of the proletariat' that was, in reality, managed externally by Moscow. Steering internally was the Stasi, an ancillary organ of the KGB. Established in 1950 as the 'Sword and Shield' of the SED, the Stasi achieved a remarkable penetration of daily life within the GDR. With 91,000 full-time employees running twice as many 'unofficial' informers (IMs), estimates suggest there was a pair of Stasi eyes and ears for every 230 East Germans.

* Ministry for State Security. The acronym was MfS.

Few visitors to the Stasi museum realize that the adjacent block, behind a series of locked doors, stores the Stasi's archives: the lion's share of 111 'linear kilometres' of files, 41 million file cards and hundreds of sacks of torn files being reconstructed with scanning software.

Those who compiled these files are long gone but nearly 1,400 people are employed by the German state here today to manage, analyse and make accessible a forty-year legacy. Walk around the windowless climate-controlled maze of shelves and soon time loses its meaning. The dry air carries the whiff of paranoia emanating from decomposing cheap paper.

'When people come to us, they can smell real history, that's not something you can get with an internet search,' says Dagmar Hovestädt, spokeswoman for the MfS Records Archive. 'People come here to try and understand.'

My need to understand East Germany's need to control everything is just part of my need to understand better my eastern German friends, most of whom experienced both the sharp and dull ends of 'real existing socialism'. Their struggles, aspirations and ambitions – often thwarted by their petty, oppressive regime – have always struck a chord in me. Not because their stories seem exotic and alien – but because of a low-level feeling of familiarity. Reading how the Soviets introduced socialist doctrine to the ruins of post-war eastern Germany reminds me, in some strange way, of the relaunch of Catholicism in post-Famine Ireland. On one level these two events, a century apart, are essentially about a euphoric minority's triumph over a silent, exhausted majority.

Until recently, I'd never made a conscious connection between East Germany and Catholic Ireland. The comparison seemed absurd on too many levels. In retrospect, though, I notice how often my ear has picked up familiar frequencies from my eastern German friends. Their inherent caution, their fear of others knowing their business, their public and private personas. No doubt they are familiar to many people in many parts of the world. But I remember one occasion in particular, when a friend told me stories of growing up in communist Saxony. There was something about his memories of social control and oppressive silence that have stayed with me. So, too, how he spoke of his lingering conflict with the vanished East Germany and his part in it both as an individual and as a part of that collective.

'I was opposed to the system as an individual but somehow supported it in the group,' he said, 'because I was aware of the consequences of not doing so.'

Ireland was far from my mind in 2016 when I visited an exhibition in a former East Berlin brewery dedicated to everyday life in the former socialist state. Following an eastern German family around, I admired the curatorial skill that lured them in immediately with familiar, vanished East German bric-a-brac: plastic egg cups in the shape of hens, polyester clothes with eye-watering 1970s patterns. Though hopelessly dated, these modernist objects were, for their owners, small plastic promises of socialist progress.

Moving on to the exhibition's second section, the family were presented with images and stories of the socialist state's mass organizations. As the rubble was still being cleared after the total defeat in 1945, these were the means of collectivization to control and re-educate the population. This was a priority for the occupying power from Moscow.

New groups – for children, artists and workers – were developed as transmission channels to shape 'socialist personalities'. Over four decades the SED oversaw this sprawling network of workplace committees, unions and youth groups that controlled work time, free time and even holidays. The official motto: 'Recruit everyone, leave no one behind.' Their dual function – participation and discipline – are, even today, a source of emotional conflict for some former easterners.

East Germany's Pioneers were the age-group equivalent of Beavers and Cubs in Ireland, for primary school children. The Free German Youth (FDJ) was a kind of communist Scouts for young people from fourteen to twenty-five that mixed camping trips with Marxist–Leninist workshops. Often these groups had the monopoly on free-time activities in a town, tapping SED party funds for outings and subsidized tickets. While just 12 per cent of all East German youths were members in 1946, every second youngster had signed up in 1961; by 1989 around three-quarters of young East Germans were in the FDJ.

From there it was a straight road to membership of the Free German Trade Union Federation (FDGB) – with 80 per cent of East German workers as members. Such indirect means of control were far more popular than the official means: just 2.3 million – out of a population of 17 million – were members of the ruling SED. Party membership was conducive, but not essential, for getting ahead. Aligning oneself with the system was – through 'voluntary' participation in mass organizations and events.

Angela Merkel knew from a young age that as a Lutheran pastor's daughter in a secular socialist state, it was far from a given she would secure a university place. Joining the FDJ as an insurance policy, Germany's future Chancellor worked as local branch secretary in her hometown, organizing a cultural programme of discos and theatre visits.

'There were few opportunities to avoid it,' she said, 'but without doubt there was a danger of being sucked in further than one wished.'

This socialist suction effect is what made the GDR exhibition so fascinating to me. I watched with growing interest the eastern German family doing the rounds, realizing too late how the exhibition replicates what the GDR did with them back then: get the frog into the saucepan, then turn up the heat gradually until it's too late to spring out.

As they progressed, the family's mood changed: jokes at the collections of everyday objects; thoughtful remarks about images of marching mass organizations; uneasy quiet when shown SED manuals spelling out how to use mass organizations to capture minds.

Through its mass organizations the SED co-opted the human need to belong and, in turn, generated a broad societal buy-in for socialism to succeed. The exhibition, I soon realized, was not a passive affair. It was challenging visitors to reflect on an uncomfortable, key question: was the price of this GDR opt-in – 'from me to we' – acceptable, given the level of complicity and conformity it demanded? The family I followed through the exhibition weren't smiling when they left. But perhaps they had new perspectives on the complicated relationship between the individual and the collective, and a state that felt obliged – entitled – to shape every aspect of daily life.

Over 130,000 people, including many former easterners, come to the exhibition annually, and Franziska Gottschling, one of the curators, says many seem enthused by what they see. 'I had a former East German woman on a tour once who was surprised by how much more positively her past was portrayed in the exhibition than she had been expecting,' she said. 'She felt her past had been honoured, not dismissed as worthless. That made it easier, afterwards, for her to discuss what was difficult in the state, and why it was good that it didn't exist any more.'

Leaving the GDR museum that day, I did a double-take in front of a huge photograph on the wall of a May Day march in 1980s East Berlin. The sea of colourful polyester uniforms and flags reminded me of something. Was it the 1979 papal visit to Ireland, which I know only from photographs, or some other mass Catholic event I experienced personally? I remember these gatherings as colourful, endless affairs: priests in cotton and polyester vestments, altar boys in their white and black gear, blue Catholic Cub uniforms, teetotal Pioneers* in dark suits and lapel pins. Irish priests and bishops would bristle at any comparison to the SED, but – alongside their spiritual message – the Church once echoed East Berlin's love of collectivization and its sense of obligation and entitlement to reach into every aspect of everyday Irish life: organizer of youth clubs, choirs, theatre troupes, gardening clubs.

Older relatives remember an even tighter level of Catholic collectivization providing a bustling social calendar. Some groups helped feed and clothe the poor, others assisted with catechetical instruction. There were vigilance committees to study the tone of periodicals, plays and films; so-called confraternities and sodalities for physicians, lawyers, schoolteachers, nurses. These groups were many things to many people but, in the main, they were about belief, socializing – and social control. One woman I know who grew up in Mayo in the 1940s remembers 'you had to go'. An older former neighbour of mine joined our parish Legion of Mary 'because they were the only ones with a function room'.

Even if there wasn't a hard religious sell, such groups created an Irish collective – on church terms. Leaving the exhibition of life in

---

* In Ireland the Pioneers were people who had taken 'the pledge' at Confirmation to refrain from drinking alcohol. While many fell away as adults, quite a number remained lifelong pioneers, sporting a lapel pin or brooch showing the Sacred Heart of Jesus as a symbol of their commitment.

East Germany, I wondered how many Irish people in these Catholic groups were as aware as Angela Merkel was of the dangers of being sucked in further than they wished. How many members of Catholic associations in Ireland found themselves conforming – even at a low level – more than otherwise might have been the case? Did being a member influence individuals' ability to see or not see, react or not react, to the misbehaviour or abuses by members of their group? Membership of such groups brought benefits to individuals and communities. But what was the cost of opting in or opting out of Ireland's Catholic mass organizations?

This was still on my mind weeks later, when I was invited to a University of Limerick conference about the GDR and Ireland. For my talk I decided to look at the respective appetites to reflect on the recent past among ordinary people in the two countries. Reviewing my lecture text now, I see it was filled with disclaimers – some typed, others handwritten at the last minute. Over and over again, I said it would be inappropriate and foolish to make direct comparisons between the two countries.

Ireland's transition from colonialism and empire to a democratic republic was very different to East Germany's journey from empire to post-war socialism with democratic and fascist periods in between. While we Irish left the orbit of London and willingly entered two new orbits – that of Rome and, later, Brussels – East Germans were sucked into Moscow's orbit, walling in citizens and shooting anyone who tried to leave without (limited) permission. No such policies existed in Ireland; if anything, its emigration valve reduced the pressure for change at home. The qualifications continued: Northern European island versus Mitteleuropa. Anglosphere versus East–West Cold War fault line. I had enough of a sense of my audience to suspect that most Irish people who had grown up in a more observantly Catholic Ireland would object to being compared to those who lived in a socialist dictatorship, hence all the disclaimers.

And yet, for all their differences, I said I could see a similarity in how two peoples – emerging from traumatic historical experiences – embraced, or renewed their embrace, of all-purpose ideologies promising salvation. Our two societies embraced cruel, crude interpretations of their respective ideologies and learned, eventually, how promises of power for the many masked a power grab by the few. As they imposed the cold, dead hand of conformity, the few made social survival dependent on conformity and self-censorship: often embracing the 'done thing' in public while saving one's true feelings and real self for behind closed doors. Our respective societies weaponized kin liability in a way that – in extreme cases – forced people to choose between family members and social status. These were two societies where the ruling elite eventually went too far, prompting angry pushback from the populace, who never remembered choosing them, freely, as their authority. Finally, I could see two societies emerging, dazed, from a time of historical, shadowy power abuses – unsure whether acknowledging these lingering burdens would bring freedom from, or capture by, the past.

The point I wanted to make was not about comparing the histories, but about how each respective set of historical memories is processed. Above all, was there a readiness or a reticence about moving beyond othering, us-and-them narratives? After years of shocking revelations, investigations and reports, I asked whether there was a way – or an appetite – to move forward without relativizing the past. What would be required to allow a broader discussion of Catholic Ireland that moves from an angry pointed finger to a reflective gaze in the mirror?

However many disclaimers I had included, when I looked up at the end of my talk I realized I had wandered into a minefield. I had asked a roomful of people who had lived through Catholic Ireland about the appetite of ordinary people – people like them – to confront their own personal pasts in a system that was imposed from above, but was sustained, I suggested, with conformity from below. I faced a wall of stony faces and a weak smattering of applause. I was not sure if I had lost the run of myself or hit a nerve.

Dr Gisela Holfter, co-director of UL's German department who invited me to talk, recalls the audience reaction as a mixture of surprise and shock. She remembers my disclaimers and remembers, too, how some practising Catholics in the audience were particularly unimpressed.

As a (West) German, educated in a society with decades of experience confronting its Fascist past, she agrees that it is good for a society to engage with its history. But the crucial difference in doing this work in Ireland is that while Germans can engage with past regimes because they have vanished, she says, things are more complicated given the regime continuity in Ireland. Only part of the old Irish elite has been toppled from power and much of what remains exerts considerable authority.

The challenge in today's Ireland, as she sees it, is separating the good and kind aspects of Catholic Ireland from the bad and the rotten. 'It's difficult because the Church was overarching in all spheres,' she says. 'And are we not always conformists, going along and falling short? Isn't that the human condition?'

Among former East Germans, Roland Jahn is the closest they'll ever come to a Pope. Instead of dazzling white robes, though, Jahn's preferred uniform is a black blazer with black shirt and black trousers. Now in his late sixties, he retains a youthful, curious gaze. His many roles and identities over the years all have one thing in common: a determination to understand the oppressive side of East German society and its consequences today. If, for the sake of argument, Irish people wanted to explore their roles as individuals in sustaining the collective power of the Church, his work – in particular, his careful, thoughtful and honest examination of his own past – could be a useful example to study.

Born and raised in the eastern city of Jena, Jahn found himself labelled a dissident because of his years of opposition to the GDR's increasingly repressive rule. He was expelled from his homeland in 1983 and, from his new home in West Berlin, his journalistic work covering civil rights marches in East Germany helped build the pressure that toppled the regime. Today, in an ironic twist, as Federal Commissioner for the Stasi Records, he is the custodian of the file archive left by the East German secret police.

A compassionate intellectual and tireless campaigner for the rights of the survivors of East German injustice, Jahn surprised many in 2014 with a frank, searching memoir, *Conformists like Us: Surviving in the GDR* (not yet published in English). In the book he exposed the private flip side of his public dissident persona. He wrote of his moments of self-doubt, fear and cowardice in the GDR: when he let down people in trouble with the authorities, just as they needed him; when he bowed to state pressure or ducked out of sight to avoid getting his family into trouble.

On the cluttered bookshelf of GDR survivor memoirs, his approach was new. Most such memoirs document real struggles with an unyielding system and its largely unpunished apparatchiks. Their authors often express anger and throw stones. In contrast, Jahn's measured book explored his own glass house. His argument: reflecting on your life, and your own conformity with an oppressive regime, is the best starting point for a fruitful dialogue with others on the costs and after-effects of such an experience.

'What consequences did this conformity have for the whole, for the functioning of the dictatorship?' asked Jahn of his life in the GDR. 'What is my part in this dictatorship?'

I read the book in one sitting, enthralled by his calm voice and compassionate approach. After three decades of important Stasi victim/ perpetrator work – which his organization drives forward – Jahn is making the case for opening a second channel to the past. Invited into this second channel are the 90 per cent of the ex-GDR population who were neither direct victims of the system, nor direct perpetrators.

These are the ordinary people who made understandable, everyday compromises – small and large – hoping to avoid attention and lead a quiet life. They occupy a largely unexplored yet universally familiar landscape of conformity, fear and regret. They are the millions of people who populate the spectrum from fearful compliance to cynical opportunism. They didn't necessarily believe in socialism or the ruling SED, but they knew that pretending to do so avoided problems and prevented unwanted social tension. As I read, I wondered if it was heresy to see parallels to our vanished, clerical republic. The public deference to the priest and the private mockery, the resigned presence at Sunday Mass. 'You don't have to be a practising Catholic to get on here, but it helps.'

When I seek out Roland Jahn, he tells me I'm not the first to see elements of their own country in his book. Every country has its unique historical burdens, he says, and every country struggles with related guilt. That is one reason why he was careful in his book to avoid 'guilt' both as term and as concept.

'Guilt is a term with a historical and religious burden, it immediately puts someone on the defensive,' he says. 'If my main aim is to learn something about how mechanisms work, talking instead about responsibility puts self-awareness at the centre, and that increases the chances of exposing the mechanisms in a more effective way.'

Anxious not to be misunderstood, he insists that nothing can take the place of legal process. Germany's post-1989 parliamentary inquiries, police investigations and trials were extremely important to those who suffered under the regime. But, in different ways, they were all limited in their scope. Three decades on, many legal battles for compensation and information drag on: for political prisoners, for athletes doped by Olympic trainers, or survivors of East German children's homes. As in other countries this is a long and painful road of witness, compensation and considerable pushback.

But a society that limits itself to legal process, Jahn argues, limits its chances of resolving the past. Without letting off those who belong on the hook, he argues for a space and an atmosphere that allows people to reflect on their past roles, big or small. Encouraging ordinary people to reflect on their own lives and deeds – and how they feel about this past today – can provide surprising insights.

'What is interesting about certain regimes is how, today, people see injustice that they simply didn't see inside the system,' he says. He remembers meeting a woman whose job in East Germany was to find new foster homes for children taken away from regime-critical parents, the ultimate punishment for dissidents. 'She says she thought at the time that she was acting for the best, and I believe her. Now she feels differently and is reflecting on why. This process of reflection is a crucial question for coming to terms with her past – and her present.'

I came to Germany ten years after unification, when the vast majority of easterners had moved on with their lives. Not everyone needs to reflect, and not reflecting is not always a sign of someone in denial. For many there was little time for reflection in the first decade after unification, as brutal economic adjustments shattered many lives. My arrival at the turn of the century came as the pendulum of memory swung to the other extreme, with so-called 'Ostalgia' – a softer-focus look back. The thirtieth anniversary of the Berlin Wall's fall, in 2019, saw the pendulum come to rest more in the middle. The battles for memory were not over, but many former ordinary easterners, now retired, are more comfortable discussing their past because they no longer have the same fear of losing their jobs.

Alongside applying to see their Stasi file, former easterners now seek out another institution, the Federal Foundation for the Reappraisal of the SED Dictatorship. Just off Berlin's Friedrichstrasse, the foundation employs researchers, maintains a library specializing in East German history, and distributes a budget of more than €100 million annually to finance history projects, events and conferences.

Vice-president Robert Grünbaum, born in the eastern city of Leipzig, says the foundation's task is to offer people opportunities to explore, in their own way and at their own pace, their younger selves in the vanished, repressive East German state. How did they respond to explicit and implicit pressures to conform in the social dictatorship? Did they accept fewer freedoms in certain areas – speech or travel – as the price for low rents, free child- and healthcare?

The foundation is careful to avoid serving up pre-cooked notions of life in the GDR, because some 17 million people all lived in their own East Germany. Everyone responded – and conformed – differently to the socialist dictatorship, just as people respond differently in a democracy.

Like the proverbial horse and water, the foundation has learned that you can't force people to approach their past, let alone drink. But giving them the option to engage with their past in their own way can make all the difference. Anyone who feels the need to go back has at their disposal a rich network of remembrance institutions and memory work. At this foundation, experience shows that an empathetic approach to the past, rather than moralistic finger-wagging, can soften hardened historical positions and excuses.

'It is far simpler for people to say that "those people up there – in the SED or a church – decided everything",' says Dr Grünbaum. 'But every day in East Germany, people had a chance to make decisions. Realizing that is a big step.'

★

Germany's decision to face its toxic twentieth-century legacy of dual dictatorships was not a given, nor will this process ever be anything more than a work in progress. In the immediate aftermath of war, in 1945, the US historian and political scientist Saul K. Padover served with the US Army in Germany. In interviews with ordinary people he despaired at 'not even a slight shimmer of awareness of guilt' for having elected the Nazis – and sharing responsibility for what followed.

'Hitler is accused for losing the war,' he wrote, 'not for beginning it.'

When the occupying Allies left, the 'denazification' process went into hibernation and West and East Germany accused each other respectively of being heirs to the authoritarian and Fascist past. In 1959, philosopher Theodor Adorno called out his fellow Germans on this, accusing them of wanting to draw a line under their terrible past and wipe it from their collective memory.

'One wants to be free of the past, understandably, because it is impossible to live in its shadow with a terror that has no end,' Adorno said. Then he added, 'The past is only dealt with when the causes of what happened then are dealt with.'

Failure to analyse the recent Fascist past, he said, was rooted in a refusal to accept how National Socialism had identified the collective narcissism in the German people after the 1918 war defeat – and exploited this to capture them.

Even today his arguments – expanded upon in the work of historians such as Daniel Goldhagen and Götz Aly – raise hackles among Germans who would prefer to frame the Nazis as 'the other' and themselves exclusively as victims of wartime suffering. They are uncomfortable when historians point out how, while some Germans were targeted and terrified in the Nazi era, the vast majority were not. Until the bombs began to drop, life under the Hitler dictatorship suited them. It was certainly more comfortable than the previous era of mass unemployment and hyperinflation.

In the post-war era, as the terrible price of Nazi-era conformity became increasingly clear, it fell to lonely figures like the West German state prosecutor Fritz Bauer to push back against the amnesia epidemic. He was a key figure in tipping off Israel that senior Nazi Adolf Eichmann was in Argentina – and his work paved the way for the 1963–65 Frankfurt Auschwitz trials. These court confrontations, involving ordinary Nazis and their crimes, exposed younger Germans, often for the first time, to the unvarnished truth of the past.

This confrontation was a key motivation for the German student revolution in 1968, just as philosopher Hannah Arendt covered the Adolf Eichmann trial in Jerusalem for *The New Yorker*. She took issue with the Israeli prosecutor's portrayal of the former Hitler aide as a sadistic monster. Dehumanizing him, she argued, fed the comfortable, undifferentiated us-and-them Nazi narrative popular in Germany – and explained nothing.

'[Eichmann] came closer to being an uninspired bureaucrat who simply sat at his desk and did his job,' she wrote. Her 'banality of evil' theory argued that petty bureaucrats played a role in the realization of the Holocaust.

The tension between duty and the individual's moral responsibility are major themes in the works of post-war German writers, from Günter Grass to Siegfried Lenz and Bernhard Schlink. But such ideas only began to go mainstream when they hit primetime with the US television miniseries *Holocaust*. Watched by one-fifth of the German population in 1978, it caused such shock that Bundestag MPs lifted the statute of limitations for murder to allow an open-ended pursuit of justice for Nazi genocide. Seven years later, Claude Lanzmann's documentary *Shoah* revived efforts to pursue surviving Nazi-era criminals. But it was only in 1985, forty years after the end of the war, that (West) Germany began to accept as its state narrative the idea of collective societal responsibility for remembering the Nazi past.

In a speech on 8 May 1985, marking the capitulation of the Nazis four decades previously, West German President Richard von Weizsäcker – son of a leading Nazi-era official – acknowledged the emotional ambivalence many Germans felt at the war's end – and since. That date meant liberation for some, he said, and loss for others. Some were relieved the air raids had ended, grateful to be alive and cautiously optimistic at the prospect of a new start under occupation. Others were distraught at the complete capitulation of the 'fatherland', embittered by shattered illusions.

With four decades' distance, he said, most Germans had come to accept 8 May 1945 as a 'day of liberation. It liberated all of us from the inhuman system of National Socialist tyranny.'

It was another thirty-five years, though, before a German head of state acknowledged, openly and frankly, the key role provided by the support of ordinary people, actively and passively, for the Nazi regime. *Us* not *them*. In January 2020, Frank-Walter Steinmeier, as the first German head of state to speak at the Yad Vashem Holocaust memorial, remembered the liberation of the Auschwitz-Birkenau death camp seventy-five years previously by closing the mental gap that still exists in German debates between the Fascist 'other' and the people who voted them into power in 1933.

'Germans abducted [Jews] . . . Germans tried to dehumanize these people and reduce them to numbers, erase every memory of them in death camps,' he said. 'The perpetrators were people. They were Germans. The murderers, the guards, the helpers' helpers, the fellow-travellers: they were German.'

Four months later, on the seventy-fifth anniversary of the end of the Second World War, Mr Steinmeier expanded on his argument. Because everyone in his country back then had been 'so deeply enmeshed in the calamity' of the Nazi era, it had taken a full three generations to acknowledge the broad spectrum of societal responsibility. His country was one, he said, that its citizens could 'only love with a broken heart'.

'It's not the remembering that is a burden; the non-remembering becomes a burden,' he said. 'It's not acknowledging the responsibility that is a disgrace; the disgrace is denial.'

In no way can Catholic Ireland be compared to the Nazi period in Germany. There can be no comparison to the singular terror and misery inflicted by Hitler's Germany on the world. Its industrialized killing of Jews, homosexuals, communists, Sinti and Roma – and others deemed 'unworthy' of life – will always remain in a category of its own. Living in the land of the perpetrators of the Holocaust, I wince when I hear the casual use of 'Nazi' as a term of insult. And I wince when Irish people – including institutional abuse survivors – draw parallels between their experiences under the Church and the crimes of the Nazis. When I can, I suggest to them that their suffering was real and unique and requires no such comparisons to stand alone in its horror.

What is worth study, however, is how Germans have leveraged the unprecedented horrors experienced by their parents and grandparents to create structures and institutions – and with them opportunities – to interrogate their individual history. If, that is, people are interested in this contested past.

Alexandra Senfft wrote two books about this big 'if'. We met while seated together on a flight to Berlin, in January 2017. She asked me what I was writing about on my laptop and I told her about the Nazi-era showgirl I had just interviewed. By the time we had landed she had told me the story of her family, and her life battling its shadows.

Her grandfather Hanns Ludin was the Nazi envoy in wartime Slovakia. During his time there, 70,000 Jews were deported to concentration and death camps. This war record cost him his life. After his execution in 1947, however, his widow began to knit a new narrative of her dead husband, 'the good Nazi'. Their daughter Erika, Alexandra's mother, lived a life of conflict: doting father or dreaded Nazi – lived lies and unspoken truths – and struggled with mental illness and alcoholism.

In the end, Alexandra believes, her mother finally cracked. Aged sixty-four, Erika died from injuries sustained after plunging into a bathtub of boiling water. Alexandra worked through her mourning by digging into her family history, work that has, so far, yielded two books, countless articles – and a new life. Her maxim: we cannot free ourselves from the shadows of our past, but facing them neutralizes their hold.

'When you know what demons you are dealing with, and when you can see them, they are not frightening any more,' she says. Choosing silence only increases the burden handed on to the next generation because children realize intuitively that something is amiss with their parents, but struggle to approach it.

Though her family trauma is rooted in the Nazi era, she sees in it a universal pattern of trauma and its after-effects. 'Many Germans struggle to reflect on how much their relatives benefited from remaining silent in the Nazi era, just as they remain silent today about child abuse or domestic abuse,' she says. 'The majority of people can tolerate quite a lot if the alternative, speaking out, has potential negative consequences for them.'

Her work – exploring yesterday's hidden burdens in the present – has not been universally welcomed. Some of her family no longer speak to her and I've attended public events where audience members have heckled her, feeling provoked by her invitation to reflect on their own family story.

For all Germany's tireless decades of work coming to terms with the past, the gold standard in international terms, Alexandra Senfft sometimes doubts whether it goes beyond public ritual to real private reflection. The 'good Nazi' lie is not restricted to her family, she thinks. The real Nazi zealots, collaborators and conformists – they always lived somewhere else. Some people reshape their conformist past into a new personal victim narrative. Others resist the idea that even small cogs keep an infernal mechanism running. A Berlin friend with a black sense of humour explains the final logic of such defensive arguments on the Third Reich thus: 'It wasn't me, it was Hitler.'

Alexandra Senfft's work brought her into contact with the late Israeli psychologist Dan Bar-On. He was a pioneer in therapy and reconciliation work with Holocaust survivors and children of Nazi perpetrators. In his career he worked, too, on promoting dialogue in conflict situations from Israel–Palestine to Northern Ireland. No matter how diverse and unique their nature, he argued that all violent conflicts create zones of silence in a society.

'The deeds and responsibility of the perpetrators are concealed, thus also the suffering of the victims [and] the role of spectators,' he wrote. 'The silence is often passed on to the next generation.'

Like Roland Jahn, Dan Bar-On believed there could be no meaningful dialogue in a post-conflict situation without first having an internal dialogue with oneself. Reflecting, acknowledging and understanding one's own complexity and contradictions creates an openness to communication and empathetic exchange with others.

'Suffering cannot be compared, there's no way to know who suffers more or less, everyone measures suffering in a subjective manner,' he said. 'There's no point . . . engaging in comparison [but] there is a point in speaking about what troubles me from the past, and how this connects to things happening in the present – that's the relevance.'

Each country deals with its past differently. Two calamitous dictator-ships in one century have seen Germany take an extensive – and expensive – institutional approach to its past, with its own strengths and weaknesses. If I were an eighteen-year-old German, curious about the GDR regime my parents experienced – their daily life or the past's leg-acy today – I can visit museums, drop into a dedicated history foundation with its own library and resource centre, or visit the former Stasi head-quarters. The complex in eastern Berlin has rebranded itself a 'democracy campus', reflecting a new educational mandate focused less on the yel-lowing files and more on their relevance today. Learning about GDR human rights breaches, as documented in the files, offers a way to sensi-tize people to spotting – and resisting – such breaches in their midst.

'Engaging with the files and this past is not about blame games or self-flagellation,' says Dagmar Hovestädt. 'It's about a society realiz-ing that it's better to talk about this past because, if you don't, democracy suffers in the present and future.'

Her boss Roland Jahn says he knows too little to comment on Ire-land's Catholic legacy. But even at a human level, he says, there is always something to be gained by an empathetic embrace of one's past. It's the next best thing to the impossibility of undoing or redoing it.

'I notice that by reflecting on my past I've sharpened my awareness in the present,' he says. 'I see conformity much clearer now, I'm much more aware of the consequences of my actions. In the end, every-thing I do to others will, in turn, have an effect on me.'

I'm walking down Adelaide Road in Dublin to St Finian's Church, home to the city's Lutheran community. I've been invited to talk about my work reporting on Germany for the *Irish Times*, but I have an ulterior motive for being here. In the community room, twenty of us around tables, I tell them about my book project and my dilemma. Is it acceptable to compare how Germany and Ireland interrogate their own very distinct pasts? No one in the group sees a problem, and many of the people here had childhoods either during the Nazi era or grew up in the post-war amnesia era.

One of the women in the group is Heidi Roseneck-O'Sullivan. She was born just after the end of the Second World War, grew up in East Germany and was fourteen when she fled west with her family in the summer of 1961 – weeks before German division was sealed. She came to Ireland in 1966, as an au pair and to improve her English, married a local man in 1968 and stayed. Heidi began working in a school and, finding herself teaching religion with no personal belief, she signed up for a one-year diploma at St Patrick's Pontifical University in Maynooth. She still remembers her shock at how much the place reminded her of East Germany.

'It was like coming home,' she said. 'It felt utterly familiar: its conformity, its enforced sameness of dress code, of humbleness and unquestioned acceptance of higher authority, and most importantly of treating their Truth like an invisible ceiling that marked the limit of all thinking.'

When (West) German Eva Molloy moved with her Irish husband to Ireland, in 1978, she remembers a tension in the air, a certain hidden sadness behind people's smiles. As for that era's Catholic Church, she remembers an immaturity on all sides: among a controlling church elite but also the conformist congregations.

'Thinking, asking questions, discussing, none of that was encouraged by the Church, something dark lay over everything,' she remembers. 'People were friendly but not really free to question or discuss what the Church and society were telling them.'

Today's empty pews are not just because of clerical abuse scandals, Eva thinks, but also a protest vote against severe clerical paternalism imposed from above. Pointing to recent votes on marriage equality and abortion that have put the country far beyond Catholic teaching, Eva adds, 'The Irish have come of age now.'

When I return to Berlin the next day, though, I notice my mind continues to ping-pong back and forth between past and present, Germany and Ireland, similarity and difference. Ambivalence is a thread I see running through our narratives: mixed feelings towards what the Germans call *Macht* and *Ohnmacht*: having power and no-power. What if your past is the tension between wanting to have power and it suiting you to have none?

Banishing Ireland's particular brand of conservative, clerical

Catholicism is a natural, overdue response to that system's intolerance, abuses and outgrowths. But this approach to our past does not resolve its legacy: not in how we lived then and not in how we live now. This past is waiting for us all, intact, in the back of our minds. Left untouched, there is every chance that many who claim to have distanced themselves from Irish Catholicism are, unconsciously, living their lives today according to more burdensome lessons.

Coming to terms with the past, everyone's role in it, is a process that is never completed. It took decades for Germans to realize that engaging with their society's past – supplementing guilt and blame of the actual perpetrators then with a wider narrative of personal responsibility to remember – improves their society's present.

Ireland's unique past requires a unique, Irish response. But it's heartening to know we are not the first to grapple with *Macht–Ohnmacht* and its complicated legacy. 'What counts,' suggested German philosopher Jürgen Habermas in 1992, 'is how the past is brought to mind. Whether one stops at reproach or one is able to withstand the horror, even grasp the incomprehensible.'

21. Coming to terms

'I had an Irish-Catholic nanny . . . I was brought up part Catholic . . .
That hero dies, it's massacred, and the self that is reborn remembers that
crucifixion. And we're doing that every day. This Christian myth at the
center of our society is very good. It's workable.'

Leonard Cohen

Here's a basic question: do we own or disown our Catholic Ireland
past? There's much to be proud of and much that summons shame.
Writing this book, I see now how much time I spent trying to get
away from the testimony of horrors. Reading the Ryan Report is a
harrowing rite of passage for any Irish person who decides they need
to know what's in it. Whether or not you've read it, or ever intend to,
it is now as much a part of our cultural heritage and identity as the
Book of Kells. When I said as much on the phone to a friend in Dublin one evening, after a weekend reading grim reports, the line went
quiet.

'You do agree that this is part of our past?' I said.

Again, silence.

'Let me get back to you on that,' he said.

As I write this, I've yet to hear back from him on this point.

That chance conversation sent my mind into a spiral. Had I gone
native after living too long in Germany? Was I mistaken in assuming
that the Irish must follow the Germans as an example for their past?
The societal consensus here is that no one alive today carries any
blame for the Nazi era, but that German citizens have a moral responsibility for understanding, embracing and presenting their history,
dark and light. But every country arrives at its own model for reflection on its past. Russia and Japan took very different paths after the
Second World War, when compared to Germany, as did Austria. A

common pattern in these countries was to highlight the victimhood and sacrifice while downplaying various degrees of criminal complicity. In the US, the struggle continues for the wider society to accept responsibility for the ongoing consequences of the treatment of indigenous people and the institution of slavery. And how many UK subjects understand or care about the real legacy of empire (as opposed to the jingoistic or sepia-tinted versions)? Looking at the decades of abuses, big and small, in Catholic Ireland – who would want to own this history?

Shaken, I disappeared down a rabbit hole and discovered just how contested the idea of historical responsibility really is. A common starting point for such journeys is the German philosopher Walter Benjamin who, inspired by a Paul Klee image, in his final essay while fleeing the Nazis, put forward his 'angel of history' theory.

His face is turned toward the past. Where we perceive a chain of events, he sees one single catastrophe which keeps piling wreckage upon wreckage and hurls it in front of his feet. The angel would like to stay, awaken the dead, and make whole what has been smashed. But a storm is blowing from Paradise; it has got caught in his wings with such violence that the angel can no longer close them. The storm irresistibly propels him into the future to which his back is turned, while the pile of debris before him grows skyward. This storm is what we call progress.

Benjamin's text caused a stir because he challenged Marxist theory, of which he was a follower, to make the case for redemption and transcendence. Coloured by his own Jewish faith, and writing in the dark year of 1940, Benjamin still believed in the power to transform the past – and correct any injustice done – by looking back on that injustice, its circumstances and effect.

A historian friend of mine at Oxford tells me Benjamin's theory is a great literary achievement – beloved of people like me on quests such as this – but one that has little to do with today's reality of historical work. Benjamin's bleak view of history, where humanity proves itself by causing destruction and a torrent of terrible events, leaves little space for historians to perceive, understand and contextualize events. And even if it did, my friend adds, their professional world is contested terrain. While there is agreement that blame rests with the responsible individual, not everyone agrees as the Germans do that societies have an inherited responsibility to remember their past in a bid to understand it.

Modern German thinkers like Theodor Adorno and Jürgen Habermas have built on Benjamin's ideas, insisting that owning our past and how we remember it is a prerequisite for meaningful engagement with past wrongs, and that critical reflection on a nation's past is the normative basis for a healthy democracy.

Of course, many in Ireland are apathetic about the Church and feel no sense of ownership of or responsibility for the horrors committed in the name of Irish Catholicism. No one can be forced to feel something they don't feel. But the complicated ties between Catholic and national identities make extricating oneself from this a difficult task. Presenteeism in the Church of the past contributed to its power. Undue deference had an effect then and creates a responsibility now.

Survivors of abuse and neglect are the victims. Those with the power carry the guilt. And what of those of us in between? Where do we place ourselves on the sliding scale between innocence and complicity? Can we separate guilt from shame, and begin exploring?

What if you saw something but chose not to see? Or only realized later the significance of something you saw or became aware of? Not everyone had opportunity, means or courage to do or say something. But even inaction then may leave people with conflicted feelings now. Where do ordinary people go with these memories, and the feelings they elicit?

The Ryan Report concludes that 'the general public was often uninformed and usually uninterested'. It's clear that many people felt they could not afford to be any other way. One lay teacher told Judge Ryan that speaking out about abuse he witnessed while working in an institutional school had only one certain consequence: 'If I report this my job is gone, where am I going to seek work?'

Perhaps this is why, when survivors speak, their testimony is soon swallowed up again by silence. That same silence eventually swamps anyone who points out uncomfortable truths about complicity in the Catholic era. We are no longer beholden to religious organizations. No more do we act or don't act, see or don't see, know or don't know, out of deference to them, but out of deference to ourselves. We don't know where to go, how to react, what to feel about such horrors and the shame they elicit. But without acknowledging these memories, and finding a forum to allow in the pain, shame and conflict, there is no way to contextualize and deal with these experiences.

The Catholic republic offered consolation for some and desolation for others. Disputing the legitimacy of the others' perspective prolongs a discussion about trees when we need to survey the wood – sexual, physical and spiritual abuse and our shared history of misogyny, snobbery and violence. All these old anxieties thrive today; they simply find new channels.

Though the fall of Catholic Ireland is recent history, several first drafts have already been written: media investigation, criminal prosecution and commissions of investigation. Further drafts will follow, as new evidence and voices come to light. But already some voices, including those excluded from Irish society in the past, are sounding the alarm. They worry that, in our struggle to come to terms with the historical wrongs of Catholic Ireland, we risk reproducing patterns rooted in the very legacy we are trying to overcome.

Some fear that Cullen-era Catholicism's controlling instincts, defensiveness and obsession with containing scandal have become – and remain – part of our national DNA. For many years survivors, their families and support groups have demanded access to personal files from institutions and access to transcripts of their testimony to commissions of investigation. Some of those blocking access, they say, appear to be operating under unreflected, inherited assumptions of power and impunity: that they alone own the past. That they, like the bishops before them, have a duty and a right to protect people's tranquil lives.

This fails to acknowledge how abuse survivors, aided by campaigners and artists, are no longer objects but subjects, and are even now moving beyond their traditional roles in the last years as victims and media talking heads. But they are working from the bottom up and many are pessimistic of ever meeting, even halfway, the top-down efforts of state and religious to deal with the past. Many holding power in Ireland then still have authority now, with no interest in exposing their pasts, and thus maintain tight control of their archives.

For many survivors and researchers this is the ultimate show of ill will, of players skilled in the language of reconciliation but, in reality, more interested in hindering rather than helping truth-telling.

Dr Maeve O'Rourke, the human rights lawyer who has crossed swords with the Irish state when working on behalf of institutional abuse survivors, has written that, 'The State's ever-expanding censorship of testamentary and archival evidence is unlikely to fully survive future litigation. Putting survivors through the intense stress and delays of litigating for access to basic information will be yet another incalculable failure on all of our part.'

State officials dismiss such claims. They say they are the ones following the rules, applying file access provisions agreed at the start of the investigation process. These secrecy provisions were agreed in part because of survivors' privacy concerns. Not all have families who are aware of their pasts. While the burden of shame they felt may have lifted through telling their story, therefore perhaps changing their mind on the need for privacy, the rules on the storytelling must remain in place for the benefit of those who might not have changed their minds.

Campaigners reply that such public servants are, perhaps unconsciously, confusing the right to privacy – which is important to observe when requested, and which can be achieved by redacting files – with an instinct for secrecy, and the unconsciously inherited Irish Catholic exhortation to avoid 'giving scandal'.

The battle over files from state and defunct religious-run institutions is just one part of a wider campaign of remembrance. The end goal of campaigners is a national institution to oversee the paper trail of Catholic Ireland. Such an institution, they say, should operate on the principle governing similar bodies in other countries: that the shame is not to have a toxic past but to bunker it.

Across Europe and around the world, countries interested in interrogating their pasts have such institutions. Poland's Institute for National Memory is working through decades of communist-era files, for the public and academic research. As we saw in the previous chapter, Germany has two bodies alone just for the East German legacy.

Canada's National Centre for Truth and Reconciliation (NCTR) was set up to make the history of its industrial schools available to survivors and families, educators and students as well as the general public. As custodian of Canada's Truth and Reconciliation Commission archive, its future purpose is to 'encourage dialogue on the many issues that stand in the way of reconciliation'.

NCTR's director, Ry Moran, calls the preservation of the archive a 'sacred obligation . . . [so] at no point in the future can people question what happened at the residential schools, so that we all may remember what we are capable of, both good and bad'.

If every country deals with its past in its own way, how can Ireland do it in a way that plays to our strengths, and reflects on specific challenges in that past, while drawing on best practice elsewhere? Living in Germany, I'm struck often at how media coverage of Ireland circles around two themes. The first is Ireland's Catholic legacy of clerical abuse scandals. The second is how recent citizens' assemblies have, in a calm and mature fashion, transformed Ireland beyond recognition.

This begs the question: why not use the latter to help with the former?

In 2016, Taoiseach Enda Kenny opened a citizens' assembly on the future of the Eighth Amendment, the constitutional provision that effectively prevented the introduction of abortion in Ireland. This grassroots approach, he said, would allow Irish society to move from a position of 'contention, even contempt' and find consensus on issues that were 'deeply complex, hugely challenging and profoundly ethical'.

If the abortion question could be approached in such a way, why not our equally knotty Catholic legacy? Such an assembly, presided over by a respected figure from outside Ireland, could hear expert testimony from all sides and allow a citizens' assembly to decide on crucial issues of contention, from file access or the establishment of an institute of national memory. And it could provide a blueprint for the future.

Assembly representatives could decide on a mandate for a reconciliation model after listening to testimony from international experts, such as sociologist Jeff Alexander, one of the world's leading authorities on cultural trauma, or Judge Janine Geske, who has done ground-breaking work on truth and reconciliation and restorative justice in the US, including with victims of clerical sexual abuse. The assembly's live-streamed sessions would take the discussions out of backrooms, out of the hands of lawyers, and into a public forum where a watching public could engage in what are divisive, emotional issues.

Such a forum could also bring to a wider audience the wealth of new Irish voices that have emerged in recent years on this topic. Academics like Emilie Pine, Susan Leavy and Mark T. Keane at UCD, who have used data analytics to interrogate the Ryan Report. Creative people who offer new ways into our hearts – artists like Alison Lowry (whose fragile glass works on abuse themes I described in Chapter 14) and a new generation of writers like John Boyne who has published two critically acclaimed and best-selling novels on Ireland's unresolved Catholic past in recent years. His 2017 book *The Heart's Invisible Furies* opens in 1945 West Cork with the collision of a priest, community and family in shunning a pregnant sixteen-year-old. Three years earlier, *A History of Loneliness* reflected on clerical sexual abuse in Ireland and its consequences for a priest, not himself an abuser, whose innocence is the product of 'an inability to confront'.

In the last years Boyne says his writing, like his thinking, has become more differentiated on the crimes of Catholic clergy. Now, more than in the past, he feels sympathy for innocent priests and other religious, judged by the actions of other members of their group. 'I would like to think a lot of people would look back now and think what I am thinking,' he tells me. 'Certainly, serious collaborators should be called out on their actions but I have come to a place where I feel constant blaming is less helpful than understanding.'

A citizens' assembly could challenge popular myths, such as the one that everyone in the Irish media embraced truth-telling like the late Mary Raftery. Her 1999 RTÉ series *States of Fear* lifted the lid on institutional abuse and prompted Taoiseach Bertie Ahern's state apology to survivors. But Sheila Ahern, who doubled as Raftery's production assistant and researcher, remembers huge ambivalence about the project in RTÉ, an ambivalence reflected in the series' shoestring budget.

The final insult came two weeks before broadcast. When Raftery opened the RTÉ Guide she discovered that *States of Fear* was not in the agreed 9.30 p.m. slot, the traditional airtime for current affairs and serious documentaries, but a graveyard slot around 11 p.m.

'Mary . . . decided that we would down tools – we were still in editing – and take all the tapes home if necessary,' says Ahern. When Raftery communicated her intention to nervous executives, RTÉ offered a 10.10 p.m. slot. 'Mary gave in on that, in the hope the audience would stick with the series and the reviews would be positive. I had never seen her so angry.'

Once set up, a citizens' assembly could try and resolve outstanding issues regarding a recent follow-up to *States of Fear*: a commission of investigation into residential, and a redress scheme to provide compensation to former residents.

Retired Fianna Fáil politician Michael Woods – who, as Minister for Education, set up both – rarely talks about the period any more. He is a friend of a late uncle and, when we talk, he tells me he is tired of what he sees as attempts to reframe his actions and disparage his political legacy.

Of particular annoyance is the claim by Senator Michael McDowell that, as Attorney General in 1999, he was excluded from final negotiations with religious orders chaired by Dr Woods. The resulting agreement limited to €128 million the orders' contribution to compensating survivors, with the state covering the remainder. The bill has since ballooned to at least €1.4 billion. In interviews and a television documentary, Senator McDowell has said that Dr Woods, by capping the orders' liability, 'effectively signed a blank cheque' – a claim Woods strenuously denies.

'The former AG is no brighter than I. What Michael McDowell says is patently untrue. His office was there at all times,' says Dr Woods. 'I was supposed to be a bit of an eejit, that they outfoxed us in every direction.'

Hearing the Woods claims, McDowell insists he and his office were 'blindsided for a considerable period'. He maintains, 'It isn't the case my office was there at all times . . . there was a secret process going on and the AG's office was only partially aware of what was happening. It was like being in a submarine where the periscope wasn't working. It only came up again once an agreement in principle was made.'

Playing catch-up at that stage of the negotiations, Mr McDowell presented a memorandum to cabinet flagging the potential risk of financial exposure by the state – which later came to pass. On one point, though, he agrees with Michael Woods: without an agreement, the result would have been lengthy jury trials, an 'avalanche of claims' and a series of religious order bankruptcies rather than compensation payouts.

Two Oireachtas committees subsequently vindicated the approach Woods took but, amid competing narratives, a citizens' assembly may be the last chance to resolve this lingering, rancorous row over what was done back then – and why.

Finally, and most importantly, a citizens' assembly could welcome survivors like Mary Lodato, put through multiple kinds of abuse in four Irish industrial schools. As an adult she wrote a PhD on survival, redress and recovery, and thinks state efforts to right past wrongs – the Ryan investigation and the state's redress scheme – ended up being abusive all over again.

Living in the UK, she works with survivors there through the medium of painting and senses their mixed feelings towards Ireland: lingering love of the place mixed with a feeling of sadness that their homeland, 'deep in its psyche, can't facilitate them'. While they are trying to ease the conflicted feelings towards their past, she sees no evidence of bystanders in Ireland being interested in doing the same. Like Paddy Doyle, another abuse survivor, she is amazed at how many Irish people think no longer attending Mass resolves their role in the Catholic Ireland inheritance.

'The emotional reality is Ireland has never dealt with this on a collective level,' says Dr Lodato when we speak. 'It's not as easy as just saying "it was Catholicism". I think there is something deeply repressive in the Irish psyche, something to do with sexuality, longing and desire.'

Of course, even if it was possible for a citizens' assembly to hear all historical, political and religious perspectives, facts are only half the battle. Another task is to reflect on the unique dilemma of modern

Irish life: how to judge and contextualize fairly catastrophic and even criminal failings, of attitude and approach, which reflected prevailing values and morals of the time but which are far from current norms, when we think so differently today. Complicating an assembly's work further is the subject we are dealing with: religion as institution and faith practice. Ireland's unique historical circumstances left Irish Catholicism divorced from reason and the Enlightenment far longer than elsewhere. With little competition, Irish Catholicism remained impervious to rational criticism or challenge.

Essential reading – for any citizens' assembly members and the wider Irish population – is *Child Sexual Abuse and the Catholic Church*, a 2012 book by Dr Marie Keenan, a UCD lecturer and therapist. Having analysed church structures and teachings and considered them in the context of interviews with priests and international research, she broadens her gaze and warns: 'As citizens and bystanders we are all in the "political responsibility dock" for allowing such individual and institutional hypocrisy to produce such cruelty and for it to last for such a long time.'

By viewing clerics and religious as them-not-us, we are 'othering' them. Yesterday's deference to 'God's holy anointed', a clerical class set apart, dovetails with conscious or unconscious denial that these religious, including the perpetrators, are Irish citizens and part of our society. Treating the past like a national out-of-body experience, and the perpetrators as 'bad apples' to be excluded, closes down discussion of the barrel – or society – in which they went bad. This approach echoes the bishops' own strategy when confronted with scandal and perpetuates the very problem we should be trying to understand: integrating the strangling roots of twentieth-century Irish Catholicism, and its representatives, into our history.

Nearly a decade on since her book was published, to far greater interest abroad, she says, than in Ireland, Dr Keenan sees at least two road blocks to owning the past in Ireland: the dominant 'bad priests/ bishops let us down' narrative, and a continued focus on individual responsibility arising from the nature of criminal and civil law.

She gives me the results of a 2011 survey on clerical sexual abuse, suggesting Irish feelings on the question of responsibility are strong, if ambivalent. Asked whether 'society would prefer to turn a blind eye to child abuse', respondents were evenly divided. Asked whether 'members of society were powerless to protect these children', 34 per cent agreed, 46 per cent disagreed. An 'ambivalent' 19 per cent said 'neither', while just 1 per cent said they didn't know.

Asked about the Ryan Report, the survey suggested huge anger that the state didn't do more (83 per cent), matched by anger at wider society – i.e. themselves (85 per cent) – for not doing more. Respondents' dominant emotional response to the Ryan Report was to feel helpless (57 per cent) and overwhelmed (52 per cent).*

Still outstanding, Dr Keenan says, are wider moral and philosophical debates on these lingering feelings, debates that would allow a society – as a collective and as individuals – to look closely at what she calls the 'continuum of knowing'. This is about where people place themselves in the narrative: victim, victimizer, bystander or someone else?

'We need the person who caused the bruise to take individual ownership, there can be no ambiguity here,' she says. 'But we need to know what it meant for all of us to be, to a greater or lesser extent, complicit – to a greater or lesser extent, knowing.'

In Dublin we have museums for whiskey, the GAA, the Famine, Jewish history, tenement life, James Joyce, leprechauns – but not for the most influential institution in Irish history. Where is the museum – for visitors, school children and the rest of us – telling the unique story of Irish Catholic faith, politics and transformation? Alison Lowry's response to the state's mother and baby homes and Magdalene Laundries, *(A)dressing Our Hidden Truths*, attracted so many visitors that its twelve-month run at the National Museum was extended by a further six months. That, and the hugely positive response in remarks left in visitors' books, suggests there is an appetite for a space to consider Catholic Ireland imaginatively.

A permanent museum of Catholic Ireland cannot be a dead place for a dead thing. It would combine, for Irish and international visitors, historic artefacts and religious art but present them in new, fresh contexts alongside objects telling the darker narrative, uniting both

* RED Express Poll carried out for Amnesty International, October 2011.

sides of the history through current historical and political debates. Given the amount of church property, financed by donations from the Irish people, such a museum would be best housed in a significant building donated by the Church. With adequate parking, Archbishop's House in Dublin might work well. A new Irish archbishop, in the more modest modern era, no longer needs a palace. Even better – there could be many museums around the country. Crucially, they would be run by foundations headed by non-Irish experts, and independent of Church and state.

In addition to museums, repurposing authentic institutional buildings, like the former Gloucester Street laundry on Sean McDermott Street, could be an additional repository of memory and site of commemoration for future generations. There have been several threats to the future of the abandoned building – including plans to sell it to a Japanese hotel chain – but at the time of writing a majority of councillors on Dublin City Council (which blocked the sale to the hotel company) have agreed to develop it into a 'Site of Conscience . . . that will seek to honour and commemorate the victims and survivors of Ireland's Institutional past'.

And let's not forget the forgotten memorials. The state has promised several already – to institutional survivors and to former laundry residents – but none have yet appeared. That's no surprise, given the contested, complex nature of remembering – expressed both in argument and silence. But that is no excuse to think they can be forgotten. One thing is certain: in the future, a decade after these memorials are eventually built, most will agree they were a great idea. But to get to that point – where they are built and embraced as essential – we still need a furious debate over the nature of the memorials. This is the point of commissioning and erecting them in the first place. We cannot have memorials until we can agree what – and who – we are memorializing.

More than twenty years on, much more is known about the horrors linked to the Catholic Church – in particular, the chains of command and of responsibility. But claims and counter-claims need a calm airing in a citizens' assembly, so that memorials – when they appear – unite, as they are supposed to.

★

Parallel to any assembly, museums and memorials, a final task awaits – creating a place for reflection. The late writer Nuala O'Faolain, herself no stranger to abuse, floated the need for this twenty-five years ago when she called out the 'spectrum of denial' at the heart of Irish society.

'Wherever there has been power and powerlessness side by side in this society of ours, some of the powerful, aided by the silence of the majority, have abused the powerless,' she wrote in the *Irish Times*. 'No inner ethic acted as a brake. Devoutness made no difference.'

The Irish default response – to talk – has given the marginalized back their voice. But, even as early in this process as 1996, O'Faolain warned that 'personal testimony piled on personal testimony . . . doesn't amount to the revolution in social responsibility that we desperately need'.

A quarter of a century later: what do we do now with the piles of testimony we have, to create something sustainable, a revolution in social responsibility?

One answer lies in the hills of Glencree, Co. Wicklow. In 1974, the Centre for Peace and Reconciliation opened its doors here and began reconciliation work with people on opposite sides of the Northern Ireland conflict. Later, it expanded its welcome to others from conflicts around the world.

The complex, 20km south of Dublin, was once a home for child war refugees from Dresden, as well as a reformatory run by the Oblate order. The centre's walls can't talk, but its staff are trained to listen. And when I contact Barbara Walshe, chair of the board, she seems intrigued by the idea of the centre helping thaw the frozen conflict over Ireland's Catholic past.

Walshe has already worked with Irish clerical abuse survivors and has first-hand experience of how they still grapple with the experience. A particular challenge, she says, is dealing with lingering feelings of disempowerment and humiliation that wider Irish society – us – once projected on to them.

Reconciliation meetings are happening sporadically around the country, she says, but it is time to move beyond the ad hoc to an organized network of healing.

'When rehumanization of the other happens,' says Walshe, 'relationships develop.'

Accepting our past for what it was – a collective experience, not an us-and-them narrative – will help us really understand survivors, forgive perpetrators and achieve peace and empathy with those in between: us. Without real interaction, and a real sense of empowerment, a long-standing pattern in Irish life continues: we assume someone higher up is responsible for everything.

As I described in Chapter 14, some survivors, artists and campaigners are seeking out gaps in our emotional defences, finding gentle ways to slip past pat explanations of our past to encourage two kinds of dialogue: with oneself and with others. In many ways they are nudging us towards the work recommended by Israeli psychologist Dan Bar-On, who pioneered new methods for approaching old conflicts, from the Holocaust to the Arab–Israeli conflict. For him, the key was dialogue – with others, but also with oneself.

'I begin with the assumption that we are complex creatures,' he wrote. 'We are made from many different parts that don't necessarily fit together, and we have to understand that complexity.'

Dialogue with others will be flat if people cannot understand first their own complexity. Only when the internal dialogue, with one's own complexities, has moved forward is a dialogue with others meaningful.

Listening to survivors – and what they are really telling us today about ourselves – is a first step in such a process. And there is no one, homogeneous message. Some are angry, others are compassionate – towards the Church and towards people in Irish society. Facing up to this complexity is facing up to our own complexity.

For this wider work among bystanders to be effective it requires, beyond Glencree-trained facilitators, buy-in from survivors, religious and, most importantly, from bishops. That, in turn, requires far-sighted financial commitment – from the Church and taxpayers – but Barbara Walshe says it would be money well spent. Not least because the positive impact of such work would be felt among those who, until now, have been left alone with their conflicted feelings about the past.

'We forget how horrendous this has been for ordinary Irish people,' she says. 'People who did whatever the Church said and felt powerless to intervene when they saw things, and now at the end of their lives wonder, "Why did I do that?" '

Three decades after the collective cellar door was opened on the destructive side of Catholic Ireland, a Glencree-led process would offer ordinary people somewhere to go with their own inner cellar conflicts.

Why go back? The question has plagued me since the start of this project. So I seek out June, Paula and Joyce Kavanagh. The three sisters are best known for *Click, Click*, their harrowing memoir of life with a tyrannical father. He manipulated his entire family into submission and sexually abused his three daughters over twenty-five years.

Just as remarkable as their first book is its sequel, *Why Go Back?* It brings together the knowledge, empathy and insights the three women have picked up on their journey. While many prefer to let sleeping dogs lie, the Kavanagh sisters believe in waking the dogs to examine their injuries.

'This process helped us find out who we really are,' says Joyce over coffee in Dublin. Paula agrees: 'It made us stronger and [helped us] become better versions of ourselves.'

I tell them of a common denominator in everyone I have met when travelling the country researching this book – exhaustion after nearly thirty years of revelations, scandals, pain and confrontation. Paula nods with recognition, suggesting this perceived lack of energy to address the past is actually a crucial reason to go back.

'We discovered that pain draws energy inwards, while empathy and forgiveness allow you to expand, grow and free yourself from suffering. In our case, going back made us our more authentic selves, it made us *us*.'

Going back is easier said than done. It raises a litany of tricky, interlocking questions. Such as: *what is the historical meaning of the victims and survivors of clerical sexual abuse?*

That, in turn, forces us to ask: *what is their place within the history of Irish Catholicism?*

And, in turn: *what was the place of Catholicism vis-à-vis Irish society?* This final question is still unresolved – and perhaps unresolvable.

Earlier in the book I mentioned the three Venn diagrams I presented to interviewees when I started researching this book, representing church institutions and Irish society. I asked my interviewees if they saw the respective circles as separate or overlapping circles, or if the Church-plus-institutions circle even existed wholly inside the Irish society circle. The idea was to invite people to say which diagram best reflected their understanding of how the Irish Catholic Church/religious existed in relation to the Irish state/people: not at all overlapping, partly overlapping or entirely overlapping. Everyone I asked answered differently, and eventually I gave up on the Venn diagrams, realizing there is not one story of Catholic Ireland but at least four million.

At some point, two dominant strands of the history of the Catholic Church in Ireland have to be resolved and braided together. One strand tells of how a religion sparked a revolution in thinking and learning on this island, sustained a people through the darkest oppression, before – in better times – it fused with national identity and helped create an independent country. Over centuries, this Catholic Church provided ritual, helped create a sense of meaning and provided leadership at times of chaos, violence, uncertainty and despair. Later, it provided healthcare and education to millions, helping transform our country into what it is today.

But a competing strand sees the modern, post-Famine Church lead a transition from a guilt- to a shame-based society. Shame was weaponized and used against individuals who contravened a strict moral code. This shame-based society was activated and steered from above but was also self-policing by ordinary people.

Sorting through this complicated legacy taxes the brains of our best historians, sociologists and psychologists. But a starting point for us to reflect on is whether the cruelty in Catholic Ireland came from layers of largely unaddressed historical trauma.

Prof Bessel van der Kolk, a world expert on trauma, identifies the 'cascade of humiliations of the powerless' – a series of historical traumas and disasters, piled on top of each other – that create both the circumstances and the moral case for an avalanche of cruelty of the strong against the weak. He describes the belated effect of this trauma on humans: remembering too little and too much simultaneously.

Trauma's sensations, thoughts and emotions are often stored separately, as 'frozen, barely comprehensible fragments'. Only a slow, methodical approach can thaw and reassemble the experience.

I wonder if that's the road ahead for Ireland? Clearing the car crash in our collective minds, a pile-up of pride and shame that has left many of us silent, struggling to deal with a conflicting narrative we simply cannot process.

Those who have lived through real conflict know that finding ways to live with it, and the complexity shadow thrown, is the only answer. When I stood with my friend Imogen Stuart in the graveyard at Glendalough, discussing the glory and cruelty of Catholic Ireland, she seemed surprised that I struggled to understand how it fits together. It doesn't, and that's the point. Ireland struggles to accept such internal conflicts and self-inflicted wounds in its past, she suggested, and prefers to cling to clearer victim narratives: 'In Ireland they go on and on about 1916. They never mention the centuries of Catholic history, the good and the bad.'

And yet Imogen has first-hand experience of how Ireland has done the seemingly impossible before: revisiting the contested meaning of 1916, working through our feelings about returning Irish veterans of the Great War, and examining the pain of civil war.

She was a member of the jury that chose *The People's Acorn* by artist Rachel Joynt, now at home in the garden of Áras an Uachtaráin. Joynt said her oversized acorn design was a metaphor for the journey of life from youth to maturity, marking Ireland's centenary of independence and 'our aspiration towards growing with maturity, optimism and wisdom for the future'. That would be a good starting point for any of the memorials promised to survivors of Catholic Ireland's cruelty.

This book is not about taking sides, or trying to square things off by rushing to a final conclusion about the significance of complex events in our contested Catholic past. It is an embrace of ambivalence, suggesting an informed, thoughtful and respectful discussion is the only way to work with the deep-rooted trauma of our Catholic legacy. Keeping the past as it is, buried in its shallow grave, leaves us stuck in a home-made limbo. If we don't want to know what's buried, or if we know and continue to deny it, we ensure that anything new we build on these foundations, over this grave, risks repeating, unconsciously and in new forms, the structural flaws of the past. Everything, from how we deal with repeated, serious failings in our healthcare system, to how we manage our housing crisis, to how we meet our obligations to those who come to Ireland seeking refuge, to our attitude and conduct towards the weak, the old, the vulnerable – much as we might aspire to fairness and enlightenment in all of these matters, without understanding where we have come from as a people, we cannot be confident of achieving either.

And unless we understand our capacity for deference, and the potential cost to human dignity and national sovereignty, our former approach to clerical leaders will simply find new outlets. Having turned our back on both religious observance and the moral authority of the Church, the Holy See is no longer the mirror in which we wish to see ourselves reflected. But perhaps we have merely transferred that craving to, and found new mirrors in, the boardrooms of Silicon Valley and the corridors of the Berlaymont.

Travelling Ireland for this book, shuttling between enemy camps, I saw two common features: a general feeling of exhaustion over the past, and a common well of goodwill to create a better outcome for all. Assuming the best of others' intentions to build on that goodwill and start a process of healing brings us back to that basic question: *are we ready to own our past?* After all, the Catholic Church may have held out the promise of eternal reward and everlasting life, but the actual institutional expression of its power and influence in Ireland was not supernatural in nature. It was man-made. Made in Ireland. By the best Catholics in the world.

Epilogue

This project began with silence. A silence inside me, as I live in history-soaked Berlin, whenever I asked myself questions about my history-soaked Catholic past – Mass, priests, parish, schools, abuse. And when I asked people the same questions in Ireland I encountered silence – or anger.

If I asked how we should remember our recent past, many interpreted 'responsibility to' this past as 'responsibility for' it and became defensive and hit back, thinking I was blaming them. Was I?

I began a journey, of reading and travelling, and learned that silence, and occasional ritualized arguments, is how most countries deal with their past. We're not that different. And many embrace silence about the past until a strategy for dealing with it seems possible. But I kept reading, and many books and authors chimed with me on the journey: historical tracts, psychological studies, trauma specialists, popular poets, obscure diarists.

I wanted to understand – and communicate – the idea that responsibility for the past is about informing oneself, about reflection and remembrance. Doing these in order to improve the present is not the same thing as asking people to accept others' blame for the past and its outcome.

One resonant book I read was *Returning to Reims* by the French philosopher Didier Eribon. He describes how the death of his estranged father prompts his own journey back to his home city and the working-class identity and oppressive family he fled thirty years earlier. Learning what happened to his father in his absence, Eribon observes himself 'rediscovering [a] region of myself . . . from which I had worked so hard to escape: a social space I had kept at a distance, a mental space in opposition to which I have constructed the person I had become and yet which remained an essential part of my being'.

He reflects on how, during his years of absence, his family and neighbours had shifted from voting communist to supporting the far-right National Front. As I read of his journey (while battling the labyrinthine language of French philosophers) I realized that Eribon's discovery was both obvious and yet, for him, profound: the French Left was not abandoned by the people; rather, it abandoned the people and, in doing so, made itself surplus to requirements. It betrayed its flock, and with it, the Left's raison d'être. The working class, with their sensitive antennae for champagne socialists, had along the way displaced the previously unmovable, dispensed with the once indispensable.

'You push something aside; you take a step in a different direction,' writes Eribon. And yet the past remains. 'We should not be dreaming of some kind of impossible "emancipation", our best hope will be to breach certain frontiers that history has put into place and that hem in our existence.'

His journey made me undertake a similar journey: to close the gap I had created, to try and understand how, in thirty years, Ireland leapt from an outwardly Catholic to a secular society. I had lived through lots of it, and was absent for lots more.

In my old parish I saw the lingering silence of clerical sexual abuse, and the unspoken taboos over religion, power and class. Travelling Ireland, I realized our talent for finessing our early Catholic history, embracing even today what flatters us, and burying what doesn't. I encountered many conflicting views and conflicted people, as well as the beauty and violence of Irish-style Catholicism. Some had been abused by it and were angry; others were angry-apathetic or unsure how they felt; some felt its comfort, and still do.

When the Catholic Church lost its monopoly on giving meaning to life in Ireland or creating a sense of community, many made the leap away from it because they could, and found new ways of framing their life and new communal homes elsewhere. But a final camp remained behind, trying to live their faith while often wary of the institution that claimed to represent it.

Like France's Socialists, Ireland's Catholic Church lost the plot and lost the people. But the needs and questions that gave rise to both are still there. The fate of the Irish Church reminds me of the start of my journey on the Dingle Peninsula, and the stone walls and vanished roof of Kilmalkedar's corbelled chapel. At the point where

Catholicism in Ireland could no longer sustain its own narrowness, it collapsed.

In *Help My Unbelief* Fr Michael Paul Gallagher wrote that the deepest truth of Christian faith is love. Many Irish know instinctively, as he wrote then, that 'the simple truth is that active love is more important than explicit faith'. But by prioritizing their understanding of explicit faith and imposing it on others, Ireland's Catholic Church denied the simple truth of active love. Not every person in the institutional Church did so, but enough of them – actively and passively, wittingly and unwittingly – contradicted this key truth at a terrible cost to others, and often to themselves. They are guilty of what Fr Gallagher calls 'the deepest denial of God . . . a refusal of love'.

And what of the rest of us? To whom did we refuse love? No matter how much we may disassociate ourselves now, most of us were members of this religious institution of achievement and abuse, and bystanders in a society that failed its most vulnerable. Enough people knew. What does it mean to know that now?

On a journey with long breaks and many detours, I found myself stopped in my tracks by the African-American writer James Baldwin, who spent his life fighting discrimination and prejudice on many fronts and on two continents. Later in life, he reflected on the cost of these cruelties, the cost of clinging to them and the cost of denying them. 'I imagine one of the reasons people cling to their hates so stubbornly,' he wrote in *The Fire Next Time*, 'is because they sense, once hate is gone, they will be forced to deal with pain.'

Accepting that pain follows anger, and curiosity can follow apathy, might help us write a mature new chapter of Ireland's history, one that is not about eliminating the Church and its failings, and our involvement in both, from our past. It will be about managing the lingering effects of what an Irish family therapist friend calls our 'unholy trinity of entanglement': Church, state and people. For her, Ireland stumbled into a bad case of triangulation. This is a term used in therapy to describe a manipulative form of communication where individuals who will not communicate directly and honestly with each other instead use a third party. It's something my friend usually encounters when embittered divorcing couples fight over children.

But we are not children. Church and state are separate like never before – though still not separate enough for some. As Pope Francis listened in Dublin Castle in 2018, Taoiseach Leo Varadkar said religion was no longer at the centre of Irish society but it still had an important place. The young leader proposed 'the opening of a new chapter in the relationship between Ireland and the Catholic Church'.

That chapter has yet to be written, and the terms of engagement have yet to be defined, but, if it is to be successful, it needs to be more inclusive and generous to all – to people of faith and non-believers – than it was in the past. Now that Ireland has flipped from a religious to an increasingly secular society, it needs to be mindful at all times of not repeating past, intolerant excesses of what Didier Eribon calls 'the confrontation between a subject and the power of the norm'.

I am well aware that the reinvention of Ireland is under way without me. I think that hit me in the last days of the 2018 abortion referendum campaign, as I watched worlds collide at the top of North Earl Street in Dublin. A small prayer group on the street recited the rosary and distributed pro-Life leaflets, while a gang of young people, blowing soap bubbles, strolled past to a pro-choice demonstration. On the other side of O'Connell Street, outside McDonald's, two young Mormons watched and waited for opportunities to proselytize. Just in front of me the wide boulevard was filled with a Falun Gong parade, an explosion of blues, yellows and smiles.

Lingering near the statue of James Joyce, an older man asked me if I'd heard of the most amazing book. 'This is higher than the Bible for me,' he said, waving a dog-eared copy of a book about the Falun Gong meditation practice embraced by millions of people worldwide. Including, it seemed, this retired Monaghan man.

'If I had only five minutes to leave the house in the night,' he said excitedly, 'this is what I'd take.'

This is another Ireland, open like never before to new ideas and practices. I'm an emigrant now, politically disenfranchised in Ireland and thus somewhat disengaged from this work of creating a different country. Born in Dublin in 1977, I have had the privilege of a relatively good education (in Catholic schools) and the blessing of a late birth. I felt the flickering flame of late Irish Catholicism, rather than the blowtorch of belief that went before. I have been spared much but deprived of other things. I can use the Catholic language of consolation and desolation without having really experienced either. This limits my analysis of a time before mine, and a country still grappling with the consequences in the twenty years since I left. I can only hope that whatever this emigrant has lost in daily detail, he has gained in perspective.

This journey has taken me from apathy to ambivalence, then anger to acceptance. Such journeys – particularly in book form – are the destiny of those who leave the homeland, and the bane of those who stay. From his Second World War exile in Brazil, Austrian novelist Stefan Zweig struggled to understand the European home he had lost for ever. The 'world of yesterday' was the greatest drama of his life, and the title of his greatest work.

Long before Hitler stole Zweig's Austria, the writer recalled his parents' lives in (pre-First World War) Imperial Austria. Their Vienna, he wrote, was a 'castle of dreams' they felt was built of permanent stone. His anger at their delusion, and their country that sleepwalked over the precipice, yields to his admission that their vanished society had 'wonderful, noble and humane elements'.

'In spite of my later knowledge and disillusionment,' he wrote, 'there is still something in me which inwardly prevents me from abandoning it entirely.'

I feel the same about Catholic Ireland, our world of yesterday. For whatever anger I harbour towards the Irish Church, echoing the anger of those whose lives were ruined by its institutional inhumanity, I see remnants of its noble aspirations through the many ordinary Irish people who tried – and try – to lead better, Christian lives.

No one can draw a line under the past, or airbrush away their role in it, but – for perhaps the first time ever – Irish people can approach their history on their own terms. That is, if they want to.

Sitting in Berlin, looking out of my window at the first buds of spring on the trees outside, I wonder – as I have dozens of times during this project – why I set off on this journey. And then I remember the silence.

A century ago in my apartment block, a former neighbour, similarly plagued by silence, in the aftermath of the First World War, also picked up a pen. With *All Quiet on the Western Front*, Erich Remarque gave voice to his fellow soldiers, too traumatized to speak or dead in the Belgian trenches. He challenged the old conservative elite's denial of guilt for the war they triggered and lost. His book was a provocation and was later suppressed by the Nazis. A society blinded by the trauma of one war walked into another.

Our history is very different as is, a century on, the world beyond my leafy street in Berlin. Yet I hope Remarque's doomed soldier, Paul Bäumer, speaks to you as he does to me: 'The silence spreads. I talk and must talk.'

Acknowledgements

This book arose from an old niggle, an *Irish Times* article and an approach from eagle-eyed editors at Sandycove.

My deepest love to my family for helping me grow, in particular during the last, challenging years. My thanks to my wonderful *Irish Times* colleagues, past and present, for pushing and prodding me. To Penguin Ireland's Michael McLoughlin, thanks for the initial approach and encouragement, and to Patricia Deevy for her protean professionalism and staggering editing skills. This book would be a much poorer read without her talent. To Shân Morley Jones for her eagle-eyed copyediting. And to the many people in Penguin's Dublin and London offices who have helped get the book into print and into readers' hands.

Special thanks to photographer Tony Murray, who went to great lengths to make possible the cover image. It's just one in the gallery of the vanished Catholic Ireland captured by him over two decades and collected in his priceless book, *Holy Pictures*.

My deep thanks to friends in Germany and Ireland for their quiet encouragement and ideas.

My endless respect to Ireland's many empathetic, educated and energetic religious, without whom Ireland would – and will – be a poorer place. Many informed this book without featuring by name, but their eloquent kindness was greatly appreciated. Also thanks to religious who are living with a burden in their past, and whose openness – and trust – was, I hope, repaid in these pages.

Equally, my gratitude to those who have come through the nightmare of Ireland's Catholic past. Many bear scars yet all were endlessly patient in sharing their unique wisdom with me. In particular, I owe a debt of gratitude to the late Paddy Doyle. Even in his last, laboured years, nothing could suppress his wicked humour and restless intelligence.

Finally, my thanks to the many nameless Irish people who enriched my journey, and those who felt the need to read this book. Ireland's past cannot be changed, but another kind of future – empathetic and tolerant – stands within reach.

Endnotes

2. The lies we tell ourselves

page 25 '. . . he had no problem with little boys': Murphy Report, 2009, Chapter 13, p. 195.

3. Into the Celtic mist

page 37 'For all we Irish': *St Columbanus, Selected Writings*, compiled by Alexander O'Hara, foreword by Mary McAleese, Veritas, 2015, p. 30.

page 43 'ruthless, unpredictable and prone to take offence': Hilda Ellis Davidson, *The Lost Beliefs of Northern Europe*, Routledge, 1993, p. 64.

page 44 'supernatural infusion . . . the arrival of Christianity': Seán Ó Faoláin, 'The Roots', in *The Irish: A Character Study*, Penguin Books, 1947.

4. Saints, scholars . . . and slaves

page 47 'Let us know nothing more profitable': Sermon 9.2 in *St Columbanus, Selected Writings*, compiled by Alexander O'Hara, foreword by Mary McAleese, Veritas, 2015, p. 74.

page 50 'whose lives were lived out': Donnchadh Ó Corráin et al (eds), *Sages, Saints and Storytellers: Celtic Studies in Honour of Professor James Carney*, An Sagart Press, 1989, p. 261.

page 53 'And since the whole thing's imagined': lines from 'St Kevin and the Blackbird', poem by Seamus Heaney.

page 55 'piling on top of something': Seán Ó Faoláin, 'The Roots', in *The Irish: A Character Study*, Penguin Books, 1947.

5. Holy victimhood

page 56 **'What wonder if our step betrays'**: 'The Penal Days' in Helen Mulvey, *Thomas Davis & Ireland*, Catholic University of America Press, 2003, p. 250.

page 57 **'especially when laced with aggressive self-righteousness'**: Liam Kennedy, *Unhappy the Land*, Merrion Press, 2016, p. 40.

page 58 **'deeply, horribly saturated in Irish blood'**: John Savage, *Fenian Heroes and Martyrs*, published in 1869.

page 61 **'priests have celebrated . . . in disguise'**: https://www.history-ireland.com/penal-laws/penal-days-in-clogher/. Accessed 31 July 2020.

page 61 **Of those who stayed, a number were killed**: Patrick Corish, *The Irish Catholic Experience: a historical survey*, Michael Glazier, 1985, p. 141.

page 62 **'minded dogs and hunting more than his flock'**: S. J. Connolly, *Religion, Law, and Power: The Making of Protestant Ireland 1660–1760*, Clarendon Press, 1992, p. 154.

page 63 **While some Irish Catholics walked miles**: S. J. Connolly, *Priests and People in Pre-Famine Ireland, 1780–1845*, Four Courts Press, 2001, p. 104.

page 63 **'religion is practised freely and openly . . . by law of parliament to make it'**: https://www.historyireland.com/penal-laws/penal-days-in-clogher/. Accessed 31 July 2020.

page 63 **'claret to treat the sheriffs in their search'**: Corish, *The Irish Catholic Experience*, p. 128.

page 64 **'on account of his extravagance . . . daily increasing'**: 'Report on the state of popery in Ireland, 1731', Archivium Hibernicum, 1 (1912), 15–16.

page 64 **In total, contemporary reports from around the country**: 'Report on the state of popery', 11.

page 64 **Even as times improved in Ireland**: Thomas O'Connor, 'The Catholic Church and Catholics in an Era of Sanctions and Restraints, 1690–1790'. In T. Bartlett and J. Kelly (eds), *The Cambridge History of Ireland*, Vol. III, Cambridge University Press, 2018, pp. 257–79 (270).

page 64 **Mankind are pleased whene'er a villain dies**: Corish, *The Irish Catholic Experience*, p. 219.

page 65 **'by one Father Tracie . . . all of Hoath'**: Rev William P. Burke, *The Irish Priests in the Penal Times*, N. Harvey & Co, 1914, p. 209.

page 65 **'four magistrates armed with warrants'**: Burke, *The Irish Priests*, p. 218.

page 65 **'unexampled sufferings . . . in the history of mankind'**: Burke, p. v.

page 65 **'cruel ingenuity . . . dragged to the scaffold'**: Clare Murphy, 'The Social Basis of Irish Nationalism, 1867–1879' (unpublished PhD thesis, Queen's University, Belfast, 1993), quoted in Kennedy, *Unhappy the Land*, p. 30.

page 67 **'vested interest in exaggerating'**: Louis Cullen, 'Catholics under the Penal Laws', *Eighteenth-Century Ireland*, Vol. 1 (1986), 22–36.

page 67 **'conception of professionalism . . . to constructive purpose'**: Brendan Bradshaw, 'Nationalism and Historical Scholarship in Modern Ireland', *Irish Historical Studies*, Vol. 26, No. 104 (1989), 329–51.

page 68 **'Tis not the poverty I most detest**: Daniel Corkery, *Hidden Ireland*, Gill & Macmillan, 1956, p. 9.

page 68 **'touchstone of how Catholics have often read'**: Oliver P. Raftery SJ, *Violence, Politics and Catholicism in Ireland*, Four Courts Press, 2016, p. 230.

page 68 **'lingering sense of displacement'**: Raftery, *Violence, Politics and Catholicism*, p. 232.

page 69 **It is hardly an exaggeration to say**: Burke, *The Irish Priests*, p. 207.

6. The little green book

page 71 **'We have just enough religion'**: Jonathan Swift, *Thoughts on Various Subjects, Moral and Diverting*, 1711.

7. The pride of Laragh

page 88 **'The wonder of it all'**: Tom Kelly, 'The making of a cardinal', *Anglo-Celt*, 19 December 2007.

page 88 'Cardinal Brady would best serve': Opinion, 'Time for cardinal to resign', *Anglo-Celt*, 16 June 2010.

page 90 Cavan's farming families were issued with ration cards . . . place names reappear: Cavan's Emergency Years. See http://www.irishidentity.com/stories/cavanemergency.htm. Accessed 31 July 2020.

page 95 'horrified, stunned and sickened': https://www.belfastlive.co.uk/news/abused-boys-dad-slams-cardinal-15073213. Accessed 31 July 2020.

8. The fall of Seán Brady

page 101 'I was expressionless': Brendan Boland, *Sworn to Silence*, O'Brien Press, 2014, p. 53.

page 101 'lost to my memory for decades': Boland, pp. 79–80.

page 102 'And if I enjoyed that': Boland, p. 83.

page 104 Canon law describes celibacy as: Canon 277, *Code of Canon Law*, Vatican, 1983.

page 104 'Male sexual identity is a primary requirement for priesthood': Marie Keenan, *Child Sexual Abuse and the Catholic Church*, Oxford University Press, 2012, p. 234.

page 105 'There were clergy who knew': Opinion, ' "Anne" weighs in on Cardinal Brady saga', *Anglo-Celt*, 7 May 2012.

page 106 The HIA report on the disgraced priest's life: https://www.hiainquiry.org/historical-institutional-abuse-inquiry-report-chapters. Accessed 31 July 2020.

page 111 'control everything . . .': News, 'A sad day as Cardinal Brady's resignation is accepted', *Anglo-Celt*, 8 September 2014.

9. Sex in a cold climate

page 115 'The parish could deem them a Jezebel': Interview with CBC TV programme *Midday*, 17 October 1994.

page 117 'traditionally silent when challenged . . . conservative Catholic moral values': James Smith, *Ireland's Magdalene Laundries and the Architecture of Containment*, Manchester University Press, 2007, pp. xiii–xiv.

page 118 **He said they 'might have been told . . . '**: The full text of Enda
Kenny's apology is available at https://www.thejournal.ie/full-text-
enda-kenny-magdalene-apology-801132-Feb2013/. Accessed 31 July
2020.

page 123 **'The story of the Magdalene laundries is not new'**: ' "Too
pretty" to be allowed out', *Irish Times*, 14 March 1998.

10. *The necessary lie*

page 134 **'direct State involvement'**: all quotations from Enda Kenny's
2013 state apology in this chapter can be found at https://www.the
journal.ie/full-text-enda-kenny-magdalene-apology-801132-Feb2013/.
Accessed 31 July 2020.

page 134 **'no factual evidence . . . ill treatment of a criminal nature'**:
*Ireland, Replies to List of issues prior to submissions of the second periodic report
of Ireland to the Committee Against Torture*, UN Doc CAT/C/IRL/2, 20
January 2016, Para 241.

page 138 **'Here the object is'**: Dr Donald Nathanson, 'Managing
Shame−Preventing Violence' https://www.youtube.com/watch?v=LZ1f
SW7zevE. Accessed 31 July 2020.

page 140 **'provides the most straightforward and convincing
argument . . . a piece of theological fiction'**: Karen L. King, *The
Gospel of Mary of Magdala: Jesus and the First Woman Apostle*, Polebridge
Press, 2003, pp. 3−12.

11. *Marie and Paddy*

page 141 **'If these sad facts teach us anything'**: Judge Mathews ruling on
the case of David Murray, reported in ' "Fixated" paedophile is given 10
years for abusing orphans and foster-sons', *Irish Times*, 18 December 1997.

page 149 **'to point the finger . . . thousands of "mes" '**: Paddy Doyle,
The God Squad, Corgi paperback edition, 1989, pp. 11−12.

page 150 **'How did we so lose our wits'**: the full text of Keating's review is
available at http://www.paddydoyle.com/tag/the-god-squad/. Accessed
31 July 2020.

page 151 **'fair and reasonable awards'**: See the Residential Institutions Redress Board, 'About Us' at https://www.rirb.ie/aboutus.asp. Accessed 31 July 2020.

12. *One in four*

page 154 **'Everyone knew'**: John Banville, 'A Century of Looking the Other Way', *New York Times*, 22 May 2009.

page 155 **'map of an Irish hell'**: Ian O'Donnell, 'Many people helped to draw "the map of an Irish hell"', *Irish Times*, 20 May 2019.

page 156 **'prison inmates and slaves'**: 'Irish church knew abuse "endemic"', BBC News, 20 May 2009.

page 156 **'wasn't an absolute knowledge'**: RTÉ: 'A Tribute to Mary Raftery', available at https://www.youtube.com/watch?v=oRNOSOEX a8Q. Accessed 31 July 2020.

page 156 **'culture of self-serving secrecy'**: 'Irish church knew abuse "endemic"', BBC.

page 159 **'In today's climate'**: The Ryan Report, Volume IV, Chapter 3, 'Society and the schools', paragraph 120.

page 161 **'the systematic cruelty . . . everyone knew'**: Banville, 'A Century of Looking the Other Way'.

page 162 **'The truth, in its delayed appearance'**: Cathy Carruth, *Unclaimed Experience: Trauma, Narrative, and History*, Johns Hopkins University Press, 1996, p. 4.

page 162 **'feel entitled to do anything'**: Vamik D. Volkan, 'Transgenerational Transmissions and Chosen Traumas: An Aspect of Large-Group Identity', *Group Analysis*, Vol. 4, No. 1 (2001), 79–97.

page 162 **'triple edict . . . whether in acts or in words'**: Michel Foucault, *The History of Sexuality*, Random House, 1978, p. 4.

page 163 **'ordinary response to atrocities . . . refuse to be buried'**: Judith Hermann, *Trauma and Recovery: The Aftermath of Violence*, Basic Books, 1992, p. 1.

page 164 **'has ongoing consequences'**: Bessel van der Kolk, *The Body Keeps the Score*, Penguin Books, 2015, p. 31.

page 164 **Their accessible study, available online**: The UCD study, entitled 'Industrial Memories', can be viewed at https://industrialmemories.ucd.ie/. Accessed 31 July 2020.

page 164 **'It became very clear . . . more widespread than that'**: Olive Keogh, 'How data analytics revealed new insights in Ryan report on child abuse', *Irish Times*, 6 September 2018.

page 165 **'Washing came in'**: Dermot Bolger, 'Home truths about our dishonest past', *Sunday Independent*, 16 May 1999.

page 165 **'Ireland made the Christian Brothers . . . an old-fashioned Irish cover-up'**: Jim Beresford, 'Ryan taboo on warped sexual training of brothers a cop-out', *Irish Times*, 18 June 2009.

page 167 **'To function as an ethical witness'**: Emilie Pine, Susan Levy and Mark T. Keane, 'Re-reading the Ryan Report: Witnessing via Close and Distant Reading', *Éire-Ireland*, Vol. 52, Nos. 1 & 2 (2017), 198–215.

13. *Between the red doors*

page 169 **'The ghosts of a nation'**: Patrick Pearse, 'Ghosts', pamphlet finished on Christmas Day, 1915.

page 172 **'with no ifs and buts'**: Patsy McGarry, 'Archbishop of Dublin defends Murphy Commission report', *Irish Times*, 21 December 2015.

page 172 **'naming and shaming'**: Patsy McGarry, 'Murphy report "highly critical", "dismissive", towards clergy', *Irish Times*, 29 October 2013.

page 178 **'something about this film . . . no room for subtleties'**: Michael Foley, 'Lack of balance in coverage of "Dear Daughter"', *Irish Times*, 19 March 1996.

page 179 **'The maltreatment of the children'**: Bernadette Fahy, *Freedom of Angels*, O'Brien Press, 1999, p. 14.

page 179 **'was created by a dominant . . . blaming of the individual'**: Crowley Report, cited in the Ryan Report, Volume II, Chapter 7, 'St Vincent's Industrial School, Goldenbridge ('Goldenbridge'), 1880–1983', paragraph 224.

page 181 **'incurred by the Dáil'**: Patsy McGarry, 'Religious order rejects calls to share redress costs with State', *Irish Times*, 3 April 2017.

page 182 **'active drive to make reparations . . . escape from the emotion-eliciting event'**: Brian Lickel et al, 'The Evocation of Moral Emotions in Intergroup Contexts'. In Nyla R. Branscombe and Bertjan Doosje (eds), *Collective Guilt: International Perspectives*, Cambridge University Press, 2004, pp. 35–55 (47).

page 183 **'Irish society, especially the Irish State'**: James Gallen, *Shame, Disgust and Contempt: Ireland's Legacy of Historical Abuse*, 2018, academic conference presentation, p. 1.

14. *We don't want to know what's buried here*

page 192 **'Excavators know this'**: Eileen McAuley, 'The Significance of Wood Quay', *Dublin Historical Record*, Vol. XXXII, No. 4 (1979), 122–28.

page 193 **'succeed in attracting the eye of the conscious'**: Saul McLeod, 'Freud and the Unconscious Mind', *Simply Psychology*, 2009 (updated 2015). Available at: https://www.simplypsychology.org/unconscious-mind.html. Accessed 31 July 2020.

15. *A stone phoenix*

page 203 **'Because of his fear of a priest's power'**: John McGahern, *The Dark*, Panther, 1969, p. 19.

page 203 **'envy, jealousy and spite would become rampant'**: J. J. Lee, *Ireland 1912–1985 Politics and Society*, Cambridge University Press, 1989, p. 645.

page 204 **'to deliberate and pronounce upon . . . their mitres glistening with jewels'**: *Illustrated London News*, 14 September 1850.

page 204 **'shrunken looks and sharpened features'**: Robert Davis, Clonmel, 26 February 1847. See https://www.libraryireland.com/articles/FamineBurncourtFriends/. Accessed 31 July 2020.

page 205 **'stir and bustle'**: *Illustrated London News*, 12 September 1850.

page 209 **'a message of self-abnegation'**: Judith Rowbotham, *Girls Make Good Wives: Guidance for Girls in Victorian Fiction*, Blackwell, 1989, p. 57.

page 209 **'as a satanic snare . . . the family'**: Joe Lee, 'Women and the Church since the Famine'. In Margaret MacCurtain and Donncha Ó Corráin (eds), *Women in Irish Society: The Historical Dimension* (Contributions in Women's Studies, Vol. II), Greenwood Press, 1979, p. 39.

page 210 **'Roman usages . . . Roman everything'**: Anne Lannigan, 'Cathedral of the Assumption, Thurles: An Historical Outline', 2005, p. 8.

page 216 **'Very much like an army'**: Interview between Eamon Maher and John McGahern, *Studies: An Irish Quarterly Review*, Vol. 90, No. 357 (2001), 70 and ff.

16. Lost in the thicket

page 217 **'The Irish priesthood'**: Archbishop Thomas Walsh of Cashel, 'The toast of "The Irish Church"' in *Record of Maynooth Centenary Celebration 1895*, published by Browne and Nowlan, 1896, p. 173.

page 221 **'has certainly not promoted the progress . . . their dwarf-like existence as giants'**: Eoin Bourke, *"Poor Green Erin" German Travel Writers' Narratives on Ireland from Before the 1798 Rising to After the Great Famine*, Peter Lang, 2011, p. 347.

page 221 **'not a university . . . the faith of their fathers'**: *Record of Maynooth Centenary Celebration 1895*, p. 165.

page 226 **'ecclesiastical imperialist . . . in meeting their needs as he did'**: Emmet Larkin, 'Paul Cullen: The Great Ultramontane'. In Dáire Keogh and Albert McDonnell (eds), *Cardinal Paul Cullen and his World*, Four Courts Press, 2011, p. 21.

17. 'The most devoted of all the children of the Holy See'

page 228 **'His Holiness is sick and tired'**: Dermot Keogh, *Ireland and the Vatican*, Cork University Press, 1995, p. 29.

page 231 **'every heart was moved . . . highly favoured by God'**: https://www.ballymenaparish.org/features/pilgrimage-to-rome-1893/94-rome-monday-20-february-1893.

page 232 **'The moment lasted only seconds'**: https://www.the42.ie/packie-bonnar-italia-90-pope-2457103-Dec2015/.

page 233 **'profound homage'**: Keogh, *Ireland and the Vatican*, p. xix.

page 234 **'we shall not really have our Jew'**: Keogh, p. 206.

page 234 **'Irish diplomats were to discover'**: Keogh, p. xxii.

page 239 **'merely a study document . . . contrary to canonical discipline'**: The Cloyne Report, Chapter 1 Overview, paragraph 1.18.

page 239 **'dysfunction, disconnection, elitism'**: https://www.irishtimes.com/news/politics/oireachtas/dysfunction-disconnection-elitism-and-narcissism-1.2884963. Video accessed 31 July 2020.

page 239 **'a Government spokesperson clarified'**: http://www.vatican.va/resources/resources_sintesi-risposta-gilmore_20110903_en.html. Accessed 31 July 2020.

18. *Wizards of Rome*

page 242 **'They are bossed and controlled'**: John Bowman (ed), *Ireland, The Autobiography: Eyewitness accounts of Irish life since 1916*, Penguin Ireland, 2016, p. 195.

page 243 **'leprosy of the Vatican'**: Paddy Agnew, 'Past popes have been narcissistic, Francis tells newspaper', *Irish Times*, 1 October 2013.

page 251 **'the most cringingly servile'**: Ronan Fanning, 'The days when our foreign policy was cringingly Catholic', *Sunday Independent*, 22 November 2014.

page 251 **'close contact with the Catholic clergy . . . people amongst whom they work'**: Bowman, *Ireland*, p. 193.

19. *Stopping the Sacred Heart*

page 254 **'Between them they succeeded'**: Brinsley MacNamara, *The Valley of the Squinting Windows*, Maunsel & Co., 1918, p. 13.

page 256 **'less an attitude of rejection . . . shallow unbelief'**: Michael Paul Gallagher SJ, *Help My Unbelief*, Veritas, Dublin, 1983, p. 59.

page 259 **'accepts an interpretation of the relationship between faith'**: Olav Hovdelien, 'Post-Secular Consensus? On the Munich-dialogue between Jürgen Habermas and Joseph Ratzinger', *Australian eJournal of Theology*, Vol. 18, No. 2 (2011), 107–16.

page 260 'But what right have we . . . the beauty of the Christian
faith': Verena Friederike Hasel, 'Glauben? Ernsthaft?', *Die Zeit*, 30
August 2018.

page 260 'fighting against religion . . . what they can discover and
learn': Synod Address, 24 October 2018. https://sjcuria.global/en/
more-speeches/204-father-general-s-intervention-at-the-synod-
complete-text. Accessed 31 July 2020.

page 265 'What was the ultimate cause': Fr Vincent Twomey, *The End of
Irish Catholicism?*, Veritas, 2003, p. 33.

20. Us and them

page 269 'There were few opportunities to avoid it': Angela Merkel,
Mein Weg – Ein Gespräch mit Hugo Müller-Vogg, Hoffmann & Campe,
2015, p. 59.

page 277 'One wants to be free of the past . . . dealt with': Theodor
Adorno, 'What Does Coming to Terms with the Past Mean?'. In Geof-
frey Hartman (ed), *Bitburg in Moral and Political Perspective*, Indiana
University Press, 1986, pp. 114–30.

page 278 '[Eichmann] came closer to being': Stanley Milgram, 'The
Dilemma of Obedience', *The Phi Delta Kappan*, Vol. 55, No. 9 (1974),
603–6.

page 281 'Suffering cannot be compared': Interview with Just Vision
portal, 16 March 2008. https://www.justvision.org/portrait/859/inter-
view. Accessed 31 July 2020.

page 284 'What counts': Jürgen Habermas, 'Bemerkungen zu einer ver-
worrenen Diskussion', *Die Zeit*, 3 April 1992.

21. Coming to terms

page 285 'I had an Irish-Catholic nanny': Mark Rowland, 'Leonard
Cohen's Nervous Breakthrough', *Musician*, July 1988.

page 286 'His face is turned toward the past': Walter Benjamin, *Theses
on the Philosophy of History* (trans. Harry Zohn), Schocken Books, 1969,
p. 249.

page 287 **'If I report this'**: Testimony of a witness to the Confidential Committee of the Commission to Inquire into Child Abuse. See The Ryan Report, Volume III, p. 287.

page 294 **'As citizens and bystanders'**: Marie Keenan, *Child Sexual Abuse and the Catholic Church*, Oxford University Press, 2012, p. xiii.

page 296 **'Site of Conscience'**: Claire Santry, 'Former Magdalene laundry to be a "site of conscience"', *Irish Genealogy News*, 21 June 2019.

page 297 **'Wherever there has been power . . . that we desperately need'**: Nuala O'Faolain, 'Nice, good folks who bear silent witness to cruelty', *Irish Times*, 11 March 1996.

page 300 **'cascade of humiliations of the powerless'**: Bessel van der Kolk, *The Body Keeps the Score*, Penguin Books, 2015, p. 187.

page 301 **'frozen, barely comprehensible fragments'**: van der Kolk, *The Body Keeps the Score*, p. 180.

Epilogue

page 303 **'rediscovering [a] region of myself . . . hem in our existence'**: Didier Eribon, *Returning to Reims*, MIT Press, 2013, p. 16.

page 305 **'the simple truth is . . . a refusal of love'**: Michael Paul Gallagher SJ, *Help My Unbelief*, Veritas, Dublin, 1983, p. 92.

page 307 **'castle of dreams . . . abandoning it entirely'**: Stefan Zweig, *The World of Yesterday*, Viking Press, 1943, Chapter 1, 'The World of Security'.

Index